Table of Contents

Copyrights...2

Dedication...3

Acknowledgement..4

Forward..6

Chapter I :   Introduction 7

Chapter II: My Story...21

Chapter III: Roadblocks To Love & Change................36

Chapter IV: Keys To Self-Love & Change 61

Chapter V: Learning The Tools of Self-Love & Healing Trade . 76

Chapter VI: Living Happily After Ever 109

Chapter VII: Spiritual Growth & Development..................... 113

Chapter VIII: Spiritual Toolkit for Healing Your Heart & Soul . 131

Chapter IX: Getting Out of Self................................ 162

Conclusion: 171

Copyrights

Dedication

This book is dedicated to all those (including my own loved ones) who still continue to suffer & struggle with addiction, depression, anxiety and the host of other psychological, mental, emotional and spiritual maladies that give us character and keep us challenged to succeed and be happy with our lot in life. And, I devote this book to helping others help themselves all over the world. May we all teach our children well, especially those in need, to find their way home.

Acknowledgements

I am humbly indebted to my beloved friends and family who have seen me through the trials and greatest challenges of my life: I owe an indescribable debt to my ex-wife Eve, my beloved children, Julia, Jesse & Noah, and to my immediate and extended family who I took hostage during the throes of my disease and malaise, and who tolerated and loved me when I couldn't love myself. I will always love you all.

A special and loving thanks to my sister, Shelley Benaroya and her wonderful husband, Dr. Haym Benaroya. I love you both dearly for all that you've done and continue to do to make my life better and brighter. You are both heaven-sent! To my mother and father, Merle & Murray who gave me life and who ferried me to adulthood. I will always be thankful for all the many things you taught me —especially love and to never give up on your dreams. My 12-step sponsor, Jim S. for having and helping me when nobody else would. To my former sponsor and dearest friend, Vee P. who passed after a valiant battle with cancer, while I was incarcerated. To all my fellows at the Shoralan Club – the "emergency room" for recovery -- in Belmar, NJ, where after nearly 20 years of trying, I finally got and stayed sober. And to all those who passed before the miracle happened, including my former sponsees, Charlie, Dave and Dave who died tragic deaths, and who left beautiful children, family and dear friends behind. You all taught me about humility and the power of our disease, as well as all the underlying causes of our addictions; you also showed me the brilliant tools of recovery that work when you work them, and how powerless we are over addiction when we don't. A special acknowledgement to Eddie Bo., Ron S., Pablo P., Neal M., Kathryn Herrmann, James Garfinkel, Toni & Matt Cerasia, Carol B., Guy Williams, Aunt Barbara and my cousins Cheryl, Sue, my niece and nephew Ana & Adam Benaroya, my other nephew, Daniel Praeger, whose wedding I missed and I who I also love & admire dearly, and several other good friends who stayed with me during my time away. God bless you both for putting up with me.

To my former literary agent, Richard Pine, who got me my first book deal when I was 25 when I falsely fashioned myself a "master of the universe." Richard, who I never properly expressed my gratitude to you back then for helping me publish "Doing Business With The Japanese," recently inspired me to self-publish and to build my own content platform on the web – which has proved to be my true love & passion. Thank you for your honesty.

To my mentors, Bob S., Tom Ingegneri and Carl Wolf for teaching me the importance of managing risk and living with emotional sobriety – even though I often failed to take their suggestions. You were all instrumental in helping me to learn my better character assets, and taught me a few important lessons on morality and ethical conduct.

A special thanks to Rob Lawrence, who I also took hostage as a former friend and business partner, but have always admired for his ability to balance and appreciate the smaller and often more important things in life. You are one of the nicest, least complicated and decent guys I know. And, to my recent mentor and former business partner, Michael Sonnenfeldt, who has been helping to guide and assist me after coming home from prison fairly shell-shocked. Your amazing integrity and charity is blessed as you are!

 A heartfelt thanks to Gay Ingegneri for helping me keep the faith and to stay spiritually fit during my darkest and now brightest days. You and Tom are an amazing power of example as to how to live a good, honest, virtuous and faith-based life. I love you and Tom both for being there for me in every respect of the word. You are true and loyal friends and I have come to call The Cranbury Inn, which you both Shepherd and keep, my second home.

To my landlord, fellow and friend, Eric Saltzman for taking me in from the storm and putting up with me all these months. I can't thank you enough as I find my way, purpose and meaning each and every day. You have made it easy to live by the beach and the serenity life here has to offer.

 To Michael Benson, who I've come to know and appreciate for his deep spiritual integrity and beliefs, and for walking the walk in his own life. Thank you for believing in me and for being a good friend and guide.

There are others, and if I have forgotten to mention you, please know that I am forever thankful. My cup runneth over to all of you! And, finally, thank you, my Higher Power, for showing me how to become Your humble and grateful servant! You have taught me the true meaning of trust and faith, as well as the power of grace!

Forward

The inspiration for this book has come exclusively from my deep pain, struggle and trauma during my time on earth. I also promised myself that I would write this book in part to honor the passing of several of my dearest and best friends who also struggled with personal and life issues like I did and asked that I use my voice to represent them in death. Charlie Cerasia, David Garfinkel and Siege Herrmann. I love you guys and have been inspired by your presence (past and present) in my life! Your collective spirit continues to speak through me and inspire me daily. Pain is the very thing, along with the daily trials and tribulations that breathe life into my purpose and passion to help others every day. I accept all this pain as well as the pleasure as my greatest teachers in this life. As my spiritual awareness grows, my appreciation for the gifts of the journey continue to sustain and help me to grow in the light and love I have been shown. Pain is truly the touchstone of all meaningful change, and I honor this as a necessary part of my growth and evolution. I also acknowledge pain and suffering as a vital part of life and character building. I am a better man because of it. As I've come to understand and deeply appreciate, everything happens for a reason, for my own good and for the very best. Life is good and keeps getting better with time, experience and deep gratitude and acceptance.

Ready To Get Help?

Let me show you how. Email me directly at
fenton@lifecoach911.com or text me at
973-885-2839

Chapter I.
<u>INTRODUCTION</u>

I've been waiting to write "Learning How To Love Yourself Even When Your Parents Don't" since the day I was born. And, that was 61 years ago. You see, I love my parents dearly, but it took me all too long to figure out what that really meant. My parents were good people: My father, Murray, has long since passed; My mother, Merle, is still hanging in there at nearly 93. God bless both their caring and wonderful souls. Today, I hold no grudges, resentments or blame.

They came to America from hard-working European immigrant families, to give me and my sister a decent middle class life. I went to wonderful schools, lived in a really nice house on Six Harrow Lane in Old Bethpage, Long Island, New York, had friends, girlfriends, was active in school, and was a fairly decent student.

But, as I matured and grew into adulthood, I ended up broken in many ways. In fact, my insecurities and never feeling good enough, loved enough, OK enough and just comfortable in my own skin, eventually brought me to my knees in desperation and then left me homeless, near death, addicted and penniless. I was full of resentment, anger, fear and anxiety that things just weren't quite right growing up, and I carried this forward well into adulthood to my dismay. I have never felt that I mattered, and no matter what I did, it seemed like I could never do enough to please my parents. So, I kept doing more and more to no avail – anything to be recognized. I couldn't fill up that broken hole in my soul with enough of anything to make me feel like I was loved and that I stacked up.

Considering where I came from, how exactly is that possible? I had two married parents and a fairly stable home life. I was one of the luckier kids – considering how many people grow up in broken homes with single parents, grandparents, caretakers and guardians.

This book isn't about my parents, though. It's about me and you. I carried these feelings of inadequacy and pain with me all these years. I never understood what I was experiencing until I became old enough to realize that my experience in childhood of emotional abandonment was more common than not. And, it hurts terribly. By the time I reached adulthood, however, the damage was already done to "little Mitchy" (my nickname as a kid). I have met many people through my own travels and struggles to realize that I am not alone, and these feelings pervade the very fabric of our lives and end up causing immense and indescribable pain and suffering.

I just wanted to be loved, to feel safe, secure, and to know that both I and things were going to be OK. Is that too much to ask when you are a five-year old? Shouldn't we feel loved and given a sense of certainty that the future is full of hope, opportunity and happiness? Isn't it reasonable that we should feel good about ourselves and our prospects for living a good, meaningful and purposeful life? Should a child have to be worried about today or his or her future tomorrow? And, is it healthy to have a child be filled with anger, resentment and fear that the way he or she is feeling is of their own making; that they, in fact are at fault? What is wrong with this picture??

While it's sad that so many of us struggle(d) with the hurt of our past, any additional suffering is optional. Today, there are so many truly amazing ways to heal yourself. I know. I've used nearly all of them to heal myself. YOU don't have to stay stuck and in hurt. _It's not so much what happened to you - as many people struggle with corrupted and imperfect childhood development; it is what you decide to do about it!_ I wrote this book to help those who still believe they are victims understand your choices and options. I know that by the time you read on, you will decide to become the victor and seek happiness as a way of life. Freedom from the bondage of your old self is right in front of you. Enjoy the journey!

The truth is, we end up victimizing and hurting ourselves for things, real or imagined, that happened to us as children. My mother grew up poor in Londonderry Ireland and later Glasgow, Scotland as the oldest child when her father suddenly passed away at 43. She was just 15 and was forced to become the primary breadwinner of her family. She scraped and saved as a dressmaker to make ends meet and to help her mother buy a house. She later built a small fashion business and helped put her brother through College, and eventually helped the entire family immigrate to the U.S. where they all ended up living happy and prosperous lives with their own families.

But, my mother always complained that her father, whom she adored, admired, and looked up to never showed her love. He never told her that she was good enough, even though she was a talented artist and designer and won awards in school. He was never able to communicate to her that she was loved and good enough as a human being no matter what. My mother never knew what it was like to be loved unconditionally. She carried these emotional scars and spiritual baggage with her entire life.

My father came from a large and loving family of 11 kids, but had a difficult, if non-existent relationship with his father, who he never talked about. Until recently, I did not even know his name. Clearly, things were not right between his father and himself. However, my father considered his mother, my grandmother, who I never met, a modern-day saint who worked herself to the bone and was incredibly charitable, always giving to the poor and those in need – even though she, too, was poor. My father was a wonderful man, big heart, seemingly happy, but unfilled. He, too, was never able to express or say these three magical words: "I love you."

I do believe my parents loved me, but could never express it in words or physical affection. Maybe it was a generational thing or an understood habit for their era in Post WWII America. Either way, it's not their fault. They did the best they could with what they knew. Perhaps my generation of Post Baby-Boomers, born in the "Love" era of the Beatles and the Vietnam War expected more. But, for me all that mattered is that I never got a hug or a pat on the back – and I always felt less than and never good enough in their eyes. It was painful and I internalized it and then ended up acting out in destructive ways, as I was never really able to heal all these years until recently.

My Watershed Moment

When I was 15, I first realized that if I didn't deal with these feelings of anger and resentment with my parents, I would never be happy. Somehow, I was emotionally traumatized.   As it turns out, becoming unhappy turned out to be a self-fulfilling prophecy. My first real girlfriend, whom I met in High School, was named Donna. She was a year younger than me and I came to love her family. Her parents were divorced, but her father was a fantastic guy and ironically, a psychotherapist – just what every teenage dude like me needs!

In fact, during my 20's, I came to realize that I had ended up adopting my friends' families – because they showed such love and affection for each other where my family didn't. They seemed stable, secure and family-centric. I liked being around them and felt OK in my own skin while at their house. That was compared to coming home to my own very stressful and seemingly dysfunctional home. I spent ALL my spare time outdoors and away from home. When I finally graduated High School, I left and never came back to visit.

So, one day, talking with Donna's father, I broke down and confessed to him how I really felt. Empty inside, driven by these feelings of inadequacy that I didn't understand and often had difficulty handling on my own. He strongly encouraged me to sit down with my parents and tell them exactly how I felt and what I was experiencing. I was so afraid to tell them the truth, not wanting to hurt them. But, I realized that if I stayed silent and accepted the white elephant in the room, I would never feel better and might even grow up to be like my parents.

So, that evening in my mother's bright yellow, cheery kitchen, I asked my parents to sit down with me after dinner – as I had something important I needed to tell them. We sat through dinner silently as I started sweating, thinking about the moment of truth that I was about to spring on them. After cleaning up the dishes, my parents both sat down with worried looks and I told them exactly what I needed to say. In tears and emotionally caught up in my feelings, which turned out to be very powerful, I confessed how I felt that they didn't love me. They never told me I was OK growing up, never said that I mattered, never used the words "I love you," never hugged me and showed their affection to me. It always seemed cold and hostile at home. I was always stressed out and took my insecurities out with food and later with binge drinking to control all the anxiety that came with my feelings. I told them that my perception of their negativity and coldness as a married couple was really affecting me and causing me to become depressed and to feel very lonely and unloved. I told them that this was no longer acceptable and that I really wanted things to change. I couldn't go on living this way any longer.

This emotional watershed moment changed all of our lives, forever. My sister, who was living away in College at the time, later learned about my confessions years later. But, my parents were never the same. As we all stood their sobbing, they confessed to me how difficult it was for them growing up and said that they, in fact, never received the kind of love and affection from their parents either. Not that their parents didn't love them. They just didn't know how to show it. They agreed that they would try harder. And, then, I did the unmentionable thing: I got up, wiped off my tears and standing there, put my arms around them both and told THEM that I loved them and that they mattered to me! And, that I intended to use these very words and those very arms to always remind them how I wanted them to treat me. It was like I became the parents to them, acknowledging my love for them and that they mattered a great deal. God only knows what possessed me or where I got the strength to carry this mission of hope and healing through.

This isn't a story about some touchy-feely kid who needed a big squeeze from his mama and papa. It's a story of emotional starvation and deprivation, and what it does to mess-up people for life. It's about internalizing emotional scars, recognizing their power and potential consequences and then making a decision to heal broken and dysfunctional feelings that prevent us from changing our lives and living the happier, loving lives that we deserve. .

I am happy to report that over the years, my relationship with my parents completely transformed to something wonderful and full of joy. We regularly say to each other how much we love each other; we embrace and show our love physically and emotionally. We share our pain, struggle, love and hope. And, we have all become good friends who support and care for one another as decent human beings. There has been a great deal of vindication as well as gratitude for a job well done. But it was a huge amount of work on my part. My story, however, has just begun. Stay with me for awhile longer!

Naturally, we all have our limitations, and that is more than OK. We are all human and nobody is perfect. We have our share of good days and not so good days. And, sometimes, when we don't get into our own way, we begin to move forward. To help each other heal and grow. This is the way it was always meant to be, but somehow we forget the importance of true love and how to communicate this effectively to each other as child and parent. So, in the absence of a normal childhood, we have to learn to love ourselves and become comfortable in our own skin.

Life is a Choice

While it might seem obvious but not always acted upon, we have a choice in everything we do. We can decide to have life "do us," or we can choose to "do life." I chose to "do life." But, it came at a price and an amazing amount of pain (much more on this later).

I want to tell you another story – something that happened to me recently and became the latest impetus for me to sit down and write this book. You see, I was driving to work one morning – about 45 minutes from door-to-door, from Bradley Beach to the Historic Town of Cranbury, N.J. where I have worked as a temporary "Inn Keeper" at the, very historic, 1780 Cranbury Inn for the last year. During the commute and whenever in the car, I love to listen to U-Tube, Ted Talks and favorite Podcasts on a variety of topics that interest me. I've also learned and trained to be a Life Coach, schooled in a variety of techniques and methods, all on my Smartphone while driving. How great is that!

This day, however, was different. I stopped the car to sob while listening to an Oprah Winfrey "Super Soul Sunday" podcast from an author and former inmate, Shaka Senghor. Shaka had just completed a new book called "Writing My Wrongs" about making amends and forgiveness... He was talking about how he ended up shooting a man to death and being sentenced to 19 years – mostly in solitary confinement - all because of the way he grew up and the poor decisions he made by not having a family and parents who taught him right from wrong and who loved him and told him so. He turned to the streets and drugs, then to the gangs and then to a downward spiral of violent crimes. He used the streets, as did all his friends, to validate his self-worth and to learn how to grow up to be "a man." He didn't know any better. How would he? He was largely left to grow up all by himself. His teacher for growing up and feeling good about himself and his world were the streets and his gang.

He found his spiritual awakening and the light of understanding and forgiveness in prison and through the mother of the slain victim as well as by his own orphan son who wrote him letters telling him that he was, in fact redeemable. Both victims offered him forgiveness for his heinous crime and for salvation to make his wrongs right. He seemed so amazingly brave and full of courage to do what he did. Despite what happened to him, he came out the other side of pain and decided to help others not experience the same fate that he did. His details a little different than mine, but with the same ending!

I understand, as I went through a similar situation and awakening, which never needed to occur. Perhaps, if I had the nurturing, expression of love and understanding and validation that I was OK, loved and good just the way I was when I was a young child, I, too, might not have acted out in regrettable ways. It took me so many years to finally figure out that I had all the power I would ever need to learn how to love myself and to know that I am just perfect the way I am. I'm good enough and loved with or without all my character defects and flaws. I just carried the deep resentments of my past and lacked the tools to effectively move forward in my own life.

Why do so many of us have to struggle with poor self-image, lack of self-esteem, never feeling good enough and loved enough, always trying to fill that hole in our soul with something that will make the pain go away? When we're children, we don't have a choice, as these are conditions of us growing up. But, as we mature into our teenage years, where we begin to have a choice and commence letting our parents know our version of right and wrong, good and bad, the dynamic changes drastically as does our reaction to all this. Later, we are the adults and, consciously or unconsciously, we make a series of decisions that determine our path and fate. What kinds of decisions have you made?

Pain & Failure as a Path to Success

Life is not a straight line – despite our best intentions. It may very well be the shortest distance between two points, but try living your life that way. Clearly, life is not linear. Actually, it hovers somewhere in between two-steps forward and one-step back, life and death, up and down, stuck and unstuck, good and bad, and happy and sad -- depending upon how you look at it. If I had to best describe it, it's very much like the dance of your normal heart beat on an E.K.G. – although don't ask me to define the word "normal." I'll leave that for you to decide!

There are times, however, when the tough get going with great enthusiasm and jet propulsion and then just fall off the edge of a cliff, like I once did. Rather than looking at life as difficult, impossible and as a failure, I choose to paint quite a different picture. And I have every reason to say so, because I came out the other side of complete failure and have lived to tell the story.

You see, I firmly believe that everything that happens to us happens for a reason, for our own good, AND for the very best. I know this seems odd and fatalistic in many ways, but let me explain: Life doesn't just happen to us. It is all part of our life plan and there are no coincidences. We work so hard to live our lives, but fail to see that most of the time we aren't really living, but are so busy obsessed with the past and worried about the future that we fail to see that life is right in front of us, here and now.

As the saying goes, life is 10% what happens to us and 90% what we do about it. I believe this to be true, full of ancient wisdom, and one of the more important lessons I have learned to date. If we do it this life thing right, we "do" life; it doesn't "do" us. The latter is where all the pain and suffering comes in. It was, it is AND it will always be this way – whether we like it or not, good or bad, happy or sad – it is all our personal cosmic game plan. Essentially, whatever happens to us is our exact and precise fate. Our spiritual healing and evolution is our primary purpose and mission in this life and on this planet. Our job is to figure out and craft the 90% that we can change and make the best of it each and every day!

Adversity has proven to be my greatest teacher. For most of my life, though successful at times, I simply wasn't very teachable. I thought I knew it all and could do it better than you. I struggled with depression, anxiety, and addiction. And, while the teacher was always there, I refused to let her in. Some people die from too much adversity -- as I nearly did. The stresses, trials and tribulations turn out to be too much.

Then, there are those who accept adversity as a way of life. They end up succeeding despite all their war scars, bruises and broken hearts they have accumulated along the way. This is just the price we pay to get where we really wanted to go. That is me. I'm a fighter, but fighting the wrong way and for the wrong thing nearly killed me twice. I should have been fighting for my own freedom – freedom from self, that is!

Today, I'm thrilled to report that I'm deeply happy, enormously grateful, passionate and living my life with intense meaning and purpose. From time-to-time, I even experience joy. I am full of hope and possibility. My soul, which had felt "dead" and empty for many years, no longer has a hole in it and is filled to the brim. Yeah, I still have moments of fear, moodiness and anxiety, but nothing compared to all those years before calamity struck. I have serenity, certainty, all my needs are being met – not always in my time, but there is nothing that I lack today. In fact, I'm just loving my new life. I am here to share this with you and to show you exactly what I did to get this way.

I'm going to teach you how to start over, despite not wanting to. Even if you've lost everything and are down and out – even hopeless like I once was, I'm going to show you how to reboot everything from scratch and to harness the many assets you already have and turn them into golden nuggets. I'm going to share with you why you must have hope. For without hope, you fail to see life's many gifts and enormous opportunities. Without hope, you will fail to make the decisions you will need to change.

But, if you don't have any hope for now, I'm going to ask you just to believe that I believe that you can. I don't just believe, but I know you can. You just have to make the decision that you are going to change everything, including yourself, and then change others in the process. Then you have to get ready to be willing, honest and open-minded to the possibilities.

Why Me?

Victim or hero? You tell me. Clearly, it's a choice that you make when life becomes difficult and overwhelming. I believe that a lot of how you think about life and its many traumas is all about attitude and perspective. Is the glass half filled or half-empty? Are things really so bad or are my feelings just lying to me. Are my emotions and feelings fact? Or is my depression and negativity telling me the truth?

If everything happens for a reason, for our own good and for the very best, then how can things really be so bad? Or are these trials and tribulations just the many important, life lessons that we are supposed to learn and grow from? Is everyone else to blame or are we accountable?

What's more, I'm going to show you how to get through nearly everything, including absolute despair and desperation. You are going to see how to inspire yourself and then to inspire others. How to instill hope in yourself, and then help your fellow man to do the same. How to be and stay happy. You have the strength to overcome just about everything – even though things might seem dim at the moment.

I want to share with you my story – a story that will make you cry, but will give you hope and inspiration that you can start your life over, despite your gravest adversities and difficulties. That is actually what life is all about. How we handle adversity and grow and change in the process.

Everyone favors a winner and frowns upon a loser. Actually, some of history's greatest "winners," heroes and prophets turned out to be people who lived through their own personal hell. But, that wasn't the end of their story. The tale didn't end until they overcame every possible roadblock to eventually succeed and prosper. And, in nearly all cases, they taught others the hard lived lessons that they had learned and were then able to inspire entire generations. People from all walks of life: Abraham, Jesus, Buddha, Moses, Gandhi, Mother Theresa, Abraham Lincoln -- all had difficult lives and were successful in overcoming all adversity – so much so that they helped changed the world. They inspire us, teach us, and help lead us on our way to our own personal victories.

It is worth taking a look at several really famous people who succeeded after first failing once, twice or many times. They each overcame all adversity despite their epic failures. Just Google them on your phone and you will find plenty. Most notable, according to lifehack.org, are Billionaire, Oprah Winfrey, who was raped and abused as a child, lost her baby at 13 and then went on to stardom, inspiring many, despite being told that her Day Time Talk Show would never make it in Chicago. Then, there's Steven Spielberg, whose movies grossed more $9 Billion and received three Academy Awards, but his first movie was rejected twice by the University of Southern California's School of Cinematic Arts. Thomas Edison was told by his teachers that he was "too stupid" to learn anything. Walt Disney was told he "lacked imagination and had no good ideas. Reportedly, he also struggled with drugs and depression as did Alfred Hitchcock. J.K. Rowling was broke, depressed, divorced single mother was rejected by every publisher she submitted her "Harry Potter" series of books to, as being unpublishable. And, finally, consider this: "I've missed more than 9000 shots in my career. I've lost almost 300 games. 26 times, I've been trusted to take the game winning shot and missed. I've failed over and over and over again in my life." Guess who made that statement? If you said Michael Jordan, who was told he didn't qualify for his high school basketball team because he was too cocky, you'd be right. Then, there are the rest of us ordinary folk who have struggled so valiantly with so many afflictions, trials and tribulations, and have lived to tell our stories. You and me!

This book is about learning how to overcome adversity and to start over at any time when the going gets rough. I will teach you how the tough get going, despite your feelings of hopelessness, depression, anxiety, fear, and incredible pain. The Human will is an amazing thing, and when combined with faith and trust and the necessary tools to learn to live a good and happy life, nothing can stop you but, of course, yourself.

We Are Reborn Every Single Day!

Every single day is an extraordinary opportunity to start over and get things right. Action and progress are what counts. Perfection sounds good, but is never what it appears to be. It is some mirage painted by the story tellers in business and entertainment. It is never real. There is no destination. Life is all about the journey. That's what we miss most of our lives and need to take stock of. Nobody but us is measuring ourselves. We are our worst own enemies. We never seem to give ourselves a break or the benefit of the doubt. We go out of our way to self-sabotage things when they start going well. We are certainly not usually our own best friend and don't always know how to take care of ourselves when we are down and out. We can't accept our lot in life and are more comfortable with the "misery" we know all too well as our reality. Really, what is wrong with this picture?

The Enemy Within

We tend to be our own worst enemies. We form irrational beliefs about the world. We struggle with negative attitudes and self-defeating thinking. We think things are bad or not good enough even when they are. We beat ourselves up for not having a good enough job or not reaching the highest heights. We are never Ok with what we have – but always seek something different, better. We want what the "Joneses" have. We think life on the other side of the fence is greener, better. Everyone seems to be happier, more fulfilled, more successful. Who are we comparing ourselves too? If you really want to know the truth, these people aren't any happier than you are. They are just as focused on externals to make them happy as the next guy. The truth is, they will end up sorry for not taking stock of the wonderful blessings that are right in front of them! Unquestionably, we are our own worst enemies. If only we could get out of our own way!

Lack of Self-Esteem, Self-Pity, and Self-Doubt Got You Down?

I've struggled most all my life with a variety of emotional, psychological and spiritual maladies. Self-doubt, lack of self-esteem, self-pity, anger, resentment and fear were my cocktail of choice (more on that later) and the usual suspects in disrupting my life, peace-of-mind and serenity.

I never let this define me, however. I was determined, with my then big ego and "I'll show you" grandiosity to become successful. I was sure that with my strong will and intense desire to succeed, I could do anything and live a life full of the fine fruits of my labors. I was willing to work hard, roll-up my sleeves and do whatever it took to break through to a more successful life than my parents had.

What Happens to People Who Don't Feel Loved Enough?

We self-destruct in so many clever ways. We act out in variety harmful and destructive beliefs, thoughts and actions. We form maladaptive ways of coping with our world. We feel the hole in our soul, that feeling of being "dead" inside with self-hurt, self-indictment, and self-loathing. We get angry when we feel our needs are not being met. We sabotage our ability to get the love and kindness we feel we need with those things that can't possibly meet our needs in healthy ways like addiction through substance abuse or negative behaviors like gambling or spending too much money. We look for love in all the wrong places and can't form healthy, life-sustaining relationships. We abuse others physically, emotionally, psychologically spiritually with anger and hostility. We even kill ourselves because we can't take the pain of not being loved or feeling good enough about ourselves. We commit crimes to get attention to falsely satisfy our needs. We rage, cry, scream out in exasperation and even take others hostage in a variety of ways just to be heard and understood.

These Statistics Don't Lie!

It is now estimated that an alarming 50 million people worldwide die each year from drug overdose and/or health related issues or complications – most of them undocumented. Suicide claims another one million victims, or one death every 40 seconds – mainly from those who couldn't find their way out from the grips of their unhappiness and dis-ease. For them, life became more painful than death!

But, this blight pales in comparison to an even bigger problem: Another two billion people struggle around the globe with depression and anxiety disorder. Of this, 220 million are children -- something that they learned from their parents or caretakers. That represents over a quarter of the entire global population of 7.6 billion struggle with pain and misery. Is that really possible? The cost to society, to our families and loved ones is beyond staggering. Clearly, the untreated "misery" business is crying out for help!

The addiction recovery industry in the U.S. alone has exploded to $35 billion in size. There aren't enough beds and addiction counselors in rehabs and detoxs to meet the escalating need from substance abuse. Another $1 – $2 Trillion more is sadly wasted each year on health care remedies that don't work. God only knows what the figures and statistics are worldwide. As the world gets more complex, challenging and stressful, more people young and old alike -- are falling victim to substance and behavior abuse, and untreated misery.

Addiction and suicide are now among the top 10 leading causes of death in the U.S. -- and that doesn't include the many others that never even make it into recovery. There are more people today struggling with addiction and drug and alcohol abuse than people who have cancer in the U.S.. Considering that the Surgeon General has stated that Addiction is a disease, those are pretty staggering numbers. This complex and incurable disease is progressive and fatal and kills absolutely if left untreated!

Addiction to opioids, and the resurgence of heroin use worldwide has reached epidemic proportions among young people. In fact, during the past decade alone, 143% more students between the ages of 18-"How to Love Yourself" have been admitted to recovery programs. Yet few schools are prepared to teach their students about the life hazards of addiction and difficulties with recovery.

Each week, I see several young people disappear and die from the many 12-step meetings that I attend. Addiction and suicide are equal opportunity epidemics, and all psycho-, socio-, economic- demographics are represented – even seniors over 60. Many of my friends share about the loss of loved ones that never even made it into recovery. And, that doesn't include the many people around us who love us that we take hostage in the process of our pain and misery. People can't handle the underlying pain and futility in their lives, and prefer to numb or anesthetize themselves to avoid dealing with reality. The fear of change keeps the addicted deep in the throes of the bondage of self. The substance abuse and misery are mere symptoms. *The real problem is usually never addressed, which is their deep life dysfunction and maladapted operating system for living that creates their overwhelming dis-ease and result in urges and cravings to use and act-out.*

"Dual diagnosis," what the medical community refers to as someone who is struggling with both emotional and psychological issues like depression and anxiety as well as addiction from substance abuse, is poorly understood and even worse – not easily or readily treated in this country – let alone the world.

There are hundreds of self-help, 12-step, cognitive and behavioral modification programs, some laser focused on rational and evidenced-based treatment and others employing spiritual and "higher power" approaches to recovery. The majority of "cures" by themselves, while helpful, don't work and last for most. Brutal honesty, accurate self-assessment, willingness, hope, raw courage, sufficient pain and an honest desire to discover our deeper spiritual truths are needed for successful and permanent change. So are learning how to ask for and receive help from others, getting out of self and a deeply rooted and acquired trust & faith in a source of strength greater than oneself. These keys to success require an-going support & commitment throughout one's life-cycle for true and lasting healing to occur.

Lastly, with the disintegration of the American family as a safe-haven for healthy emotional, psychological and spiritual growth and development, overall personal dysfunction, depression and anxiety disorders are on the rise. Combined with our overall addiction to texting, video games, obsessing on the web and with email, we seem to have lost the art of "human touch" and healthy eye-to-eye communication between people. Our kids no longer talk to us and to each other. They don't play outside in nature and the neighborhood like the baby-boomers once did. In fact, author and speaker, Simon Sinek, talks about many of the social and emotional dysfunctions of the Millenial generation – soon to be the largest segment of the population. The extended family and the family structure no longer exists in many homes – as many kids grow-up in single parent families or with caretakers or grandparents. More than 50% are victims of divorce. And, things are bound to get worse before they get better. I see evidence in the rooms of substance abuse recovery every day and also in my life coaching practice. Things are not good out there in happiness land. In fact, they are really bad and even frightening!

Education, love, compassion and helping others, along with the willingness and making the decision to change, is what's missing and in great demand. This book touches on them all and focuses on the tools this author has learned in order to adapt and stay alive and get happy through the school of hard work, hard knocks, pain, enormous struggle with pain and failure. I think by now, I should have been awarded a PhD in pain and suffering! But, I would exchange it any day for a golden heart of happiness I got free from all my hard work that I'm about to share with you!

What Does It Mean to Struggle with Feelings of Not Feeling Loved?

The best five-letter word I can think of is that it "sucks." Being depressed, anxious or feeling lousy about just about everything, including me, is not fun or liberating. While I'm not big on labels, when feelings or more permanent states of depression and those butterfly and insane feelings of panic and anxiety strike and define my experience and day, I know today that these are important signs for me to really check my motives, see what is going on underneath those feelings, and to challenge them for misbehaving and thinking that they can rule my life. It's also a signpost for me to call my circle of friends and advisors to get perspective and to get out of my own head – that little committee upstairs in that feeble brain of mind that keeps chattering nonsense to me!

Feelings aren't facts and that is by far the hardest thing I have had to learn. Logic, feelings and emotions don't mix and if they do, somebody is lying about their version of the truth. I can honestly say that when you are feeling depressed, sad, and uncomfortable or even feel like jumping out of your own skin, you must change your strategy and take a time out to see what is really going on.

There are so many great tools that I've learned to manage my fears, states of depression, moodiness, uncomfortability that keep me from acting out in harmful and negative ways. For example, I've learned to recognize the warning signs and triggers that make me feel "squirrely" and restless, irritable and discontent. I have also learned to take a time out and think the feeling through. What's more, I've learned to create better feelings and states of mind in the first place to avoid having to become overwhelmed by negative feelings. They are most usually all bogeymen anyway, and I know now how to call their bluff when they surface every now and then. Before this, however, they once consumed me and directed my thoughts and actions – which were mostly always bad. But, I have also learned to honor them and know that they are signs from a higher power of sorts to get right with my true purpose and motives in life. So, today, feelings are like traffic lights that get and direct my attention and then guide my actions.

As I continue to believe and preach, pain continues to be the touchstone of all meaningful change and has turned out to be my greatest teacher. Once I stopped fighting the feelings and emotions that surrounded all my painful experiences, I learned to accept them, question my motives and better understand the lessons that I was meant to learn from the specific experiences. I have learned to accept and move through painful moments in life as part of growth and evolution. When I get out of the victim role that leads me to believe that others are making me feel pain, I stop pointing the fingers of blame and allow those fingers to point right back at me. I need to examine more closely what is going on with me that am making me feel this expression of pain and what is really going on underneath the pain that is causing it. Most always, it is my irrational thoughts and beliefs that are triggering these negative feelings and I am ALWAYS the problem. So, acceptance of life as it is, not as I would have it or believe it should be, is always the answer. More on this later.

Please note that I am not a doctor or psychiatrist, though I have gotten to know quite a few in my day. So, I don't pretend to be able to diagnose your particular problem or issue. Nor can I tell you that your level of serotonin, endorphins and other "happy" neuro-transmitters and naturally produced chemicals in your body are low and deficient. I can, however, identify with your feelings and your many experiences with those feelings. I can also tell you how I have learned to manage these feelings to create better and more positive and rewarding outcomes. So, stay with me for a while.

What is Feeling "OK" Really All About?

I have come to believe that we weren't born in this life to stay suffering. Suffering and pain are states of mind – albeit important ones just like joy, peace-of-mind, serenity, and authentic happiness. Some people are able to naturally feel ok with themselves. For many of us, it is something that we must learn and create – as it doesn't come naturally for whatever reason – most of which I find unimportant lately. I can say that it is not my preferred state and mood of choice – being miserable that is.

I know that feeling OK is a verb, an action word of sorts. It takes work to create self-esteem and self-love, but once you learn how to use the many tools available to you to induce and change your states without mood-altering substances, you can change your thoughts, your beliefs and your states of mind and your mood fairly easily. You can also work to create long-term and even permanent happiness by changing everything in your life – and I mean everything!

The important question is, what do YOU really want in your life. As a certified Life Coach and student of empathy, compassion, humility and gratitude, and an observer of the human condition, I can tell you that the story you are telling me right now about yourself speaks volumes to your ability to satisfy your basic human needs. There are six big ones – four physical and two spiritual, and how you address them will ultimately determine your base level of satisfaction with life. We will spend more time on this later.

But, suffice it to say that once you begin to understand the negative and positive patterns in your own life, and then develop the level of honesty, open-mindedness and willingness necessary to change, you will be able to make the important decision to do things differently. Misery IS optional and besides physical causes, which may need to be addressed separately or may even be exacerbated by out of control emotions and beliefs, most of your negative and destructive feelings can be replaced with positive habits and good orderly direction that will create more happiness and fulfillment in your life and for those around you.

So, in short, feel love for yourself comes from a series of small decisions you make every day. You choose to be happy or sad. Yes, circumstances are part of this, and it is ok and important to feel your feelings. But, when you let them take you hostage, you are in trouble and you are no longer in charge of your own destiny. Now, your life is doing you. Not a good or enviable place to be. And, I do understand and feel for you. But, ultimately, you have to decide how you choose to live your life. Not me, your physician, psychiatrist or spiritual teacher. You are in control here. Not just occasionally, but all the time.

It's like looking at yourself in the mirror and saying that you must go on a diet and join a gym -- something that you perhaps promise yourself once a year on New Year's Eve. You really must know that looking good, being healthy and living a balanced life is work. It's not free. You have to exercise those muscles every day to reach and sustain weight loss, a firm and healthy body. You need to form new habits, routines and rituals. You need to do the same with your feelings and desired state of mind. If you want to be happy and feel comfortable in your own skin, you have to build those muscles that can help you to achieve and permanently sustain those goals AND your expectations. It's practice and a lot of it makes perfect!

<u>**How It Works**</u>

Here's how this book of self-love and self-healing works: First, it's, really very simple, but you will have to roll-up your sleeves and do the work. I will be with you every step of the say. It will take a great deal of honesty, open-mindedness and willingness for you to fully engage in the process of change. There are five major pieces to my "system." The **first** piece is knowledge, identification and awareness of the problem. My goal is to get you to open your eyes wide open and take a hard look at yourself. In the **second** section, we look at your roadblocks and then the positive keys to change. In the **third** section, we spend a great deal of time getting to know the real you and then examining the specific tools and strategies that I use to effect real and lasting change. The **fourth** section takes us past our anger, resentment and self-loathing to learn how to meet our needs in a healthier, permanent and self-sustaining fashion. Here, we explore how to satisfy our needs to heal our souls and begin on a spiritual journey to will keep us happy forever. And in the **fifth** and final section, we learn how to give this gift of self-love and deep joy to others who are still struggling. We learn how to give away what we were so freely given. We learn how to love others as we have come to love ourselves. This is where the permanent change takes hold and deepens. This is where you finally get free from your own past and step into the light of healing that will create true meaning and purpose in your life.

Now, I'd like to tell you my story, which shook me to the core of my being and changed my life forever!

Chapter II.

MY STORY

Everyone kept telling me that I had all the 'right stuff': Life is all about winning – we just need to make our own success. With hard work and unyielding effort, perhaps, life can be really good and we can make the best of it on our own willpower. I thought these to be immutable truths, but I was sadly mistaken!

I bought into a good part of this lie: The first sentence proved to be true. Life is beautiful and a gift – which took me far too long to understand and appreciate. But, the rest of this paragraph led me down a garden path that nearly killed me. My all too boastful pride and ego, collective fears, overwhelming insecurities and a general addiction of "more" drove me to leapfrog my inertia as a kid and catapult myself to what I thought was personal & professional success. After an initial burst of "success" during my 20's and early 30's – I believed that my forward momentum would simply last forever; that I could do no wrong and that this inflated balloon of "success" would never burst. I also convinced myself that I could and would continue to accumulate more toys and money, and make my parents and family proud. Little did I know, my definition of "success" was an illusion, and would never bring me to real and lasting happiness?

I tell this painful story and bare my soul to you in the hopes of helping others who also struggle making their own lives and success work. I am confident that my own tornadic, chaotic path to happiness will resonate with many others. My illusion of "success" finally turned on me and forced me to face the music.

Life was just happening to me. Sure, I thought I was the driver, but didn't have the knowledge and equipment to navigate it on my own. Before I understood what happened to me, I ended up very sad, addicted to drugs and alcohol, broken in jail, miserable, angry, anxious and very confused. I've done and accomplished so many wonderful things: Education, career, family, journalist, published author, successful entrepreneur, family children, house in the choice burbs, great schools and all the many trappings that go along with a "successful" life. Just how exactly could all this have happened to a guy like me? Beatles legend, John Lennon, reminds us that "Life is what happens to us when we're busy making other plans" He was so very right!

This year, I turned 60. Sadly, I paid dearly for this misguided stupidity during my 50's. This past decade proved to be a first class and stunning disaster, with me jumping off the cliff of life with no rope, except just enough with which to hang myself. I don't remember much of it now, as I ended up living in an utter haze on 15 medications, drunk, disabled, penniless, homeless and hopeless. I became an incurable Alcoholic & Addict, was terminally pissed-off and anxious, and fell into a deep and disturbing depression. My kids and ex-wife were afraid of me. I became riddled with anxiety, full of rage and cratered into an incredible and hopeless state of sadness. I eventually became the kind of guy and neighbor you would NOT want to hang around with on most social occasions and at cocktail or dinner parties at your house.

My fall from personal and professional grace was swift. Alcohol had become my master and gravitational pull downhill.   At 56, I ended up in Federal Prison. Around this time, I nearly died twice from acute alcohol poisoning and was no longer able to cope with life. I wished for the end to come fast as only the dying can know. I was bitter and angry. I lost my family and friends, my wealth and status, but mostly I lost myself to my untreated misery and disillusionment.

One of my many problems was that I chose to live in the problem, in an incredible state of denial, not understanding that my life had become an out-of-control ping pong ball -- without purpose or direction. I kept chasing after the holy grail of fame, fortune and success. Despite all my hard work and best efforts, I was simply lost and clueless as to how and why things didn't work out as planned. I must not have been given the instruction manual as a child on how to live a good and happy life. I certainly did not choose many things wisely!

When all things failed, I blamed my parents, my wife, my children, my career, the government, and my business partners - everyone but myself for my failures. I falsely believed that good intellect, keen instincts and unending drive would get me where I needed to go: Upwards and onwards, rich and famous, happy, successful and accomplished. Again, I was dead wrong.

Then I so rudely discovered that I would be going to prison. It was like a bad dream – a nightmare actually. It came on top of nearly 10 years of living a life and doing so many very important things wrong and unconsciously that landed me there. I finally came to the end of my "old" life with this massive crisis looming over my head and decided to change; to change everything I thought important to me and how I went about living my life. My life had finally gotten so bad that finality struck me as a possible reality. So, in an act of desperation, I chose to make a new beginning and to scrap the life that I once thought so wonderful, successful, important and precious and start anew.

The truth is that I was never truthful about my real problems and addictions with all the medical doctors, psychiatrists, addiction counselors or therapy professionals that tried to help me. Yes, they saw my pre-cirrhosis liver numbers and rapidly declining physical, mental and emotional state, looking on in horror as my condition and symptoms failed to improve. It's not their fault. They tried valiantly to fix me. But, how could they ever help me to get better and "recover" from whatever I said ailed me if I never told them what my problem really was: I didn't really understand what was causing my problems in the first place!

That's when everything changed for me – from the inside out! It was time for a complete overhaul and to reexamine everything – to create a new beginning as if it were going to be my last. At least, that's how it felt to me. I finally took an honest look in the mirror and realized that I didn't like what I saw. Strangely enough, for me, prison saved my life, because if I didn't receive what I refer to as my "Adult Time Out," I clearly was doomed to a sad and painful death of my own.

Prison was my rude and necessary awakening. My "bottom," and the accompanying pain that hung on to me like a bad smell, had not yet gotten unbearable. I needed to suffer some more, to go out and do more research and development on life until that "aha" moment finally clicked following my arrest.

Through the serendipity of ending up in prison, I discovered that I no longer had to live my life this way any longer – as an insane person who could no longer distinguish right from wrong, truth from deceit. I began to transcend all the pain I was experiencing, because, quite frankly, I just couldn't take it anymore. My life skills and strategies, including over 20 years in and out of 12-step recovery, detoxs and rehabs, along with lots of therapy and spiritual exploration simply weren't working.

So came the beginning of the end of my old life and the beginning of something entirely new. I discovered that I actually had a choice – that there really was a way out of this mess for good and that I didn't have to struggle and suffer the way I once did. As I began making better choices and surround myself with willing mentors, advisors and coaches, my fear and anxiety began to subside. Finally, I began living in the solution and slowly the problem began to fade away!

The choice to change everything in my life proved to be the best decision I ever made. Following an emotional, physical, mental and spiritual breakdown, I finally awoke to my own truth. In a fit of repeated humiliations and desperation, I discovered that the answers to my happiness had nothing to do with external factors, but I that I could change my life and its many outcomes by choosing to be happy from the inside out. I came to realize that with better choices, and a lot of re-education, there was nothing I couldn't handle or do.

If I was to be truly happy and free from my mangled and unhappy past, I had to drop the corrosive rocks of anger, resentment, doubt and self-pity which had been formidable and painful roadblocks to my happiness. I had to focus on the recovery of not just my alcoholism and addiction problems, but also my dysfunctional personality and life. I had to relearn everything I thought important, take a hard and serious look at myself and start all over with a clean slate. I had to forgive myself and others, clean house of my dysfunctional and old beliefs, attitudes and behaviors. What's more, I had to take responsibility for and ownership of my life and actions, and no longer live in my own fantastic and delusional head. This was the beginning of a long, windy and strange trip I could not have possibly anticipated nor planned for.

This physical, mental, emotional and spiritual transformation is a process and there is no longer any destination or fixed time schedule. It involves the WHOLE person – not just our thinking, emotions or spiritual condition. There is, however, a deep sense of urgency to make up for what I often see as "lost time." I know that believing this statement brings additional risk, and that I need to slow down. I say this because I wasted most of my life misguided, not knowing right from wrong, good from bad. I did know that despite my successes, I was like a tornado whirling through the lives of everyone around me – causing constant friction and chaos. If only I knew then what I know now, perhaps things would have been different. But, sadly they weren't. So, now I do know the difference and have made a conscious choice to do everything differently.

Allow Me To Introduce You To Your New Life!

Making life work and living it well are both an obligation and a choice! Acknowledging your own pain and struggle, and then making the decision to take the necessary actions to achieve your true potential, to capture the brilliance, value and virtue of your own life -- this is your destiny. We must all use our time here on earth to grow and help others before our time runs out.

Yet, many of us don't know how to "do" life well. We get caught up, trying to get to the greener grass on the other side of the fence -- not fully knowing why and with what consequences or rewards. Many of our fellows are struggling and are clamoring for help. Our youth and people of all ages are challenged with terminal unhappiness and are dropping like flies from the dis-ease that is our user-unfriendly earth. The opioid explosion and other addictions are continuing to fan the flames of emotional and spiritual malaise. But, you certainly don't have to be an alcoholic or an addict to know what it's like to struggle! In our tumultuous and ever-complicated world, life can be plain hard.

If only getting the life we really wanted was so easy and we could just fix it all now on demand. Looking over the fence, we see others succeed in relationships, love, work and personal and professional pursuits while we find our own life to be so unacceptable.

When we look back after many years, much of our life seemed so unplanned -- uncharted. The truth is that we made many choices – little, small ones either consciously or unconsciously that got us here.

The Things We Need To Fix:

Let's examine some of the areas where many of us struggle to see if you can identify with some of the facts, feelings, challenges and emotions. They may not all apply to you, but some things might stick to you more than others:

- ✓ **Lack of Self-Esteem/Poor Self Image:** We often feel less than, not good enough, insecure in so many ways.

- ✓ **A Hole in Our Soul:** There is just something big missing from our life. Our essential needs are not being met. We feel empty and alone, even "dead" inside, and without solutions to fixing the hole in our soul. We often can't put our finger on it, but it hurts, we are lonely and don't feel loved or love-able. We hurt in so many ways and just can't figure out how to fill the empty void – this very sad and hopeless feeling.

✓ **Never Comfortable in the Moment:** Obsessed or stuck in the past or anxious, worried and/or fearful about the future.

✓ **Full of Fear and Anxiety:** We're often full of fear and anxiety. Sometimes it seems irrational and we can't seem to control it.

✓ **Anger, Resentment, Jealousy, Self-Pity, Self-Doubt** and a host of other negative emotions are often present and getting in our way. It often seems overwhelming and we don't even know where to start to fix them.

✓ **Restless, Irritable & Discontent:** We're never satisfied and nothing seems to feel right, fit or make us happy. We have never had the confidence or strength that we could be happy and successful.

✓ **Depression, Anxiety, Sadness:** Yep, we have struggled from time to time and maybe are even there right now. Our depression has occasionally gotten bad enough that we thought about or considered hurting ourselves. We are often anxious and even sad and can't help but feeling this pit in our stomach or tears of frustration.

✓ **Self-Centered & Self-Absorbed:** Our primary focus and obsession is on us and our problems and needs. It's often hard to think about the needs of others.

✓ **Overly Sensitive, Childish & Grandiose:** We are very touchy over what people think about us. We aren't always the most mature in the way we react and process life and we think we are more than, perhaps, we really are.

✓ **Egomaniac with an Inferiority Complex:** We tend to be headstrong in our opinions and presumption of grand stature, but right underneath our frail surface, we're crying like babies and very insecure. If only our bark was really as loud as our bite, then you might actually have to contend with us.

✓ **Bitterness, Remorse, Blame:** We're getting older and feel it is too late to change. Our lives came up short and we are so mad and angry at those that are responsible! Life has been so unfair to us. We do a lot of blaming and everyone else seems at fault.

✓ **Uncertainty:** Everything seems so uncertain and unreliable. Our life is constantly in flux and unpredictable.

✓ **Not Fulfilled in Job or Career:** We are successful, but never put it all together. We don't know exactly how to create a clear path to get where we think we should go. We either don't have the skills, education, knowledge or wherewithal to move forward in our jobs, careers and we really don't like what we do for a living. Or maybe we're unemployed and can't even get or keep a job.

✓ **Relationships:** Not happening in this department either. We want love so badly, but just don't know how to find or keep it. Our relationships never last very long and if they do, they seem inadequate and unbalanced. We might even be lonely.

✓ **Significant Other:** We should be in love and be loving to our soul mate. What's with this and why has this not happened? It all seems so unfair!

✓ **Friends:** Don't have many and the ones we do have are just lacking.

✓ **Family:** Dysfunctional parents or siblings — we are always arguing and feeling hurt and unloved. If only we could fix all the conflict and negative emotions.

✓ **Self and Self-Image:** We are mostly insecure and uncomfortable in our own skin. We have an inadequate self-image and struggle with self-pity and never feel we are enough. We are often uncomfortable with so many things. We hate the way we look, wish we were thinner, bigger, more handsome or pretty, smarter, funnier and popular with everyone. We are just unhappy with ourselves and wish we could change.

✓ **Direction & Goals:** Our lives seem to have taken us somewhere unexpected and unwanted. We thought we should have ended up somewhere else, with someone else with something different. We don't really have much direction nor do we have goals that we can achieve. It feels like we are rudderless and will never achieve our destination.

✓ **Feeling Misunderstood:** We don't feel understood by others and this upsets us and feels unfair.

✓ **Externals:** We want to be richer, have more things and success, perhaps be famous or be someone that others recognize or admire. We struggle with the disease of "more." If only I had more money, a prettier girlfriend, a better job, a hotter looking car, more popular friends, had more vacations in more exotic places…then my life would be better and I would be happier and complete. Nothing ever seems to satisfy us for very long., no matter how much of it we obtain.

✓ **Success:** If only we were successful like someone else -- this one or that one. I'm going to get there someday, even if it kills me.

- ✓ **Abuse:** We either punish ourselves by beating ourselves up, abusing drugs and/or alcohol or an addictive pattern or behavior or we abuse others perhaps emotionally or maybe even physically.

- ✓ **Religion or Spirituality:** We resent or don't care for the religion of origin and don't really believe or know how to connect with God. We'd like to, but our prayers are mostly the fox-hole type out of desperation. Our prayers never seem to get answered.

- ✓ **Happiness, Serenity, Joy, Peace-of-Mind?** Missing in action - if it even ever existed. Maybe we remember being happy as young children, but, now we feel stuck in a rut and find happiness and peace-of-mind fleeting and impossible to sustain!

Does any of this resonate with you? If so, you are not alone. Much of the world struggles a little or a lot with some or even all of these feelings and emotions from time to time or quite often. Unhappiness, getting stuck and not feeling fulfilled in life is way too common. Life is so darn complicated and the pain never seems to end. Everything just seems a struggle with no end in sight. This is not how I want to live, but I really don't know how to change my situation. I've tried so many things, but nothing works for long or at all. There's got to be a better way!

Time for Change

Each breath you take today is the best time to change – a golden opportunity to repurpose and reboot yourself and your life. There is every reason to have HOPE and to believe that things can change. NEVER give up that wonderful sense of hope! I didn't and neither do you. All it takes is a decision and a leap of faith. You have everything to gain and nothing to lose – except for your misery which I will happily refund. You have every reason to have hope and to believe that there is something better waiting for you. But, first you need to summon your trust and faith that with great and concerted effort, you can and must change. And to that end, I've written this book to save you from yourself. You've already made the decision to reach out and ask for help.

So, put down the bat, give yourself a much deserved break and spend the next few days together to learn "How to Love Yourself." Let's take your deep-seeded pain and despair and transform it into positive action and meaningful change. Together, we can and will make a difference in your life and the lives of others. The rest of our time on this planet is yours and mine, as we still have our lives to live on purpose and to teach our children and loved ones well for future generations.

No doubt your present pain and struggle resonate deeply within you. Together we are going to consider and make a series of new choices and decisions that will finally help you break free from the yoke of self-abuse and inaction that has kept true joy and happiness from your life. What you will find in the pages ahead is a unique message of hope and positive action. Share it with those you love and who love you. Take responsibility for how you feel and what you do and how you think, because these are three of the most important things that you CAN control. May you all surrender to the deeper answers within and to a happier, more joyful beginning!

"How to Love Yourself" reveals the many lessons we have learned from life's blunders, mistakes and humiliations, and details those attitudes, thoughts and actions we must continue to initiate daily in order to finally live good, purposeful, productive, meaningful and happy lives permanently.

My hope and wish for you is that you seize this powerful opportunity to get real with yourself. To look honestly at the many choices you have made that got you where you are today. And to harness the courage to identify and confront those areas of your life that you are not happy with and that are begging for attention and to change them once and for all.

Learning To Live In the Solution!!

"How To Love Yourself" is about exploring and adopting achievable solutions to life's greatest dilemmas, and learning how to live a good, happy and fulfilling life on a daily basis. It is not about focusing on the problems that brought us here – but rather the motives and choices we made that brought you to seek new choices and make new decisions to change.

What does a solution-focused life consist of? How do we get to have and continue to grow such a good life? How do we avoid once and for all relapsing into old and unhealthy and potentially fatal attitudes, beliefs, thinking and behavior? And, finally, how do we actually make these changes and let go of our past? That's job number one and what we are here to answer together.

The Help We All Need, But Are in Denial of or Just Too Proud To Accept

While I do believe that some people are authentically fulfilled and happy, most of us ordinary folk struggle with bouts of unhappiness or disappointment in the daily course of our lives. Some of us are better at dealing with these moments than others, and some of us just don't know how to deal with the trials and tribulations that seem to always cling to them. Perhaps they were just born that way and there's nothing they can do about it. They "stuff" their problems under that big pile under the rug and just do life the best they can. We all know the kinds of dis-ease that come from that futile, unfulfilled life of mental and emotional hide and seek.

Others need professional help or are starving for love, attention or validation. Many feel empty, alone or unfulfilled, without purpose and meaning, without direction or are isolated without a support network. Maybe nothing seems to go your way. You feel like you got a raw deal and somehow life is nothing but a struggle. Some days you feel OK and things are manageable. But, maybe these feelings are fleeting and few and far between – a more routine pattern of your life. Maybe your unhappiness or inability to cope like "normal" people do has caused you to abuse alcohol, drugs, sex or you gamble, or to turn your frustration into rage and anger that you often inflict inwards towards yourself -- anything to provide that relief that you so desperately have come to call your friend, your place to go, your escape.

And, maybe your life has gotten so bad that you can no longer stop these negative and harmful behaviors which have led to general turmoil and self-loathing. You so hate the world for doing this to you! Everyone else is to blame. You are in such a state of denial. And, maybe nobody knows of your unhappiness or misery. Not even your doctors or shrink, your spouse, parents or children. Not even your best friend, although they probably suspect something is deeply wrong and disturbing you. They are all so concerned for you! Little did you know how much your problems affect them, too.

Eventually, your "problems" become a state secret that you will go to the grave with. Nobody will ever know and you will die a proud and noble death one day. Or maybe you've already considered death as an option. If only luck and fortune would come your way and soon. Then, it will all be OK. Or will it ever be? How utterly insane, but real is this thinking??

The Power of Love & How It Helps Us to Heal Our Lives and Sustain Us

Love is always the answer. More books and poems have been written, music has been written, songs have been sung, art has been painted or sculpted, lives have been lost, and gifts have been given in the name of love than perhaps any other commodity on the planet.

Love is the universal language of the heart and it is eternal. It is an action word. The more you have or grow love within yourself, the more heal yourself and heal others. The healing power of love is amazing. It is perhaps the most powerful and effective antidote to the many ills that mankind suffers with. Sadly, we often have to look hard to find it in this seemingly cruel, impersonal and heartless world. Everything often seems so negative out there – from the news, to politics and government to the still warring nations, people and systems that are supposed to help us. Terrorists and terror reign supreme and guns can't always silence them. They hurt in their heart and are misguided by their own soul sickness and lack of loving nourishment. They are acting out in horrific and abysmal ways.

All we need is love. If only it were so simple. We struggle with so much isolation and loneliness, technology, the great facilitator of economies, social networks and people, can also create the walls that separate us from one another. We find ourselves so connected to the internet and to our emails and text messaging that we often forget to look each other in the eye, face-to-face, human-to-human, soul-to soul.

The ultimate answer to the pangs of aloneness and separation is love. To feel love and to be able to be loved. It can solve even the most complex of maladies. When people speak from the heart and not the head, everything seems to change. The negativity and misunderstanding between people quickly melt away under the incredible healing heat and power of love's amazing grace. Truly love is divine and God-given.

The heart and soul are very connected. We will spend a great deal of time on how to build a really healthy relationship with both of them, as the soul lives and speaks through the heart. And, the heart and soul are divine flickers of the eternal and incredible grace that our creator wants us to have and to feel. It is very natural to love and be loved, and it your God-given right. Nobody can deny you this experience of incredible satisfaction and infinite joy that comes from the act of love. Not sexual, but the grace of God, the divine energy in the universe that makes us who we really are.

Feeling loved and comfortable in your own skin is truly an inside job. The only way to get love is to give it. That is the shortest distance between the two points of misery and happiness. So, in order give love, you have to feel loved and good about yourself in the first place. You have to build self-love first and then you can build enough trust and courage to start to show it.

So this simple, yet complex book is about learning how to love yourself no matter what. Whether you are a hermit, incarcerated in solitary confinement as I once was for eight days, hate yourself and everyone else around you, or the President of the United States and master of the free world, you must learn to love yourself and to then give that love to everyone else you can. This is how you will heal yourself and the world. One person loving themselves one person at a time.

The Basic Components of this Five-Step Program to Love Yourself:

Repairing the heart and learning how to build self-love requires that we learn new skills while working hard to heal our soul – the source of all love. Healing our soul is our primary purpose in life and on earth. When we don't feel good about ourselves or are constantly in pain and struggling with negative feelings, we have work to do. Negative feelings come from negative beliefs and result in harmful and negative actions. Nothing good comes out of a sense of poor self-esteem than, perhaps, our desire to no longer feel this way. Absence makes the heart grow fonder, but pain is the touchstone of all true change. Pain is not a good thing, but is necessary as a way to understand what we need to do to change our pain to joy and happiness.

So, let's examine the five key pieces to feeling good about ourselves and feeling loved by others and ourselves:

Self-Love: We all need to feel loved. This is a basic human need and is our God-given right. If we don't feel loved by others, we are separated from this vital life force which makes the world go around. The result of this separation or absence of love in our lives is our feeling that we are just not OK. We blame ourselves and everyone around us for not allowing us to feel love in our lives. We don't understand how powerful this feeling less than or not good enough to justify getting love, so we try to replace this feeling of inadequacy with things that will never satisfy us. That is how people become addicted to substances and maladaptive behaviors. That is why people end up hating themselves and others. When this basic human need is not met, that of love and connection (more on this later), the basic human operating system is disrupted and runs out of gas. Love is the fuel that we all need to feel a part of the world and having our love tank filled up is critical to our long-term survival and happiness. Science has already proved this all out to be true. Only we can fix it by making the decision to change.

Self-Worth: Our sense self-worth, or that we are worthy of feeling significant and worthy of praise and consideration by others has a lot to do with how we feel about ourselves. We learn self-worth from our parents or guardians growing up. It is both learned and manufactured internally within us. Our D.N.A. is pre-coded with love, but we have to first get it and then build upon it.

When we feel this emptiness and sense of self-loathing that comes from not feeling good enough, we try to fill the void by doing harmful things. Often the absence of self-worth is self-loathing, which is horribly negative and potentially fatal if not intercepted.

Self-Esteem: Self-esteem is another skill that we learn from growing up. When we are not told
That we are good enough, pretty enough, smart enough, sexy enough, we start to implode and feel less than, not good enough in the eyes of others. We seek their approval, but don't get it. The only way people who lack healthy self-esteem can build it is by learning to do esteem-able things. We have to discover on our own that we are, in fact, good enough and don't require anybody else's approval. We can learn to build our self-esteem by doing the things that make us feel good about ourselves each and every day. This is a big part of the inside job that is ahead of us.

Self-Care: People who don't like themselves or don't feel they are not good enough or deserving of love have a difficult time learning to be good to themselves. They don't feel deserving of the self-image that they really want and crave, but can't get from others – especially their parents. So, self-care is how we learn to be good to ourselves and to take care of our essential needs. Not only is this a critical part of our need for self-preservation, but it is the only way that we can help build the self-esteem, self-love and self-approval that we need to replace those feelings of insecurities. We will also learn to change our beliefs so that we can chase the bogeyman away that is caused by our negative feelings. Again, we will learn that feelings aren't facts, and often lie to us.

We will learn a variety of healthy ways for us to care for ourselves and become the most important person in our lives. It's not about being selfish, but about being responsible to ourselves and the others who rely on us to love them. It's very much like the metaphor of putting on your oxygen mask on first before putting on your child or loved one. What good are you if you can't breathe? You certainly can't help another when asphyxiation is knocking at your front door. Love is like air. You need to secure it first yourself and then you will have enough to spare for everyone else.

Validation: YOU MATTER! "I'm OK, You're OK," the 1969 bestselling self-help book by Thomas Harris, talked about the transactional analysis method of healing therapy for solving problems in life. What it really boils down to is satisfying a basic human need to know that that you are at your very core – your essence – good and acceptable in your eyes and the others of your peers and loved ones. You need to feel OK to survive and thrive in the world. You need to know without hesitation or doubt that <u>YOU MATTER</u>. If you don't feel OK, you will overcompensate finding ways to make yourself to feel OK. This state of not feeling OK and not worthy of praise as a going human concern causes people to be insecure. It also causes many of us to stay miserable out of fear, become depressed, anxious, hopeless and even abusive to ourselves and others. Maybe addiction to substances or behaviors or even suicide become good looking or necessary options.

The price we pay as individuals and as a society is enormous when our inability to be validated by others in life is withheld. Our parents are the first place we find validation. When we feel that we are not loved or loveable, we can never feel validated. When we are told that we are not good enough or worthy enough, this creates an enormous hole in our soul and we will never be able to feel it. I can't tell you enough how my own inability to be validated by my parents affected me to the core. It altered the course of my life as a child and I paid dearly for not feeling valid as a going human adult in many ways.

Learning How to Fix Those Things That are Broken:
Your Heart, Your Soul, Your Life

So, "Learning How to Love Yourself is going to help us learn how to fix the very things that you feel you are missing. It is this feeling that you ARE loved, esteem-able, worthy of praise and serious consideration by your peers and loved ones, that you are good enough, smart enough, good looking enough and capable enough that we are going to fix and change forever. I am also going to show you how to drop the very heavy rocks of resentment, anger and fear that have blocked you from being your best and most loveable self.

You never have to feel this way again. You will see how to forgive yourself and others for perceived harms done. I know, because I went through my own personal transformation to heal.

Today, my life is good and I have and continue to fill that huge hole in my soul and void in my life that I thought would never be repaired.   All the tools are available and ready to go. You just need to make a decision that you are both ready and need to change the way you feel forever. Once you start to apply these tools and exercise the new muscles, new routines, habits and rituals that we will explore together, you are going to feel the change. And, I assure you; you will be happy with the results and wondered why you waiting so long like I did. Save yourself the years of pain and agony that I experienced and give this gift to yourself and everyone that matters to you today.

The Power of Choice

We choose all the time – every day of our life. Many of these choices are unconscious and others conscious. And, many small choices accumulated to become part of bigger, more global or macro choices we made in the past -- choices like how to think and feel about ourselves, how to define who we are to the world, how to relate to others, how to take care of ourselves, the best way to identify and satisfy our dreams and desires, how to love and be loved.

We also choose to be victims when things don't go our way. When we become unhappy because our needs as human beings were not being met or we felt the world wasn't treating us the way we believed we deserved, we got angry, depressed, remorseful, became anxious revengeful and maybe even acted out in harmful or abusive ways. It's those very choices – both good and bad – that got us here to ground zero. We can't go back to change the past, but we can spend the time to understand our choices and how they led to our chronic unhappiness, and then choose to make better ones going forward.

Our Failure to Satisfy Our Basic Human Needs

While all humans have basic needs, it wasn't until Abraham Maslow "invented" a way to describe them that our inability to satisfy them was finally understood. In his "Theory of Human Motivation," Maslow described a hierarchy that included his observations of humans' innate curiosity. At the top of the pyramid is our need for Self-Actualization, then Esteem, Love & Belonging, Safety and, at the bottom, Physiological – a basic description of the pattern human motivations generally moves through.

The goal of all these basic needs is for us to achieve our highest potential as humans – Self-Actualization – or the opportunity to become our highest potential selves where our true purpose in life is fully grown and achieved.

According Life Coaching gurus, Tony Robbins, Chloe Madanes, Magali and Mark Peysha (my Life Coach Teachers), we all possess six core human needs. Those needs are for Certainty, Variety, Significance, Love & Contribution, Growth and Contribution. The first two are seen as needs of the personality and the last two are spiritual needs. Our emotional, spiritual and mental and psychic needs are more internal. Our physical, material and social needs deal with externals. Much of our dysfunction and unhappiness in life can be attributed to our inability and failure to satisfy these basic needs. When our choices result in unhappiness, a feeling of not being understood, not being sure, not having satisfactory options, we get stuck or feel that we're not making a difference in our lives and our world, the result is feelings of anger, rage, sadness, even depression and anxiety. That is our signal that it is time to examine our past choices and to make better decisions with more successful choices. All of this is within our power and ability.

Take a moment to ask yourself with brutal honesty, what area(s) of your life are you not happy with? What's lacking? What do you really want that you don't currently have? Is it love, self-esteem and self-worth, confidence, a feeling of accomplishment, joy, more and better relationships, more financial security? Maybe it is just peace-of-mind, and sense that everything is going to be alright, no matter what! I know with certainty that you already know the answer to this question. Perhaps, you just haven't been able to put it into words. Together, we are going to explore a number of ways to get you just want you need and want and to help the pain to go away for good.

Your Inalienable Right To Be Loved and Happy!

Love and Happiness are such a sought after, yet elusive commodities. It's OK to be feeling angry and unloved, but it's not OK to stay feeling this way. The choice to love and be happy or stay in misery, lonely, angry and victimized is a choice that we make every single day. At some point, we have to give up the fight to always be right and commit to change.

Everyone deserves to feel loved and to be happy and to be comfortable in their own skin, to have hope and to not be living in fear, to feel safe and be OK with their lot in life, to feel a sense of joy and accomplishment and self-esteem, to feel like they've made a difference in their world. Most importantly, EVERYONE deserves to be loved and to be able to love others. Not all of us feel this way and before it is too late, I'm going to show you that not only do you deserve all of the above, but you CAN and must have it. Under one condition if you're willing to roll-up your sleeves put down the bat and trust me long enough to take you through a journey that changed my life and could very well change your life, too. I've been through the ringer from childhood through my adult life, and I felt like certain days were going to be my last. I nearly gave up hope, and then finally crashed and burned. After so much excruciating pain, I gave up fighting and surrendered to a better way of living. I realized that I had to start living my life on purpose as if it were going to be my last. Because that's when the moment of clarity that I didn't have to and simply couldn't live this way any longer finally took root. I needed to change everything and keep focused on only those essential things that were going to free me from the pain of my past and lead me to greater joy and happiness. I've found that formula for living and now and I am happy to say, it works well when I work it! I'm going to share it with you in the hopes that you, too, can start living your life fully and not keep fighting the changes that can save your life. For me, it's a work in progress and one that I MUST practice and live honestly in all my affairs and in every aspect of my life every day.

Ready To Get Help?
Let me show you how. Email me directly at
fenton@lifecoach911.com or text me at
973-885-2839

Chapter III.
ROADBLOCKS TO LOVE & CHANGE

Now, it's time to get to work: Let's take this time to examine what exactly are the more common impediments to changing those things that are no longer working in your life and result in pain and disappointment. The more I focused on people's roadblocks, the further I discovered that there were a mountain of roadblocks that affect people from taking those important next steps to freedom and happiness. Most are fear-, self-centered or denial-based, but we have all learned to call them different things. While they all may not apply to you personally, the ones you can identify and relate to are important because their very existence blocks us from growth and change. So, let's try to understand the specific issues that may pertain to you. These are the ones that matter and identifying with them will help you to better see what it is that you need to work on going forward:

Fear

Excessive worry and fear kills and destroys happiness and prevents self-fulfillment. The first step in the process of changing everything in your life is appreciating and understanding that most of our actions and behaviors are fear-based. Fear is our old enemy, and we are too fearful of changing what we know has worked in the past. There are a thousand forms of fear. We are afraid of so many things that we can't necessarily put our finger on: all the "what ifs", second guessing, and lack of certainty of most everything. What if we get it wrong? What are people going to think about us? Our lives are full of free-floating anxiety in such a way that we can never be happy, and if we do it, are fleeting, temporary and not our natural state. Beyond the need for survival, flight or fight from our cave man days, the illusion of fear is both a self-imposed mirage (a figment of our imagination and a projection of the ego) and simply unwarranted and not real

I come from a long line of worry warts on my mother's side. Looking back, I now see how fear controlled their lives. My mother, her mother, my aunts, uncles and cousins were all full of anxiety and unjustified fears. It literally shaped and controlled their lives and mine, too. With all this worry and fear, how could it ever be possible to enjoy life? Or stay focused on the important things we're supposed to learn like loving ourselves and our fellow man, and making a difference in the lives of others and the world around us, let alone being able to experience happiness, joy or peace of mind. I didn't have time to think of these precious things as I was always too busy worrying or sitting in my anxiety and insecurities. Our family was always too miserable and afraid. Escaping reality seemed like the only good choice for me at the time. Sadly, living with anxiety and fear is tragic and has killed many people and maimed so many others. I was one of those people and I am telling you outright that you DON'T have to live this way anymore! When I'm prodded to think about it, which used to be often, when was the last time worrying about nearly everything ever had a positive pay-off? Mostly never! In his best-selling book, "Don't Sweat the Small Stuff," author Richard Carlson offers dozens of simple solutions for reducing and even eliminating worry from our everyday lives. I strongly suggest you study this excellent and easy to read book – as it just might help to change or even save your life.

We spend so much wasted time sitting in fear of our own shadows that we lose sight of what our real purpose and mission is for the day, week, year and stage of life that we risk not accomplishing most everything "important." Then, we end up sitting in our anger and feelings of resentment that we didn't accomplish what we needed to do or failed to get where we thought we had to go. We fear that we're going to lose something we already had or won't get something we think we really need or are, perhaps entitled to.

As the saying goes, "Tomorrow is a mystery, yesterday is history, and all we have is today." But, few of us really end up living in the day, in the moment, in the present and here and now. If we did, we would actually be living our lives on purpose and we wouldn't live in this senseless state of worry and fear. As President, F.D. R. often reminded, the only thing that we have to fear is fear itself." It's the bogeyman that we are afraid of. Nine out of 10 times, the things that we fear the most never come to pass. It ends up all just being a projection of our unrealistic expectations or irrational thinking (subjects we will address in greater detail later in this book).

But, dropping our fears is not so easy, and that is one of the very goals of this book. Once we learn to challenge those often negative attitudes and self-talk – all those irrational beliefs that lead to our fears, we start the process of setting our self-free of them. We become more able to become the master of our own destiny and to see things clearly for what they really are, not as we have so often wrongly imagined them. We learn to trust the process of Good Orderly Direction. No matter what happens, WE are always going to be OK, no matter what. We begin to pay attention to those very things that matter the most to us on a daily basis. One day we look back, and we are happy with the results. We never have to fear anything again.

Self-Centered Fear

This character defect also falls under the category and roadblock of fear, but it is unique in the following way. Our selfishness, self-centeredness are typically the root of most all our problems and perceptual distortions. When we are so hyper-focused on our own needs and fear of either not getting something we think we want or losing something we already have, we begin to spiral down into a negative pattern of Ego-based fear. All fear is Ego-based, but EGO is at the root of much of our dysfunctions as human beings, and we are going to work to eliminate our selfish fears and associated misery.

Self-Defeating Fear

All fear is self-defeating with the exception of, perhaps, healthy fear. Healthy fear is measured and predictable and in moderation can act to propel us to manage risk and situations that might otherwise harm us. Healthy fear is a basic human instinct that keeps us alive and protected from real harm. It is necessary for the survival, safety and continuation of the human species. All of creation shares this basic instinct.

But, when our perceived fear exceeds its survival function, it then tips the scale to the unhealthy side. With fear as the driver of our beliefs, thoughts and behaviors, we can't win. Overcoming negative and harmful fear requires us to have some faith that the outcomes of our beliefs and actions will turn out OK, even if we do fail at achieving our goals this time around. Fear is negative and not usually real. So, as we progress on our journey to change, we will find tools and methods to better help us manage our fears without the use of mind-altering substances. Fear is a reality of life, but it doesn't have to harm us or prevent us from reaching our goals and achieving our true purpose in life.

The Gaping Hole in Your Soul

When our soul and basic needs are satisfied and fed, we develop a sort of soul sickness. This is an important sign that you need to take a time out and fix those very things that are creating the symptoms of emotional, mental and even physical pain. The latter three are all signs that something deeper is misaligned inside you. We are going to explore how to better take care of your essential needs as a living human concern and fill up your soul with meaning and purpose. This is one of the primary goals of this book, to fix once and for all those things that are creating this feeling that you are just failing at satisfying your needs and can't seem to find a way out of your pain and struggle.

Ego

Defined as a person's sense of self-esteem or self-importance. Also coined by Freudian Psychoanalysts as the personality's translator between the unconscious and conscious mind – directly responsible for reality testing and a sense of personal identity. We typically refer to the ego as "Big." But, in its most healthy state, it is serves a really important – in fact vital function as the mind's emotional reality regulator.

For most of us less than perfect humans (meaning most all of us), we refer to ego as something that is not functioning well and has outgrown its intended purpose. Perhaps it is excessive or over the top. When we say someone has a "Big" ego, we think of someone who thinks they have a greater sense of self-importance than others. Someone with a big ego has a distorted sense of self-importance and often their presence can suck the air out of the room. It can be a turnoff and result in alienating others. To me, it also shows a lack of humility, not being right-sized and can be a damaging roadblock to one's change, as well as a blind spot in one's own perception of their world and their role in it. It can lead to an unhealthy sense of entitlement and a host of other emotional and mental disorders. Many of our character defects and roadblocks to change result from unhealthy egos. It is something we need to get our arms around and heal.

Rationalization and Justification

Most humans are irrational in their approach to life. As you well know for yourself, we can rationalize and justify just about anything. If there's a will, there's a way to get what we think we want or need – even if we hurt ourselves and others in the process. Most of us weren't just born with logical minds like that of a scientist. We will make ourselves believe whatever truth is convenient for us at that time.

This has a lot to do with dishonesty and lack of integrity. If we can lie to ourselves because it is easier and less painful than dealing with the truth or doing the right thing, we are capable of much more. What about stealing a candy or grape from the supermarket. Or how about "fudging" the truth on our taxes. Or what about not returning that phone call because we didn't really like the person any way and they were never very nice to us. Or what about taking out our anger in some passive-aggressive way with our wife and kids because we had a bad day at work. They should know how hard our life is. Or we can have just one drink or cheat on our diet – nobody will know anyway. We all have quite the list of rationalizations and justifications for the things we do. We get so accustomed to doing it, that we don't even realize that we aren't being fully truthful. It just becomes habit – and not necessarily good ones. This is human nature. Or is it??

Pride, Grandiosity & Big-Shot-ism

While taking pride in one's achievements and sense of self-esteem is both important and healthy, it can also get in the way of one's happiness when it becomes oversized and serves as a block to seeing other ways of doing things.

People with Big ego's can also be grandiose – impressive or magnificent in appearance or style -- especially pretentiously so. Perhaps they are excessively grand or ambitious – the operative word being "excessively." Someone who is grandiose thinks too much of themselves, their accomplishments and self-worth, which can also interfere with one's need to change things in themselves that no longer serve their intended purpose.

When a person is too prideful, grandiose or is considered to have a "big" ego, they can also suffer from what we sometimes refer to as "Big Shot-ism" which turns people off and keeps positive change out. Big-Shot-Ism can also lead to one relapsing to old and destructive behaviors and addictions if they are involved in an addiction recovery program.

Self-Doubt

Another classic and serious roadblock to change is self-doubt. Fear and doubt originate from the personality or lower consciousness and feed on negative energy that is required for it to sustain itself. Unlike enduring and positive qualities that are generated from the higher energy of your soul -- like love, tolerance, wisdom, respect, compassion and empathy -- fear and doubt, along with uncertainty, will block any sunlight of change from your life.

Self-doubt arises when we struggle with poor self-esteem and self-image, perhaps suffer with depression or anxiety and, are generally insecure with our abilities to see our lives through difficulties, challenges and obstacles that continue to get in our way and knock our self confidence. This is fairly common, but understand and recognize its negative and damaging nature to open and allow you to adopt more effective and successful strategies and tactics to move forward and growing in your life.

"Don't Tell ME What To Do!!"

A toxic combination of Pride & Ego, needing to always be right and a sprinkling of arrogance mixed in. The end result is stubborn resistance to listening to others (lack of open-mindedness), and a sense of believing that you always know it all. "How dare you tell me that I don't know what's best for me!"

Many of us struggle with not wanting to hear or listen to others for so many reasons. My suggestion to you, if you are someone who identifies with this character defect and roadblock to change, is to start realizing that you don't know it all and that there might be more than one way to do things. Perhaps your way just doesn't work and you need to begin to listen and learn from others who have had success in areas that you haven't. What do you have to lose, but except believing that you might be vulnerable and not perfect! I believe that these are false beliefs and a serious roadblock that you need seriously examine and look at changing if you expect to change your ways and get different results! Try not to shoot the messenger, but focus on the message itself. It's not always about you or the person you believe is out to get you!

Self-Pity

That constant false reminder that I am not good enough and that the world should feel sorry for me. Poor me. I am and should feel pitiful. I should just wallow in the mind trap that tells me that I'm just not good enough or worthy of praise or recognition. If you had my life and my problems, you would understand how I feel. Rubbish! If you continue to feel sorry for yourself, you WILL be sorry and things WILL continue to get worse! Now, quickly get off the pity-pot and forget everything you know. You ARE good enough and deserving of all the goodness that life has to offer. So get out of your own way and just believe for a moment that you don't have to feel sorry for yourself any longer.

Guilt & Shame

Who doesn't feel guilty about how they may feel about a situation, an attitude that have about a person, place or thing or some behavior they wish they hadn't engaged in? When you really think about it, feeling guilty is nearly always a reflection of past behaviors (or lack thereof) or something you're contemplated doing in the future. Is there really anything you can honestly change about the situation?

If not, stop feeling guilty over it. It's done, history, already in the past. There are three things you can really do about negative feelings: Say something, do something or accept it. But, don't sit in your feelings and negative self-talk – as this too will get you nowhere but unhappy. Feeling shameful about something you did or said or even felt is unfortunate. But, the only thing you can really do to take away your feelings of guilt and shame is to apologize for your past actions and/or change the way feel, think or act in the future. Feeling ashamed about things that have already happened or might happen is all on you. You CAN and must change many things in order to not experience guilt and shame. These are huge roadblocks to change. I strongly suggest you recognize when you are experiencing these feelings. As we will explore later, these feelings are not necessarily facts or healthy to entertain. There are better and more rewarding ways of dealing with this type of negative self-talk. We WILL learn how to handle both of these in a way that creates positive action and far more satisfying outcomes. Again, feelings are not facts!

Resentment

Perhaps one of the biggest and most dangerous roadblocks to change along with self-pity and fear, are resentments. Untreated and deeply rooted resentments can quickly lead to anger, conflict and a repeated pattern of unhappiness. A really strong an untreated resentment can burn a hole in your soul as well as your stomach. *"Holding onto anger is like drinking poison and expecting the other person to die." –Buddha.* If left untreated long enough, resentments can lead to acting out in very inappropriate ways and with bad endings. We like to hang on to our resentments because that's often what we've come to learn and expect. It feels good to wallow repeatedly in our anger and disappointment that we either didn't get what we felt we deserved or were entitled to or were wronged by others. How dare they treat me like that. Don't they know who I am? I wouldn't treat my best friend like that. I've always been generous with them, I deserve better.

We will painfully discover that the root of all our resentments is self-inflicted. We have false expectations of others and perhaps ourselves. These often turn out to be pre-meditated resentments just waiting to happen. We set ourselves up for disappointment. We blame others for things that are in our control.

Further, we will learn that the crazy act of holding on to these resentments is completely self-inflicted. The other person(s) don't have these resentments, but we hold on to them for dear life and love to stew about them – sometimes for the rest of our lives. What's with that? That is insane. Why? We are in complete control of these irrational beliefs and the thinking that leads us to harbor these resentments in the first place. Once we come to understand that we are completely in the driver's seat, we can learn to let these old resentments go and not allowing them to develop in the first place. We will focus the blame on ourselves for allowing them to happen in the first place. We will begin to see that resentment for any period of time is both insane and potentially fatal. We will come to appreciate the need to rethink the way we think and act which will lead to a feeling of empowerment and success without repeated blame and disappointment.

Resentment is often rooted in past pain: having your heart broken, being cheated on, and feeling abandoned or mistreated, being abused or violated. You might resent yourself for choices you've made, or flaws that you perceive in yourself. You might resent the universe for the death of a loved one, or for its random chaos that often seems unfair.

Remorse

Many of us get stuck in feeling remorse for things that we either have or haven't done. We feel badly that we didn't do or accomplish something that we set out to do, didn't put in the necessary effort and got not so great results. Perhaps we disappointed our loved ones or didn't tell the truth. Maybe others got hurt. In doing so, we ended up hurting ourselves, because we still hang-on to these useless feelings and negative self-talk.

As we will explore in greater depth, feelings are not necessarily facts and often cloud our judgment and thinking. Guilt, shame and remorse can easily create inappropriate or incorrect beliefs that lead us to think and act a certain way. This in turn can lead to unsatisfactory outcomes that can disappointment us and others. If you struggle with remorse, there are strategies we will learn to better manage our feelings by correcting our beliefs, attitudes, values and thinking and behavior. When we live in remorse for the past, we are stuck and not living to our fullest potential in the moment. Nor are we able to let go of old behaviors that lead to feeling remorseful in the first place.

Lastly are those feeling of shame, guilt and remorse that we experience from having made a host of bad choices and decisions. I certainly have had my share! Lamenting about what is now in the past is never very fruitful and easily interferes with our ability to move forward in a positive way in our life. We have all made poor choices and decisions in our life, but we will explore ways to deal with these subsequent regrets and learn how to reframe these unfortunate experiences as learning lessons in our lives. We can't revisit the past to correct them, but we can change our attitude and perspective on dealing with these memories today and tomorrow. It all falls under dropping the wreckage and old baggage of our past.

Dishonesty

Honesty is perhaps the most essential attitude and asset to true and lasting change. On the flip side, dishonesty is one of life's greatest offenders and is full of lies and deceit to ourselves and others. Who are we really fooling when we are being dishonest? And, what is dishonesty to you anyone? Is it OK to tell a white lie? How about manipulating others to get what you want or to hide something you are afraid will put you in a poor light. God forbid people think less of you. Do you just exaggerate or "stretch the truth? Maybe you only fudge the truth when it's convenient or you think that it won't harm the other person, but will conveniently help you.

For me, a life of dishonesty and self-deceit nearly killed me. It hurt many others – some that I love dearly. While I knew all along that I was being dishonest about so many things, after a while, it became a well-grooved habit and it's just what I knew and was familiar with. To me, it was normal to not fully disclose the reality and all the facts of my life at any given and important moment in time. Who's going to really know the difference if I leave out certain facts or details? The sky was sometimes falling and this Chicken Little didn't think it necessary to tell my family I was in serious trouble financially, emotionally, with substance abuse or that I was incredibly or possibly even fatally unhappy and suicidal. If I tell them, then they will know!! Imagine that!! Who would ever want to share those darkest secrets that I swore I was going to take to the grave.

I believe that I grew up this way. I learned to be dishonest from an early age. My mother, who I love and cherish dearly today, and have long since reconciled my differences and childhood resentments with, taught me that it was OK to steal food from the grocery store and to exaggerate the truth about many things. I never learned about the ethics and virtues and need to be honest, so my life of dishonesty was left unchecked for many years.

There's a saying in 12-step recovery programs that "you're only as sick as your secrets." This has proven true with me. The more I hid from others, who loved me and could help me, the sicker I became. After awhile, it was hard to tell what the truth was and what a lie was.

Being brutally honest with myself and sharing my dishonesty with trusted others in substance abuse recovery and through 12 step recovery programs has taught me much more about the need to be honest. It is vital to be brutally honest with yourself and others if you ever expect to recover and stay recovered from this life-long illness.

It is a painful process to get honest with yourself and others and often takes a lifetime of habit change and full disclosure. The best metaphor I can use to illustrate the process of getting honest is like this: It's like peeling away the layers of an onion.

Denial

Like the river in Egypt (the Nile), denial that you have a problem is potentially deadly. Nobody likes to think that they are flawed (God forbid) or are less than perfect. But, out and out denial of reality – yours or someone else/s – is tantamount to the highest form of dishonesty or blatant blindness. I consider it a mild form of insanity.

There was a great story I heard as a newly recovering alcoholic about a man who peaks his head out of his storm shelter after a tornado only to say "everything looks grand, ma." Meanwhile, the house and the entire surrounds had blown away in the storm, but he just chose not to see it. Denial of an addiction, of a life threatening struggle, of your unhappiness, of your emotional struggles with life, of your terminal disease or general state of anxiety and depression is a serious roadblock to change and possibly survival.

Analysis Paralysis

Some of us have a tendency to be our worst own enemy and get in our own way by over-analyzing and scrutinizing everything to death. Not that managing our risk in all important decisions is not a good and wise thing to do, but we can get carried away in the process. We become so fearful that we haven't learned everything there is to know about something, fact or situation that we forget that we eventually need to take action and make a decision to do something, say something or just accept that we should pass on taking action for now.

This process of having to control everything about and related to every decision we make can lead to what I fondly call "analysis paralysis." It's a brand of fear that without our own intense and personal scrutiny of every little detail, pros and cons, assets and liabilities, that we will make bad and scary decisions. We see many people do this and the end result is continued inertia and inaction - a general inability to move forward and process the information we have gathered to make a balanced and informed decision about something.

While I have a strong tendency to make decisions quickly and with general ease, I have also been known to make poor decisions and to not fully think things through or at all! I'm not suggesting taking this path. My point is that if we spend all our time analyzing every detail to death, nothing ever happens and we fall further into fear and disappointment. Again, when things don't change, they don't change. And, this is not always good – especially when we come from the unhappy family!

Rather than making this a roadblock to your own change, be mindful of this often negative pattern and ask for help in evaluating situations and decisions to best help you build a decision-tree or framework, or just to generally simplify the process and learn from others' experiences with similar situations.

Terminal Uniqueness

How many of us struggle with the fact that WE are the only ones struggling with a particular life or personal issue. As if we were the perfectly unique and different snowflake from all the others. When we come to falsely believe that we are the only one with a problem or challenge, we unintentionally isolate ourselves from the legions of other that have gone through similar, if not identical struggle. It is these very people who are most qualified to help us.

As we come to understand that of all the billions of people on earth, it is likely that many people have experienced the very things that we most need help and perspective on. We are never alone in our problems, and certainly there is so much available experienced and willing help that we can access anytime when we need it the most.

Co-Dependency

A favorite roadblock of mine, co-dependency is a label that one should be careful to use. It can best be described as an over dependence on others to make decisions, to find our own happiness and to live our lives independently. Through extensive analysis, I discovered that I had been co-dependent on my ex-wife for doing those things that I found hard and she found easy — like having healthy relationships, making friends and keeping them, making plans for our social life, taking care of the kids and their many needs and responsibilities. She was so great at many of these things that I found it way too easy to rely on her to just take care of this part of my life while I allowed myself to become addicted to work, my own need for success and acceptance in the professional community. I would easily work 80 hour weeks and not pay attention to our personal, social and our own marriage because I was too busy being a "good" provider — some standard that I imposed on myself.

It took me way too long to understand my over-dependency on her and even former business partners for my success and happiness. But, now, while I have worked hard to fortify those areas of my life that I once found difficult with new skills and the elimination of my own roadblocks to change. I am a work in progress, but I feel fully responsible for my actions and the results. I am no longer overly reliant on anyone for my fate or outcomes. I feel wonderful, independent, and free from those negative bonds and general fear and anxiety of failure and even success. I am so much more focused on the process than I am of the results.

Stubbornness

Many of us take pride over our supposed "stick-to-it-iveness," our tenacity, our amazing wherewithal to see projects through our way. What we don't necessarily see is our inability to let go of our old or "right" way of doing things. We insist that things must be done this way or they are going to fail. Since, we never fail at anything (lol), we will persist in our stubbornness until you either die or just go away. We all know the stubborn ones, and often don't even try to approach them. But, our stubbornness is a serious roadblock to growth and change, and as a general attitude and way of doing things, doesn't work most of the time. So, if you are known to be stubborn, start to develop an open-mind and willingness to try things differently. Because, most likely, YOUR way didn't work when it was needed the most.

Lack of Acceptance

We will spend a great deal of time on the concept of "Acceptance" – perhaps one of the most important techniques and ways of life that can change your life and so many of the accompanying maladies. We all know what lack of acceptance is: Often evidenced by stubbornness, being opionated, inflexible, blind to reality, in denial and slow to change. Lack of Acceptance is a serious roadblock. We will later discover how the development and adoption of a general attitude of acceptance can change your life and possibly even safe it from further disaster. Acceptance, in my humble opinion, is one of the best ways to help open the eyes of the blind, deaf and dumb – figuratively speaking.

Unmanageability

When things are unmanageable, they are generally not in your control. When your life is no longer in your control and is spinning out of control, you might refer to your situation as being unmanageable. Not a good place to be or a state of life to be praising. Out of control is never good, unless you are a magic carpet ride, and this is not a Disney movie, so please move unmanageable to the "con" side of the balance sheet. Addicts and Alcoholics learn a great deal about unmanageability of our lives when the power of mind altering substances takes control of our life experience. Powerlessness and unmanageability are two fundamental truths of an addicts/alcoholics reality. There are also many emotional, psychological, physical and spiritual illnesses that might contribute to one's life being unmanageable, but it is important to recognize this condition for one to then find the help necessary to move towards a state of manageability – whether those remedies are internal or external.

Arrogance

The act of obnoxious display of ego and bad attitude; the lack of gratitude or humility; a general state of thinking that we know it all and can do no wrong – because we are perfect. That's arrogance. It is part stubbornness, part defiance and doesn't work in a world where we seek to be happy and free from the wreckage of our past. It's a non-starter and is nearly guaranteed at some point in your life to get you nowhere fast – while keeping you terminally unhappy! So, if you were ever told that you were arrogant, you were probably not told that you were obnoxious and had an ego problem. Now, consider yourself on notice, if this poor character quality applies to you!

Unrealistic Goals & Expectations

This applies to many of us well wishers and terminally hopeful people. Many of us don't have a realistic sense of how to set achievable long- and short-term goals and as a result, form unrealistic and unachievable expectations for ourselves and others. This, in turn, leads to disappointment, poor self-esteem, negative attitudes and many other life disrupters. If you struggle with setting realistic and achievable goals, you've come to the right place, because we are going to learn appropriate strategies to set and achieve whatever your goals you establish for yourself more appropriately and with better results.

Distorted Sense of "Success"

Not necessarily a roadblock, but I put this one in this section because I have struggled with my own concept of personal and professional success in my own life. I can tell you from direct experience that it would have saved me so much pain and grief if I had just understood and appreciated what true "success" is. For me had a lot to do with Ego, grandiosity, approval and validation from my peers and material achievement – all distortions of true success. It will mean different things to different people, but defining your own sense of life success is important to understand and achieve. And, we will explore what this means for you today and how you can redefine this more appropriately and with greater realism and satisfaction for you.

Being Judgmental

Many of us love to judge and label others. We feel the need to put everyone in their proper bucket in our eyes so that we can better make sense of our own lives; to compare ourselves and to size other up as to good or bad, better or worse, like or dislike, love or hate, keeper or throw in the garbage heap. Judging others is both a waste of time and very damaging to forming good judgment and sustainable relationships – let alone peace-of-mind, serenity and true happiness. We will need to get out of the judging business, as there are many more qualified souls than us judge. None of us is qualified or tasked in life to be judges of anything – let alone one's own character!

Stinking Thinking

Another way of saying possessing a bad attitude and a small way of thinking. Also, the state of mind that an alcoholic and addict possess before they hit their own bottom. Even then, bad attitude and stinking thinking can linger until the person finally cries wolf and begs for help. This frame of mind leads to distorted and often twisted beliefs and thinking, and will hamper one's ability to build a sustainable bridge back to life. The little committee in your head is telling you lies and making you miserable. I'll show you ways to shut it down for good and make it stay away, so that your thinking becomes more rational, your beliefs more logical and your feelings and emotions more manageable.

Negative Self-Talk

This is our way of telling ourselves that things will never turn out well. Those little voices in our head will literally convince us of that the sky is falling and that things will never turn out well or as planned. So, why even bother.

When you think negatively about most all things, it turns out to be a self-fulfilling prophesy, and things are pretty much guaranteed to fail or not go your way. Negative out, negative back. This is a basic law of physics and energy.   It is really hard to stop our negative thinking, but we will come to see that it is largely based on fear and insecurity. There are ways to change our negative attitudes and dispositions to more positive and effective ones that result in better outcomes. Some people who think negatively are sometimes called "Awfulizers" – as that is usually the result of their negative thinking – things turn out awfully. However, if you were a good reporter, you would soon discover that things usually never turn out the way we think they will. But, our minds trick us into thinking that the worst will always happen.

Knowing It All

I put this right behind Stubbornness and Arrogance. What it means to me is that people who believe that they know it all really know very little and are falsely convinced of their grandiose vision of reality and the truth. Nobody likes or admires a know-it-all and some people would refer to people who display this attitude or disposition as being foolish. Not a good way to attempt to change your life – since you must already know all these answers to all your problems and hence choose to remain miserable and ill at ease.

Self Sabotage

When things seem to be going great or perhaps we have successfully adopted some positive change in our lives, some of us, without realizing it, have this urge to pull the plug and blow up the good works of our progress. When we unconsciously set ourselves up for failure even though we desire positive outcomes, we are self-sabotaging ourselves. I'm not a psychologist or a criminologist, but it would seem to me that an unconscious desire to fail, to ask for trouble or create harm and/or avoid success says a lot about our inability to live and good and balanced life without negative consequences. Setting ourselves up for failure despite our true desires for better outcomes is something a lot of us do and need to be aware of, if we expect to stay out of harm's way and achieve purpose and meaning in our lives. Easier said than done, and perhaps better left to the psychological experts to assess and help remedy.

Anger

Many of us struggle with "anger problems." I have struggled with effectively managing my emotions, which sometimes led to anger and damaging consequences to both myself and others. If unattended, anger can eventually escalate to emotional and even physical violence – either self or other inflicted. As my life spun further out of control, my anger and frustration escalated. I have since learned many of the excellent spiritual and behavioral tools to manage and eliminate anger in my life. I am happy to say that with hard work, I no longer struggle with states of anger anymore. Frustration, yes, but erupting in inappropriate ways both towards myself and others, no longer. If you struggle with anger, stick around, as we will introduce strategies and techniques for minimizing and even eliminating such states of self-induced terror later on.

Poor Self-Esteem

Feeling "less than," never good enough, insufficient or inadequate are all feelings that result from a poor self-image or sense of self. Many people struggle with this state of mind, and most always it simply isn't true, but we don't think we deserve the recognition of being good enough. Having a sense of poor self-esteem can be very damaging to achieving inner peace and happiness in your life. We will learn that by reframing our lives and doing esteem able things, we can build confidence and a strong foundation for feeling good about ourselves and our lives today and everyday going forward.

Emotional Oversensitivity

I was perhaps one of the most emotionally oversensitive people I know. My distortions about how people thought of me, what others' true intentions were towards or about me, and taking things out of context or feeling hurt is something I struggled with all my life. I am happy to say that after my "re-education," I came to see that my reactions to many things were emotionally charged and distorted. I learned to challenge my often irrational and emotionally charged beliefs and I have since learned to see the world and my experiences in a more balanced way. I don't get so bent out of shape about most things anymore. We will work together on eliminating this roadblock to change in your own life.

Irrational Thinking

I was never taught to think rationally. Why is this important? By not learning to challenge false beliefs, are thinking creates negative emotional outcomes like anger or resentment when things don't go our way. While a part of this Therapeutic Community in prison, I learned how to challenge my many false beliefs to create less emotionally-driven thoughts and feelings. I discovered that by not giving power to my often irrational thoughts, I could create far more satisfying outcomes and not get so bent out of shape. We are going to explore this really nifty gift called the rational challenge in a later section. If you practice it, it is almost guaranteed to get you really good results over time.

Rage, Self-Loathing, Jealousy and Bitterness

When our anger is so pent up and has nowhere else to go, it often surges inward, and we begin to punish ourselves for things that we just can no longer control. We act out inappropriately and aggressively towards others with rage. We even rage against ourselves internally with feelings of self-loathing and bitterness. It's all a part of the hate and vitriol that comes from living a life out of control and un-purposed. This path of self-destruction can be fatal if not caught in time. Often, we need an intervention by family members, doctors or other professionals before it is too late. We no longer have and may even never have the life tools to cope. I've seen many people die unfulfilled, angry and bitter. What a sad and futile way to end your time on this earth! It all seems like such a waste.

Defiance

Also akin to arrogance and stubbornness, Defiance is either a conscious or unconscious attempt to passively or aggressively challenge authority or those who love us most. It is a way of acting out negatively and usually results in bad consequences. When we are defiant, we are telling others that it's our way or the highway, and we know better or frankly don't care about what others think, feel or do. Our ego keeps us in the right and we don't pay attention to the possible negative consequences of our actions or lack thereof. Being defiant can lead to serious damage and even death and misery if left unattended or unchecked. Defiance can also lead to not trusting and finding one's true self and real purpose in this world. It's OK to be right, but not all the time!

Impulsivity/Impetuousness/Immediate Gratification

Got to have it now, bigger, better, brighter, more please! How many times have we pulled the trigger in making decisions without thinking things through? I, for one, have long struggled with over-exuberance and quick trigger on reacting before thinking – a potentially deadly and damaging impulse.

It's like seeing a juicy cheese burger with bacon, pretty girl woman, ice-cream, the buffet line. Sometimes I just can't resist, despite my need to. Learning to take that pause that can give one time to consider the consequences before snapping a decision or judgment seems to be absent from some of us. I can make a decision in a heartbeat without often thinking things through and it has gotten me into trouble, into addiction, intense sadness and eventually desperation and prison. The fact is that sometimes it is so very hard to resist – we lack impulse control.

So, in ""How to Love Yourself"-Hour Reboot," we are going to learn how to take the pause that refreshes and saves a lot of heartache and grief. We are going to learn to step back, think and consider, reflect and then decide or choose otherwise. This is a filter that needs to be learned and practiced and is a real and proven roadblock to the road to long-term happiness.

Needing To Always Be Right

Another form of defiance and, perhaps, ignorance, is that some people are so insecure or stubborn that they always need to be right about most everything. Not recognizing our serious limitations as humans can be fatal and very frustrating. Not exactly a way to make friends and influence people. Most of us don't love to be around know-it-alls or those who always need to be right and win an argument.

Generally arises from some form of insecurity and the only reason to note it is that we can't be willing and open-minded to change if we are always right – because then things never change! More importantly, I've learned the hard way that I'd much prefer to be happy than to be right all the time – or always win an argument!

Lack of Power

That is our collective dilemma in attempting to WILL our way to healing and wholeness. Life's trials and tribulations often rob us of our power to solve some of our thorniest and most difficult issues. It is important to recognize our own limitations in trying to solve these challenges on our own. It's not that we are literally powerless, but it is the misuse and often misguided use of this personal power that keeps us in a vicious and repetitive cycle of pain and disappointment.

Once we learn how to get out of our own way, we can and will explore and adopt many techniques for harnessing this amazing power within us. It is not an external power, but rather an internal power that generates from our souls and then intelligently draws all the available energy from our physical and emotional selves to achieve our goals and actualize our full potential.

I Don't Need Anybody Else's Help

How many times have you heard yourself and others plead that they've got this. They don't need yours or anyone else's help, thank you! Pride, ego, knowing it all, not wanting to seem vulnerable or weak, having an inferiority complex and not wanting to seem stupid or incapable, being socially insecure and being afraid to ask for help – all lead to blind ignorance. Whatever your reason for thinking that this is a good idea, you can leave it at the front door and forget about it! Really, who doesn't need help from time to time?

My father, God bless his soul, never thought he needed anyone's help. My father also hated doctors – which I understand is not all too uncommon. At the end of his life, he refused to go to a doctor even though he wasn't feeling well and wasn't himself. He became sluggish, had stopped dancing and teaching others ballroom dancing, was always tired and just wasn't himself. He'd rather struggle and suffer in silence. That was what men did.

My sister and I finally forced him to see a doctor. And, low and behold, he ended up being diagnosed with Stage 4 lung cancer and died within six weeks of his diagnosis. The doctors insisted that he waited too long and that they could no longer help him. My father, who was vital and extremely fit and healthy for his 86 years, was so very angry that he could no longer enjoy and be with his beloved children, beautiful wife, grandchildren and many friends. He felt robbed of his right to live. He had taken such good care of himself. Certainly, he didn't deserve this dreadful fate.

How sad and difficult to explain to any reasonable person who knows full well that my father could and should have seen a doctor six to nine months earlier. Perhaps asking for help when he really needed it could have given him more years to put his life in order and to focus on those things that mattered to him most – much like what we are all attempting to do right now.

I tell this story because many of us protest that we can do everything ourselves. I learned as a journalist early in my career that it's most important to get the facts and build an intelligent perspective on whatever issue or subject you are grappling or challenged with. With the internet and Google today, information and intelligence on just about everything is available at your fingertips. Information on just about anything is so readily available and free.

What's more, so many people have had had relevant, real life experience on just about every subject. Chat groups and special interest clubs are evidence of this. But, if you're a loner, too smart or just have other biases or vulnerabilities about asking for help, this is the time to re-examine all your assumptions and to get out of your comfort (or is it dis-comfort) zone and ask for help when you need it. You would happily do the same for anyone else who asked you, and you would feel good about it. Well, on the flipside, people love to feel needed and wanted and are happy to help you when you need it. This is also an important part about getting out of self and staying out of your own way. I think you now get the point!

Getting Out of Our Own Way

We are typically our worst own enemy in the change business. We try so hard to harness all our physical and intellectual resources to solve our problems, but we end up actually causing more harm than good.

From my experience, until I learned how to stop trying to do everything on my own and understand my own limitations, I was unable to ask for help and get it. Call it stubbornness, fear, willfulness, grandiosity, stupidity, whatever label works best for you. Earlier, I introduced this big concept of surrendering to win. In order to succeed in areas of my life that I was wholly unqualified to improve on my own, I had to get out of my own way and surrender to the people who were most qualified to help me the most.

External Focus of Control

What I mean by this is that some of us have a tendency to put our focus on the external things in our life such as making a lot of money, being successful at work or in your profession, having a beautiful spouse or important and wealthy friends or, perhaps, acquiring lots of expensive "things." When we place our attention on getting things as opposed to looking inside of ourselves to fix and heal those things that we struggle with, our attention is turned from the external world to inside of ourselves. That's where the true power is and where the healing needs to occur: Inside ourselves. The stronger we get inside, or under the hood so-to-speak, the better we begin to feel and act on the outside. So, if you are one of the many people who place a high priority on acquiring and having things in order to make you feel better, you've come to the right place. Because, in time, you will come to understand that your real wealth is hidden deep inside of you. And, once you've discovered your own hidden jewels, your sense of accomplishment, completeness and satisfaction will allow you to stop looking on the outside to make you feel better. You might then very well become the wealthiest and wisest person alive! So, stick around. The journey to your own riches is just beginning.

Isolation/Loneliness

When I'm struggling in my own life, I had a tendency to want to be alone, by myself, in my own private Idaho. It was safe inside all by myself, and no one could bother or hurt me there. Feeling isolated and/or lonely is a symptom of a much deeper problem. And, the existence of it in your own life is a good indication of your inability to cope with some larger issues that you may be struggling with.

Ironically, I have since found that one of my go-to strategies in solving the feeling of aloneness and isolation is to get out of myself and be around and engaged with other people. Easier said than done, but, trust me, it works. We will spend considerable time later learning how to "tell" on ourselves when we're getting into a place of isolation and how to use the tools of "How to Love Yourself"-Hour Reboot to find our way back to sanity, security, serenity and becoming once again a vital part of the human race.

While I still love to spend time alone with myself, today it is by choice and not by default or out of weakness. I love my privacy, where I can go deep within and find peace-of-mind and serenity, but this is what gives me the strength to both help other people and in doing so, helping myself to life's many blessings!

Poor Risk Assessment & Management

People used to comment on how amazed they were at my ability to make decisions so quickly. At times, I even amazed myself! While I do have some facility and agility to move through issues quickly, I often shortchanged myself by not fully assessing the pros and cons of each decision I made. When it comes to making important decisions, don't be too quick to jump to a decision without taking the time to evaluate the possible consequences both good and bad. We often look only at the pros or good potential outcomes, but fail to fully vet the possible negative ones. So, making hasty decisions and judgment calls can easily lead to disastrous consequences if our thinking isn't balanced.

Today, I use what I call "My Personal Board of Advisors" before making any really important decisions. I need the balance and perspective of others to process my often rapid-fire decision-making process. But taking the appropriate time to gain a more balanced perspective on important issues, generally keeps me out of serious trouble and out of the red zone of life.

For many of us, good risk management is an acquired skill, but one we must learn and get good at if we are to continue to grow and change in a positive and meaningful way – whatever age or life-stage we might be in. Here's where the Know –It-All needs to learn a great deal about humility and knowing how to ask for help.

People Pleasing

As a formerly insecure person with low self-esteem, I was sure to make to let everyone know – including those with more perceived power than I, what a dutiful and skilled servant I was. How very capable of taking care of things I could be and how reliable and dependable I was. It never occurred to me that nobody ever asked me to "perform" on command. I had so internalized this need to please others that I forgot to take notice that I never focused on pleasing myself. I was always so concerned what others thought of me that I forgot sometimes why I was doing what I was doing. I never felt comfortable with being in the #1 position, as I was socially insecure and uncertain of myself.

Why is this so important to note? If you struggle with feeling an excessive need to please everyone else, take a serious look at your motives for doing so. Why are you doing what you're doing? What do you really have to gain except, perhaps, being very helpful and thoughtful of others. They may or may not appreciate your noble efforts and you are very likely to be disappointed by their lack of sufficient acknowledgment of how very good you really are.

An aspect of being a people pleaser is being co-dependent on others for your self-esteem. Stop looking at others to make you feel OK, and start looking and what you need to do for yourself to make yourself both feel and be better. The only person you really have any control over is yourself, and you can't expect others to do this for you. If you do, you are cruising for some serious disappointment and future resentments.

So, if you find yourself needing to please others to make yourself look and be OK, know that you have some internal work to do to understand and correct this. The only motives and actions you need to be concerned with are your own. You will reap tremendous and permanent rewards by just being beholden to yourself and your own standards of accomplishment. You don't need anyone else's approval to know that you're good enough. You are good enough and that is ALL you need to know – whether you feel that way today or not. Things will change going forward as you learn how to better do the esteem able things that actually will make you better all around!

Sweating the Small Stuff

Perspective is a lot and many of us lack this invaluable asset. We spend so much time pining away over small and inconsequential decisions and issues that we often miss the larger picture. We get lost in the sauce or become a small tree in a big forest. What's going to happen if I don't finish this project now,

figure out the formula for resolving this problem, forget to turn off the outdoor sprinkler, having balance
my checkbook today, am 10 minutes late for a hair appointment, forget to tell my son or daughter to
take care of a minor task, didn't read the instruction book for the new App I just downloaded on my
phone, didn't lay my clothes out from the night before, and the list goes on.

So, ask yourself, how important is it really? What's the worst thing that could happen? You need to
build a healthy perspective on where does the resolution of this issue or problem fit in to the general
scheme of things for your day, week, year or life. Is not ordering dark chocolate for the birthday cake
going to ruin your Grandmother's Party? Is being five minutes late going to ruin your day?
Now, I'm not suggesting you ignore all the details all the time. Rather, I'm suggesting that you place a
priority or sense of importance on the many "To Do" items on your list for today and not ruin your day
feeling that this might be your last day. Ultimately, mastery of small things can lead to big successes in
life, but many things are simply not ruining your day, serenity or peace-of-mind over!

The Committee in Your Head

Call it White Noise or the never ending chatter in your brain. However you refer to it, it's just a lot of
excess brain chatter and very distracting to our true mission. No doubt, we all experience. It. Try to
consciously turn off these voices and incessant conversations that your mind seems to have on its own
without your permission. Try to consciously and purposely quiet your mind and see how hard it is to
experience silence. You will find it frustrating.

Not only are these voices a distraction, but they never permit you to have peace-of-mind when you
need it the most. I often think that there's a bunch of insane people upstairs in that brain of mine, and
they just won't shut up and listen to anything I say. It's obsessive and drains my energy.

I don't allow these "people" who love to chatter in my brain to rent space anymore, and I've learned to
practice methods that quiet the mind and allow me to process my life in a far more enjoyable fashion
without all the clutter. There's enough of that on the outside. I certainly like to have more control of it
on the inside.

Later, we will learn how to quiet the mind and allow your own true internal dialog to reverberate loud
and clear without the chatter in the head.

Blind Spots

We all have them! This might very well be another way of describing denial. The things we don't see in
ourselves that other people are happy to point out to us. These are the very things – often referred to
as our character defects -- that we need to become more aware of so that we can correct them and not
allow them define our day. My blind spots were many --including not being a good listener and
spending more time needing to be heard than actually listening to others, being late, allowing my

uncomfortable feelings to initiate my addictive behavior, isolating, allowing my life spokes to get unbalanced, working too hard, not spending enough time taking physical and emotional care of myself, not investing in important relationships and expecting them to just happen. We all have our own lists, but typically we aren't even aware of them.

Becoming aware of our blind spots will allow us to learn strategies for minimizing and even eliminating these devilish defects and detractors from our lives.

Medical/Psychological/Emotional Issues

While many of us are impacted by a host of issues affecting our overall well being and ability to achieve our full potential, some of these issues are best addressed by the professionals most equipped to deal with them.

I certainly don't want to ignore the importance some of these issues or conditions may have on our ability to live our lives happily. I am not professionally or legally qualified to offer help or solutions to many of these problems which Doctors, Psychiatrists and psychologists and other professional designations often diagnose. Nor am I a big believer in labeling people or conditions, as doing so can do far more harm to a person than good. But, for some of us, these issues are real and present us with serious challenges on a daily basis.

If you have been diagnosed by a professional with one or more of these issues, welcome to the club. I have personally been labeled and struggled with depression, anxiety, addiction and have been treated and medicated by those professionals who have clinical or relevant experience in those areas. I have personally taught, counseled, sponsored, mentored and befriended so many people that take claim to one of these many labels. I have also successfully dealt with most all of them with excellent results.

While depression, anxiety and addiction were and, to some degree, are an important part of my story, I am happy to report that I have successfully dealt with and managed my own respective "conditions" through a variety of methods — among them spiritual, physical, emotional, behaviorally and through prayer and meditation, yoga and intense exercise and therapy. So, I have experimented and have found solutions to not allow these to be roadblocks in my own growth and self-actualization as a human being. They still exist, but do not debilitate or prohibit me from living a full and wonderful life today.

What's more, those issues that presented many challenges and "tests" in my own life have proved to be incredible gifts that allowed me to grow all that much stronger. The trials and tribulations that I experienced as a result of my addictions, anxiety and depression in the past have perhaps been the cornerstones that allowed me to become the person I am today — overall much better equipped to deal with whatever life throws at me and to continue to grow personally, spiritually and emotionally without the use of mind altering substances or other crutches.

The purpose of singling these issues out here in this book is simply to help you best identify and address those issues that you may struggle with and to find the right professional help to deal with them as appropriate. My goal is to help you grow and become the person you were always intended to be – happy, joyous and free from the debilitating issues that have held you back from reaching your full potential in the past. Again, if you need help, please get it immediately for any medical, emotional or psychological issues that you may be struggling with. You don't need to be embarrassed or afraid to ask for help and there are many well qualified professionals who will be happy to assist you.

- ## Common Disorders & Technical Labels:

  - ✓ **Medical or Psychological Disorders:** You may be struggling with a serious physical and/or mental issue like old age, cancer, AIDS, heart disease, Alzheimer's, an accident, a stroke or something worse. These are conditions that are best tended to by medical professionals.
  - ✓ **Depression:** A mental health disorder characterized by persistently depressed mood or loss of interest in activities, causing significant impairment in daily life (Mayo Clinic). I have long struggled with depression and have been treated with emotional and medication help. I am now stable and thriving.
  - ✓ **Anxiety:** A mental health disorder characterized by feelings of worry, anxiety, or fear that are strong enough to interfere with one's daily activities (Mayo Clinic).
  - ✓ **Addiction:** A brain disorder characterized by compulsive engagement in rewarding stimuli despite adverse consequences – a behavior that is both rewarding and reinforcing (Wikipedia). Always involves a "substance" or emotional/behavioral issue.
  - ✓ **Abuse (Physical & Emotional):** Sadly, many people – both men and women, have experienced either bodily or emotional abuse. Many are too embarrassed and afraid to admit it. It has clearly impacted your life in very negative ways and you deserve and require immediate help from health and psychological practitioners in order to stop what threat may still exist or what is left behind. It is more common than you think.
  - ✓ **Dual Diagnosis:** is the term used when a person has a mood disorder such as depression or bipolar (aka manic depression) combined with a problem to drugs or alcohol. —two separate illnesses that each requires its own treatment plan (dbsalliance.org).
  - ✓ **ADD/ADHD:** A chronic condition including attention difficulty, hyperactivity, and impulsiveness. Can be helped, but not cured can last for years or be lifelong – usually exists in children, but can also affect adults (Mayo Clinic).
  - ✓ **Bi-Polar:** A disorder associated with episodes of mood swings ranging from depressive lows to manic highs. It is very common (Mayo Clinic)
  - ✓ **Antisocial Personality Disorder:** A mental health disorder characterized by disregard for other people. (Mayo Clinic)

- ✓ **Schizophrenia:** A disorder that affects a person's ability to think, feel and behave clearly. Considered complex but treatable (Mayo Clinic).
- ✓ **Anxiety Disorder:** A mental health disorder characterized by feelings of worry, anxiety, or fear that are strong enough to interfere with daily living and quality of life (Mayo Clinic).
- ✓ **Insomnia:** Persistent problems falling and staying asleep. Can be caused by physical, psychological, emotional and behavioral problems (Mayo Clinic).
- ✓ **Obsessive Compulsive Disorder:** Excessive thoughts (obsessions) that led to repetitive behaviors like agitation, compulsive hoarding, hyper vigilance, impulsivity, meaningless repetition of words, repetitive movements, ritualistic behavior, social isolation, compulsive hand washing or showering or repetitive flooding of thoughts (Mayo Clinic).
- ✓ **Borderline Personality Disorder:** A mental disorder characterized by unstable moods, behavior and relationships. It is considered very common (Mayo Clinic).
- ✓ **Psychosis:** A mental disorder characterized by a disconnection from reality. (Mayo Clinic
- ✓ **Dyslexia:** A learning disorder characterized by difficulty reading and reversing of words, numbers and patterns – very common (Mayo Clinic).
- ✓ **Post Traumatic Stress Disorder (PTSD):** A disorder characterized by failure to recover after experiencing or witnessing a terrifying even. Very common and readily treated. (Mayo Clinic). Soldiers returning from war where violence may have been prevalent, domestic violence and family dysfunction, a car or other serious accident or other physical, psychological or emotional trauma. I once experienced this from my experience in prison. It can be treated within a matter of months.
- ✓ **Phobias:** Can be divided into specific phobias like social, agoraphobia. An adverse reaction to certain animals or insects, natural environment, blood or injury and specific situations. Common: Fear of spiders, snakes, and fear of heights or being closed in to small spaces (Wikipedia).
- ✓ **Other:** Of course there are hundreds, if not thousands, of "conditions" that affect us all physically, emotionally, psychologically and spiritually. So, what? The point is that most all of the more common treatments we experience either ourselves or see in others are treatable, if not completely curable by the army of physical, mental, emotional and even spiritual counselors and specialists. I have included additional resources and contacts for your review in the Appendix if you need additional assistance or want help immediately.
- ✓ **Dealing with the Professional Community:** First, know who does what and what they actually can do: **Medical Doctors (MDs)** are specialists who have completed advanced education and clinical training in a general or specific area of medicine. **Surgeons are** doctors who treat diseases with surgery. **Psychologists** have a doctoral degree (PhD) in an area of psychology, the study of the mind and human

behavior. **Psychiatrist/ Psychotherapist/Psychoanalyst** are a medical practitioner specializing in the diagnosis and treatment of mental illness. **Psycho pharmacologist** is a Psychiatrist who specializes in medication management (today also a licensed **Nurse Practitioner** can administer medications). A **Therapist** is skilled in a particular type of therapy or treatment. A **Counselor** is a person trained to give guidance on personal, social or psychological problems – usually has a Master's Degree (Web MD).

✓ **Issues of Being Wrongly Labeled and/or Diagnosed:** Health care professionals use diagnostic labels to classify individuals for both treatment and research purposes. According to experts, there are clear benefits for the professional community, but the labels that are used also come with stigmas and stereotypes that we as consumers typically distort and misunderstand. The intensity of any condition can vary to very little (trace) to very prevalent (extreme). Mislabeling people with x or y condition can have detrimental and permanent impacts on the people who are being labeled – often falsely so. This is so unfair to those who are mislabeled and targeted in hurtful ways and also is a form of personal discrimination. Be sensitive and take the time to understand each particular situation with compassion, empathy and with an offer to help in any way that you can. Research the "condition" on the web and learn as much as you can about the particular situation to minimize misunderstanding and potential and unintended damage. Labels can create enemies, animosity, hate, resentment, anger, anxiety, depression and a host of other negative feelings and emotions to those that are struggling. Be sensitive and appropriate always and remember, science may have come a long way, but it, too, has its limits to knowing with certainty what is really going on with people who struggle with these supposed maladies. People in glass houses shouldn't throw stones!

Science and Technology Are Great, but They Alone Can't Fix You

Science and technology are human inventions, and granted, are just amazing -- perhaps even inspired by the divine nature of all things. All human beings, even Doctors, Therapists, Psychiatrists and Psychopharmologists, have their limitations, however.

Science, modern medicine and technological innovation are collectively amazing advancements and masterful achievements for mankind, but they alone can't fix all your deepest pain and hurt. This is where the creative intelligence and the divine and healing nature of spiritual energy come in. By harnessing this infinite healing power, we all have within, we can climb mountains and solve just about any problem and even affect the outcomes of amazing science.

Chapter IV.
KEYS TO SELF-LOVE & CHANGE

Change is hard, but always worth the effort and the initial discomfort. Once you get started and get past the fear of not knowing what's ahead, the process of change becomes contagious. The positive results you get, sometimes two steps forward and one step back, are very seductive. You feel good about yourself, your momentum and feel you are moving forward. As we discussed earlier, change is also necessary to getting to where you want and need to go. If nothing changes, then nothing changes and this is simply a non-starter.

We are all "wired" differently, and our emotional and mental DNA is unique. It is important to recognize that one size never fits all. Knowing yourself and your unique ways of processing your life experience is important, as we all experience our world differently – even though there is a remarkable degree of similarity. But, know your uniqueness so that you can best apply the keys of change to your particular needs and way of doing things. There are many ways and solutions to get to the same place of serenity, peace-of-mind and enduring happiness and growth, so keep an open, ready and willing mind!

There are several key & essential ingredients you must begin to focus on and this section will help prepare you to take a positive attitude and keeping an open and non-judgmental mind to looking at yourself and the many tools and strategies available to you to best change your life for the better.

The Power of Change

While away on my incarceration journey, I was blessed to teach a number of Adult Education Courses in addition to G.E.D. High School Equivalency. One of my motivational/inspirational favorites was called "The Power of Change." Little did I know I would end up writing this book, but I suppose that was my fate and path, and I was just beginning to explore how to best communicate this program of actually changing one self. It was a fun course to teach and I learned a great deal as a teacher, as I was also a willing student who got to share with hundreds of other inmates who were on a similar journey in their own lives.

One of the many things I learned was that people change at different speeds and there are so many ways to get to real and lasting change in one's life. What I discovered was for the more profound changes to occur, pain was often the touchstone of significant change and motivation as was the presence and belief in a power greater than oneself. We call this "power" many things, but I refer to "him" as God, Creative Intelligence, Divine Energy, and the Universal Creator of all things. Aka, the, the man upstairs, King of the hill and other displays of affection and absolute respect and reverence for anyone except yourself.

The other component that is necessary is willingness and motivation. And, naturally, the thing that brings change into reality for all of us is trust in others; trust and faith in the process that changing actually might work, and not judging the results before experiencing it for oneself. Change becomes real when we acknowledge and accept it as part of our new reality. It's an expansion of energy, perspective, knowledge, understanding and, of course evolution and growth of consciousness.

The impact of change varies depending on the goal and expectations, but success, while real, is often incremental. There is no fixed time table to change. It can happen immediately like in an "aha" moment, or it can take a lifetime or two! We can seek to change a behavior (usually a bad and inadequate one), an attitude, a belief or a way of thinking. Change is often iterative, incremental and not like a flash of intense lightening that produces miraculous and complete change and increased awareness. For most of us, change occurs as needed and wanted. It can be painless or painful, but it is usually permanent – although it can be experienced as two steps forward and one step back with a lot of frustration. But, it is about progress and not perfection and we are not being the speed of change. Remember, change is best experienced at a comfortable pace, and is never a race – as there really is no destination except for "better" than before.

The power of change is real and can be incredibly wonderful and life changing as it has been for me. It always involves risk and taking a chance. But, if you believe as I do, all change is for our own good and for our ultimate benefit.

Change is an Inside Job

Nobody can make you change but you. You hold the power and keys to massive and positive change in your own life. If you truly want to transform your current life into an amazing, new and happier life, you have to do the work. Nobody else can do this for you. The tools are all here. But the effort must be yours and yours alone. There is much help available to you along the way. But, the most important and worthwhile journeys in life are done alone with you and for your benefit. You may not feel this now or thought I'm out of order for saying this. But, I can tell you that I have done the dance of life alone, with my own will – often unconsciously – but with profound effect. It is not always clear to us why we are where we are in life, but it always for your own good and for the very best. This I believe with all my heart and soul and it has become one of my own greatest truths. With enough honesty, open-mindedness and willingness, there is nothing YOU can't do and you will be on the ride of your life as you do so. Nobody can make you change. But, you have the all the power you will ever need. I am going to help you to access this power. Are you ready yet?

Speed Up And Slow Down!!

One major caution, however. And, that is we all change at different speeds. Some are quick to change, others take more time. Don't beat yourself up if you feel you are falling behind. You are not! Just ask for help and be patient with yourself. If you have sufficient willingness and honesty, you will get there in due time! Again, we are not in a race, but just trying to keep a steady pace.

Time for a Major Attitude Adjustment

In my opinion and from direct experience, the key to opening up the door to change is drastically changing your attitude. Attitude is everything or at least the first step to change. When you decide that nothing is going to change, it won't. Taking a different and positive attitude (which we will discuss at greater length later in this book) is the first and foremost step to real and lasting change.

Once you start to get out of your perennial state of self doubt and self inflicted inertia, you must begin to focus on being hopeful, courageous and willing to do whatever it takes to make the difficult changes in your life.

Change is both necessary and an unfolding process. Once you've made the decision to suspend your negative beliefs and learn how to become more positive, you will begin to create a different and new experience for yourself AND for those around you.

Positivity is contagious and comes back to you in tremendous ways with real and permanent benefits, as long as you focus on keeping your positive attitude in front of you!

Life is 10% what happens to us and 90% what we do about it. That being the case, the big difference between 10% and 90% is ATTITUDE!

Honesty

We have already looked at how dishonesty can be a huge roadblock to change. So, focusing on being brutally honest with yourself and others can be the very key that opens the lock to seeing your life for what it really is and listening and learning from others what you need to do to make an unhappy, unfulfilled life into one that is happy, productive, meaningful and transformative.

Understanding the importance of honesty and taking daily inventory of your own acts of dishonesty – whether in your intentions, beliefs, attitudes, actions and behavior – was the way you learned how to get honest. Pain was also another profound motivator as was an interest not to harm either myself or others anymore. Learning how to be honest has reaped huge rewards in my own personal transformation, and has provided me with so many positive and life-changing rewards. So, as hard as this may be for you, and as deeply unconscious you may be of your own dishonesty, changing your attitude and keeping an open-mind can make a huge difference. Getting honest is a process, but you have to want it. With steady progress and taking your own honesty inventory, you will see the rewards of having good, sustainable relationships, respect, integrity and a host of other positive character traits will lead to better self-esteem and get far better results to a happier and more meaningful life in the future. Be patient with yourself, and don't forget to give yourself a break when you fall into moments of dishonesty. Just keep correcting yourself and the new habit will be formed. I once heard, "divorce your old story and marry the truth."

Open-Mindedness

Whether you believe it or not, keeping an open mind that things can change for the better, despite your own failed attempts to do so, can and will make the difference in allowing change to happen in your life. Having a closed mind limits your ability to grow and change .You are your own worst enemy - as Archie Bunker refused to acknowledge in the sitcom, "All in the Family." A stubborn and close-mind kept him in ignorance and denial.   What do you really have to lose? Some of us refer to negative self talk and thinking fraught with resentment, anger and self-pity as "stinkin thinkin." Defending yourself with a closed-mind comes from thinking that you are always right, or perhaps it's a defense mechanism for keeping people out. Some people are very change resistant as that takes work and involves risk. Close-mindedness rears its ugly head from Pride and EGO and is guaranteed to disappoint you in the long run. Yes, in the short-run it will keep you insulated from "outside" forces and will also steal your opportunity for happiness and positive change. So, suspend your stubborn beliefs for the next "How to Love Yourself" hours and keep an open-mind. Just take the leap of faith that I just might be right. I will happily refund your misery if after persistent practice of living on purpose fails to show meaningful results.

Willingness

Unlike animals, only man is born with free-will. Many of us allow our wills to exceed their normal functions. The result is that we become willful, pushy, stubborn, aggressive, grandiose, over powering and even obnoxious. The proper use of our free will – which is a gift from our higher power, is that we have the unique ability to choose. Choice is a freedom and an obligation. Used correctly, our willingness to try new things, experience the unknown, stretch our imagination and expose ourselves to potential positive and powerful change requires a belief that we can succeed to be happy, joyous and free and to live our full potential as human beings. We have to want something badly enough to be willing to take the necessary attitude and actions to achieve that which we set out to do. Willingness, like other positive character assets, is an essential component to winning in life.

I put this before hope, because it is, perhaps, the most important, fundamental key to change. If you BELIEVE that you can do or achieve something, you may have already won the battle. Belief is a very powerful prelude to action. So much so, that it makes almost anything you believe you can do or achieve possible. Being convinced that something is possible and achievable brings one to a state of readiness and goes beyond possibility. The more you believe that something is possible, the easier is the task of actually achieving it.

When you believe in yourself, you are displaying self-confidence. When you believe in others, you are encouraging them and giving them the confidence that they might lack to achieve their own goals.

On the flip side, if you don't believe, then most likely all bets are off. Failure and disappointment are sure to follow. The lack of belief is part of the negative self-talk that holds us back from being our best self possible. Being in dis-belief can paralyze one from taking any action. So, as we put our best foot forward and learn how to take a positive, CAN DO attitude, believe in yourself and watch the miracle or your own personal transformation take place!

Hope

Hope springs eternal, but not with many of us who have lived negative lives. So, first things first. Let's face it without hope, in my humble opinion, all bets are off. Chances are meaningful and lasting change is difficult at best without a clear sense of hope. While many people struggle from a self-imposed state of hopelessness, it is a choice and state-of-mind. Your life becomes a self-fulfilling prophesy of negativity and despair. You remain in the thankless rut of misery that you falsely believe you were born into and must maintain the rest of your years. After all, this is all you've ever known. But what if you stubborn thing were actually wrong? What if things might get better? What if you might actually change for the better? If you don't try it, you'll never know and you don't really have much to lose, do you? Hope is the basic framework that allows change to occur where it needs to. If you live in a state of hopelessness, then you can't expect anything to change. But, once you stop blocking this feeling of hope to emerge and play an active role in your life, everything changes and finally, the process of change can finally begin. You may not feel all the change overnight as good things often come to those who wait, but change you will and if you stay positive and avail yourselves of the attitude of gratitude and living in the positive in your life, you will have hope. In fact, I'm telling you now that you have every reason to be hopeful, even if you failed to feel better in the past. Never give up the battle and have faith that you will have hope that things will get better. Because they will. They did for me and for many others that will tell you about the miracles that occurred in their own lives. But, hope is both essential and eternal, for once you acquire this quality, you will always be able to muster enough hope to allow change to occur. There is a reason and truth to the saying that "hope springs eternal," because once you take the leap of faith and start to develop hope in your life, and you see the positive results that can come from this, you will never go back to be hopeless again.

<u>Courage</u>

Some say the opposite of fear is courage. Regardless of what comes first, fear or courage, courage is one of the essential ingredients in the larger recipe for change. For those of you who are not familiar with The Serenity Prayer, (the original long version was written by the American theologian Reinhold Niebuhr) the short version goes like this: "God grant me the serenity to accept the things I cannot change, the courage to change the things I can and the wisdom to know the difference". If we have no courage, we will never be able to identify, walk through and change difficult situations or problems in our lives. With courage comes hope and strength. It takes power and strength to have courage and this is something we must muster up in order to effect real change. Fear is what prevents the power of having courage to surface. Working on letting go of our fears and clearing the path allows us to gain courage. The rest of it has to do with changing our attitudes about fear and courage. Why is it that other people seem to have courage and we struggle with finding it? Somehow, they have succeeded in developing this wonderful quality and a result have been able to move forward with their lives. Does that make us a weakling and a wimp? No. Everyone has the potential to have courage. At some point of our lives we have exhibited courage or we wouldn't be alive. The courage to go forward despite our misery and feelings of sorrow and inertia, there have been time in our lives where we had and displayed courage and as a result of working through our fear, we did something important that resulted in something even better. So, I ask you to go visualize in your mind's eye those times in your life where you did so and remember this as a point of reference to how you can show courage to change in your life today. You CAN do this and now you MUST and WILL do this. Just know that and never say never!!

It's one thing to have the courage to change something and another thing to actually take action. So, I ask you again, have you had enough pain yet? If is, and you have the positive attitude that allows for courage, you then must turn it into action and to do that you have to be willing to do those things that are going to make you feel better. If your memory and experience of your pain, discomfort and suffering is finally great enough, you might actually be willing to do something about it. This time may come now or it may come tomorrow, but you have to be willing to walk through whatever it is — whatever fears or doubts you possess in order to do this. So, suspend your doubt and fear and take a leap of faith that everything will work out well. So, ask yourself, what's the worst thing that can happen? You return to your old sorry state of misery? Not a bad bet to make if you are a betting man.

So, let's break this down. There are three key components to this statement. The first talks about "Acceptance of the things we cannot change" as the reality of many situations that we, as humans, are powerless over like the weather, the time of day, natural disasters, the color of our eyes, the traffic , our parents and many other things; The next section talks about having the courage to change the things we can. It takes courage and much strength and determination to change and stayed changed, and with a "Can Do" attitude, anything in our lives is possible. And, the third piece of this wonderful and mindful prayer is "having the wisdom to know the difference." Wisdom is required to fully understand with a mature perspective and usually direct and repeated experience, the full implications of our actions and behavior. So, having the wisdom to know the difference Our Will and the given reality of our life conditions leads to more peaceful acceptance of many often frustrating and challenging situations. If life is 10% what happens to us and 90% what we do about it, the wisdom is the main way we have willingly accept that some things in life can't be changed by human will alone. We can choose to be "right" all the time or "happy." Practicing acceptance in your life can lead to an experience of peace and serenity. I choose to be happy today. My Ego and grandiosity would have it otherwise!

It's one thing to have the courage to change something and another thing to actually take action. So, I ask you again, have you had enough pain yet? If is, and you have the positive attitude that allows for courage, you then must turn it into action and to do that you have to be willing to do those things that are going to make you feel better. If your memory and experience of your pain, discomfort and suffering is finally great enough, you might actually be willing to do something about it. This time may come now or it may come tomorrow, but you have to be willing to walk through whatever it is – whatever fears or doubts you possess in order to do this. So, suspend your doubt and fear and take a leap of faith that everything will work out well. So, ask yourself, what's the worst thing that can happen? You return to your old sorry state of misery? Not a bad bet to make if you are a betting man.

Acceptance

So, let's break this down. There are three key components to this statement. The first talks about "Acceptance of the things we cannot change" as the reality of many situations that we, as humans, are powerless over like the weather, the time of day, natural disasters, the color of our eyes, the traffic , our parents and many other things; The next section talks about having the courage to change the things we can. It takes courage and much strength and determination to change and stayed changed, and with a "Can Do" attitude, anything in our lives is possible. And, the third piece of this wonderful and mindful prayer is "having the wisdom to know the difference." Wisdom is required to fully understand with a mature perspective and usually direct and repeated experience, the full implications of our actions and behavior. So, having the wisdom to know the difference Our Will and the given reality of our life conditions leads to more peaceful acceptance of many often frustrating and challenging situations. If life is 10% what happens to us and 90% what we do about it, the wisdom is the main way we have willingly accept that some things in life can't be changed by human will alone. We can choose to be "right" all the time or "happy." Practicing acceptance in your life can lead to an experience of peace and serenity. I choose to be happy today. My Ego and grandiosity would have it otherwise!

Nothing has worked and we have reached the end of what seems like a long and futile journey. What is the point of continuing on like this and beating ourselves up anymore? A now famous story by an Alcoholic Doctor of the hopeless variety appears in the AA big book on page 417 of the Fourth Edition. I think it brilliantly illustrates the irony, frustration and wisdom of the experience of acceptance in one's life. It has proved true for many and countless others who spent much of our lives beating our heads against the wall with our sheer force of our wills and narrow-mindedness. It goes like this: "Acceptance is the answer to all my problems today. When I am disturbed, it is because I find some person, place, thing, and situation – some fact of my life – unacceptable to me. And I can find no serenity until I accept that person, place, thing or situation as being exactly the way it is supposed to be at this moment…Unless I can accept life completely on life's terms, I cannot be happy. I need to concentrate not so much on what needs to be changed in the world as on what needs to be changed in me and in my attitudes. Acceptance is not submission; it is acknowledgement of the facts of a situation. Then deciding what you are going to do about it.

Coming To Know Our Limitations

We'd all like to think that we're Superman or Batwoman, but we're not and that is just for science fiction fantasy or the comic books. And, we're certainly not God and the Boss of all things. As hard as this was for me to understand, I finally realized that I can't change other people. Nor is it my change in life to do so. We're just human and in the eyes of "The Great One," we're all equal and exactly the same.
The only thing I can change is me and my attitudes. That is a lot and enough. And, coming to understand, appreciate and practice this takes time and also surrendering to the uncomfortable process of change. We have to learn to let our need to manipulate others and our world go or we will never be happy!

Asking For Help

Let's face it; we all need help from others to best work through life's many challenges. Some of us have partners and good friends, family or children. Others know how to ask for help when they need it and to listen to it even when they don't want to hear it.

But, that is not us. We are too proud, too stubborn, too always right and way too defiant. We'd rather isolate ourselves and prove to the world that we can solve life's problems on our own. Nobody should know our business. I have always solved my problems, so why not this one? Besides, my pride and ego tell me I have all the answers I need. I could never show you how very weak and vulnerable and perhaps "helpless" I really am. Then, what would you think of me? And, what's even worse, what would I think of myself.

It is these very negative and ill-informed, frankly pointless questions that our negative self-talk tries to defend. We are our own worst enemy. If we could just get out of our own way!!

In this book, we will explore in depth the need to bring others into our lives. To not live alone and on our own. To know when and how to ask for help. It's out there, many people would be happy and honored to assist us and mentor us back to health and happiness. In 12-step recovery programs, we find our way back to healthy and purposeful living by asking someone to sponsor us in the 12-step program of recovery. Whatever our specific issues and problems, someone has been through it before. There is no point in re-inventing the wheel and we need to rid ourselves of this pointless and harmful "terminal uniqueness" that propels us to do it everything on our own by ourselves.

Perhaps one of the most effective recovery programs in the world, the 12-steps of Alcoholics Anonymous, which has been translated to virtually over 100 self-help programs dealing with a thousand form of addictions, that has proved time and again that the fellowship of people like us with common problems and treatment issues can better work together to solve our personal and collective problems.

For me, it was a necessary bridge back to a better life. Quite frankly, I largely attribute this program divinely created by two struggling and hopeless alcoholics, Bill Wilson and Dr. Bob back in 1935 to helping me to relearn my life with something I fondly call Good Orderly Direction – something I failed to learn growing up. First, through the rooms of 12-step recovery and then a sponsor and many mentors, I finally learned how to live life and get out of my own way.

When the Student Is Ready, the Teacher WILL Appear

How true this has turned out to be. One has to be ready for change, and until that time, he or she will continue to resist or deflect those things that could and most likely would benefit him or her most. I have experienced so many "Aha" moments of discovery and sudden realization in my own life, and each time I realized that I was finally open to and ready for some new truth or pearl of wisdom. I experience an epiphany or sudden realization that something I haven't heretofore understood is true and finally makes sense to me. For me, this often revolved around the experience of pain, intense frustration or discomfort, but as I learned slowly and often begrudgingly, when I began to trust the process of change, a new window of opportunity took place.

It is never too late to have an "Aha – oh yeah, now I get it!" moment in your life when suddenly understood or never got before -- a powerful and exciting, new reality. These serendipitous moments of clarity can be powerful gateways to new and important experiences and levels of awareness. It's all about growth, and as I look back, there were always teachers and guides ready to help and the moment I was truly open and ready, they were there happily guiding me to some new truth or realization. Today, I experience "Aha" moments regularly and happily, as I am very open to change and discovering new truths in my life. Sometimes, we call these miracles – and indeed they are!

"Don't Worry, Be Happy!"

The talented lyricist and songwriter, Bobby McFerrin, wrote this now famous song "Don't Worry Be Happy" some 30 years ago. It resonated with all of us a few years ago, because we all know how very hard it is to both not worry and be happy at the same time. Clearly, everyone wishes this were always true all the time. If only we didn't worry and were always happy. What would or could this eternal state of mind really be like? Allow me to share some of the lyrics that still play on in my head:

"Here's a little song I wrote
you might want to sing it note for note
don't worry, be happy
in every life we have some trouble
But when you worry you make it double
don't worry, be happy…"

Ain't got no place to lay your head
somebody came and took your bed
don't worry, be happy
the landlord say your rent is late
He may have to litigate
don't worry, be happy."

What a great way to think, believe and act! I need to be reminded that whatever life challenges come my way, it is always important to have a good, positive attitude and to know that no matter what, EVERYTHING is going to be alright! This belief and attitude towards life eliminates so many roadblocks to change.

Facing Your Fears

America may be the home of the brave, but for many of us, we are scaredy cats when it comes to facing our fears. We talked about Fear in "Roadblocks to Change". We all have them to varying degrees. But, the only way to grow is to move through our fears and to face them square on. There is no way around it and it takes bravery and courage to do so effectively. You don't need to face these all at once, but you do need to prepare yourself for good, positive and beneficial changes in your life. So, once again, as the saying goes, "No pain, no gain." While it doesn't have to be painful to move through your fears – as most all of them are imaginary and simply the boogey-man in disguise, it does require a strong enough desire to realize that facing our fears also translates to dropping most all of them once and for all and for good.

So, you will come to realize that these fears are not facts and can easily be dispelled with experience and perspective. So, jump in, the water's fine!

Life Is a Journey

One of the fundamental precepts to learning to live our lives on purpose is that it doesn't need to happen all happen in a day. It takes time to develop a good and meaningful life, as well as to make the many iterative changes along the way. Some days we will see big changes, other days we won't feel any at all. Or it may seem that we have take two steps forward and then one step back.

It is important that we realize that this process we are attempting to go through, while being looked at in a "How to Love Yourself"-hour period for shock value, is going to happen over time and with varying results. Enjoy the ride, as that is exactly what it is. There really is no destination. Each day never stays the same. As we come to realize that the joy of life is in the here and now and letting go of the past, no longer fearing the future, we come to appreciate the joys and gifts of each and every day. And, here like a snowflake, no one day is ever the same as another. We finally get to smell the roses and observe their amazing beauty. Life just keeps getting better with time.

Building a Durable Foundation

One of the benefits of learning to be patient with ourselves and others is that constructing a masterpiece takes time. It also has to happen in steps. You can't put on the roof and insert the kitchen without first building a durable and lasting foundation. Let's do the job of changing our lives right the first time. Otherwise, we will be doomed to rip it down and start all over again.

As a chronic relapser back in to my addictions, I now understand the importance of changing everything and taking the necessary time to build my life correctly from the ground up. For me, that means building a solid set of beliefs and values, good moral character and acting and behaving in a way that is responsible and positive. It also means taking care of all the precious pieces that make up my life like my physical health, emotional and spiritual health, feeding my head and educating myself, and being a solid card carrying member of society by being an active part of the world around me. These are the solid stones on which I can layer the rest of my building and my life. At the end of the day, come good days and bad, my house will endure for eternity and be a gift for many others who will come to live in it.

Making a Decision

The first step to change is actually making a conscious decision to change. I can only assume that you if you've made it this far, you have a pretty good idea that you both want to and have make a conscious choice to make important changes in our own life. If that is so, congratulations! You have taken the first step to receiving the many wonderful benefits that lie ahead by choosing wisely!

Becoming Accountable

I believe that being and staying accountable for the things we think, believe, intend, do or say – for how we treat ourselves and others is entirely our affair and responsibility. Being brutally honest with yourself on the accountability front is a huge step towards growing up and becoming a positive example of change for others.

How many times to do we find ourselves blaming others, letting ourselves slide on taking responsibility or those things we either need to do or did – thinking that others will pick up the slack. We have this built-in forgetter to our commitments to ourselves and others. It is OK to let things slide this time. But is it? Are we still that child that needs to be scolded or are we the adults here?

I'm all about results and they don't lie. So, when you make a commitment to do something, just do it! If you won't, then don't expect others to do it either. Where does that leave you? Probably in the lurch and later feeling guilty that you didn't own up to your side of the bargain. And, the only place that this leads is to regret and disappointment.

Life Is a Practice Test

Each and every day of our lives prepares us for something bigger, better and at a higher level tomorrow. It may not seem that way, but when we drop our need to always be perfect and perform on cue and at peak performance each day, we come to realize that it's OK to not be perfect, to make mistakes and to learn from them and improve the next time. The point is to not keep repeating the same ones over and over.

The concept of "practice makes perfect" makes enormous sense. Each day we refine our aim, our technique, and our style and look forward to the many rewards of daily improvement. When the day is done, we can thank the power of the universe for a job well done and for another opportunity to improve tomorrow. We never know when our big performance will come, but when it does, we can give ourselves a pat on the back for a job well done and well rehearsed!

Trials & Tribulations

I have become keenly aware of the importance of both trials and tribulations as the result of experiencing so very many of them in my own life – especially in the last 10 years. Each experience of pain and suffering, struggle and judgment is our higher power's way of getting us to change for the better. To grow and to become conscious of these difficulties as huge opportunities to learn something new about ourselves and to see those areas of our lives that need improvement. They are not punishments, but rather random gifts to pay attention, because each new challenge and difficulty is an opportunity to improve and grow. Pain is truly the touchstone of all change in our lives.

When we reframe our focus from feeling that we are being punished each time our wits are tested or we experience difficulty and discomfort to high-level signals that we need to look deep inside to see what we are doing wrong, the problem becomes an opportunity to turn what appears to be a negative into a positive.

Stepping Out of Your Comfort Zone

Nobody said lasting and permanent change was going to be easy. Nor is changing anything worthwhile comfortable. Prepare yourself for the ride of your life. Be brave and stay positive. Your glass is half-filled today, not half-empty. You can do anything if you apply yourself.

Doing the same, old thing produces the same old results. Keeping an open mind and showing a willingness to try new ways of doing things might actually surprise you. If you don't try, you'll never know. If you don't know, you will never know what you missed. You already know that you life is missing some essential skills and strategies that will help you to break out of your unsuccessful way of doing the same old, disappointing thing.

Try, Test, Experiment, Take Calculated Risks

To that end, the way we learn new things in life is by exposing ourselves to trial and error. I love learning new ways of doing things and discovering new truths. The way I got there is by taking chances. While it is important to think things through before jumping off a cliff, you might also learn a great deal about gravity and the body's amazing ability to heal itself.

Build Perspective, Get Information & Knowledge, Educate Yourself, Read & Learn With Passion

What we are trying to do here is to build a new framework for living our life, and it is important to become an explore, learn as much about this new way of life, talk to people who have been through the pain and struggle and have successfully come out of the other end of the dark tunnel changed people. To that end, gather information, get the facts, educate yourself, learn and read with a passion and build a new perspective on what it really means and feels like to live a meaningful and purposeful life. Be hungry for the truth.

Become an Observer of Life

As a reporter and journalist early on in my career, I was taught to ask questions and in order to build perspective on any subject I was tasked with writing about. I love to research and explore on Google, in the library, or even by interviewing people. But, some of my best research is done by observing not just what people say, but what they do.

Nature and life is a magnificent laboratory full of secrets and strategies that are free and readily at our disposal. Become an avid watcher of people, of patterns, of the news, of nature and always stay a student in the process of discovering deeper levels of truth and understanding. I can sit in nature all day long and be amazed at what I learn. Our surroundings are inviting us to learn about them. Predispose yourself to becoming an observer and constant student. Be curious and explore. Open yourself up to a new adventure each day and stop prejudging what you think you are supposed to see and learn. You'd be amazed at how just being present for all the many experiences of life around you can teach you so many important things.

Hope and Inspiration

Hope springs eternal and as discussed in "Roadblocks to Change" section earlier, the lack of hope that your life and circumstances can get better is a sure sign that you have given up before the good fight. Being and staying hopeful is the necessary invitation for miracles to happen in your life. It is the flame on the candle that becomes brighter with time.   And, it is this flame that illuminates your way to positive change and to good things today and tomorrow.

Life is full of inspiration – especially when I open my eyes to the many brave people who have come before me and who were inspired by others and even their own, incremental improvements. These are my life's heroes and I am awed and amazed by their strength and fortitude to both take action and see the positive side of their journey, despite life's many obstacles and challenges. Stay inspired and always full of hope. You will be amazed at how the well of good fortune never runs dry.

"Just Do It"

One of the best advertising slogans and branding vehicles by any product or corporation ever, Nike coined this phrase, and most of us find that it still rings true today. Stop getting in your own way, find your own momentum and just go for it – whatever you heart desires or passions burn. Never look back and never have regrets for trying and doing new things in your own life. This is something my father taught me at an early age. There is no time like today to take responsibility, own your life as it is and go for the gold in whatever you choose to do. Live with vitality and a thirst for whatever you do!

Lighten Up & Don't Take Yourself So Seriously

If only I could have internalized this concept when I was younger, perhaps my life wouldn't have turned out to be such a heavy weight and a burden at times. I need to always remind myself to lighten up and not take myself and my life so seriously. Nothing is that important that it is worth being miserable over or dying for.

Identify, Don't Compare

As we embark on our "How to Love Yourself"-Hour Reboot journey, it is really important to try to identify with others' experiences and feelings, and not to compare these to our own. We are not in a race, and it is important to be part of the collective experience by being able to show empathy and compassion towards others. We are not the standard to which everyone needs to be compared. But, we will learn a great deal about ourselves by seeing common experiences in others. This will also help to open up our heart, get out of self and become an important part of something much larger than ourselves.

Further comparing ourselves to everyone else will be sure to disappoint and create resentments. Everyone has their own unique set of strengths and weaknesses. The only one you need to please is yourself and what others do or compare is really none of your business. We want and need to turn the focus of attention on ourselves. In time, you will develop your own acceptable standards and this is how you will learn to measure yourself. Comparing ourselves to others is all part of the negative self-talk that we want to avoid and that we will address shortly in the next section.

<u>Take the Pause That Refreshes!</u>

When in doubt and you're not sure of your motives, take a time out and give your situation a pause. By taking a time out and stepping away – even momentarily -- from a difficult situation, this may save you from later embarrassment or humiliation. How many times can you remember saying something, doing something or sending something via email and then regretting it? I'm sure you can relate. So, pause before reacting and give the moment some inner thought to create the best possible outcome that won't come back to haunt you later.

Chapter V:

LEARNING THE TOOLS OF THE SELF-LOVE & HEALING TRADE

Making a Commitment to Making Life Work

The first steps to change are first making an actual decision and then a commitment that you will exert the necessary psychic, emotional and physical energy, as well as marshal the necessary physical and psychic resources to effect positive changes in your life. You are not going to have all the answers to all your problems today. The truth is, you don't need to. All you need is sufficient trust and faith in the process that you will be guided through. You will ultimately have complete control over the decision to pick and choose those tools and strategies that might work best for you. So, stop all the unnecessary worrying.

These are action steps that will get you to the starting point. Have you had enough pain? Is your life unmanageable? Have you tried other approaches and didn't get the results you were after? Are you ready to try something entirely new? Then, now is the time to choose to heal and grow and commit to do WHATEVER is required to take the actual steps to get you where you know you really want and need to go. Upwards and onwards, bigger and better, happier and more fulfilled, towards the light and away from the negativity and defeat that you have all too well known. Are you now fully committed to change??

Treating the Whole Person

All the many tools we will explore now are meant to treat the whole person. What do I mean by that? We are not just our body, our mind, our five senses, our thoughts, our personalities, our feelings, passions, desires, and our souls. Our lives consist of a complex ecosystem of body, mind, spirit, heart, interconnectedness to family, friends, society, our country, to nature and other beings, the world and planet and finally the infinite universe. Everything is connected and you can't treat just the mind, the body or the soul separately without impacting the other parts.

So, change and healing can only occur when we treat the whole person. Not just our past, our future fears, our physical ailments or symptoms, our spiritual malaise or mental impairments. Please keep this in mind when choosing any method, strategy or treatment.

Life is all about balance and wholeness. My particular healing process took place from the inside out – from the healing of my inner soul that needed and continues to need attention and growth, to allowing my body, mind and emotional self to be healed. My body and internal organs were pretty beat up from

all the years of abuse. I was an emotional and mental basket-case and nothing seemed to be working.
As my soul began to heal, the body and mind followed. I felt better physically and mentally as I started
taking care of my spiritual and emotional needs. As I continued to heal on the inside and outside, my
life and all the many people and parts of my outside world also began to heal. This is the story of my
life, and can be a big part of your story too!

Humans are ingenious with their inventions, potions and remedies for coping and easing pain. Some of
this is hocus pocus and some of it is valid. It's often hard to distinguish the charlatans from the true
healers.   Pain comes in many forms, but it almost always hurts. The mind and willpower have given
birth to a wide variety of imaginative salves and solutions. But the common denominator is that pain is
almost always uncomfortable and creates dis-ease emotionally, spiritually, cognitively and, of course,
physically. And pain affects not just us, but all those we love, care for and associate with on the outside.

We are all familiar with the legions of mental, emotional, spiritual and physical healers and practitioners
who we happily pay to help us ease our pain and discomfort. Born out of necessity is the army of
specialists for just about any ailment that you can describe. Our society is very pain adverse and we will
often pay just about anything to ease our pain and secure expert advice.

Despite the professional armies of pain "healers" that exist in just about every country through a litany
of institutions, science and the experts are fairly clueless about the true causes and conditions to our
discomforts. Most treatments treat the symptom and not the root cause. The exceptions appear to lie
with many ancient therapies – mostly originating either from Mother Nature or from Asia. These latter
remedies focus on treating the causes and not so much the symptoms, as is true in most Western
medicine.

I've long been a "searcher" of cures and for the truth. I've been more successful recently with getting
the truth. After 60 years, I've come to the frustrating conclusion that there are many paths to the same
solution. Depending upon your specific D.N.A., level of belief and willingness, different strokes will work
for different folks. But permanent relief is work and a work in progress!

What has finally worked for me after repeated trial and error is a combination of therapies and
techniques. More recently, my searching has paid off with more spiritually based healing of the very
deep type. I endured an incredible and ridiculous amount of pain and suffering to find out that what
works best for me is prayer, meditation and spiritual psychology – which are a fairly new, and highly
unappreciated and ignored field of exploration in the rising Age of Aquarius. I've combined that with a
strong dose of cognitive behavioral therapies, 12-step spiritual guidance and the spiritual side of my
religion of birth and choice – Judaism. I still cling too much of Buddhist and Hindu practices and I pray
and practice transcendental meditation daily. I am a devout believer in a universal creator and creative
intelligence – divinely inspired in the universe.

What's more, I now take really good care of my body and emotional health and have let go of my past traumas and have finally begun to really enjoy and honor my life. My attitude is positively positive, passionate and awesome!

Let's take some time to explore the different methods and practices that are out there. I will do my best not to bias any of them and will suggest that you explore and experiment with your own "mix" of methods and strategies. But, please do focus on combining the best with the best for your own unique situation and personal needs. There are more than enough professionals to help you dive deeper into anything you choose. You need to be the judge, but research, try and test and then discover what works for you best.

The Importance of Self-Care

I don't know why people often aren't as kind to themselves as they are to others. Perhaps, it has something to do with not recognizing our own blind spots. We seem to always know what's best for others and are quick to point these certainties out to them, but when it comes to looking at our own needs, we seem to come up short on wisdom and taking good care of us.

What kind of care am I talking about? Care of our emotional needs, our physical needs and wants, our psychological health, or basic physical care. And, perhaps as important as all of these combined, the care of the soul. This latter area of self-care is toughest for most of us because we can't see and feel what it is that we need to be taking care of. How do we fill that "hole" in our soul? What is our particular soul sickness?

There is a need to take care of the whole person, which includes both the physical and metaphysical -- things we can touch and those things that we feel or sense but don't fully know or have the skills to wrap our arms around. We will discuss in a while the need to develop and maintain a lifestyle balance – which includes all these and other pieces. Humans are part of a micro and macro ecosystem and any weaknesses in the chain affect other parts of the system.

Clearly, if we don't take proper care of ourselves, and keep in repair those parts that are getting worn or cheated, then we will pay handsomely for this negligence in other ways later. Things like getting physically ill, emotionally challenged, depressed, anxious or a host of other more serious psychological and emotional ailments. Perhaps we'll have a mental or nervous breakdown, or just feel like we're getting closer to our breaking point. Like the body, we can only push those other parts of ourselves so far before they break or begin to show wear and tear. Then, there's the mind-body connection where say an emotional illness can later manifest in physical ways – making us even sicker. When the soul is not taken proper care of, the emotional, mental and physical parts of ourselves suffer. So, be good, considerate, thoughtful, loving, caring and kind to your body and your soul, to yourself. When you feel worn out, rest. When you feel sad, allow your feelings to direct you to the source of the problem. While our feelings may not be fact, they are signposts to the areas of our lives that need healing. Get to

know yourself, your capacity and limits. Know when to say no and when to ask for help or perspective
Learn to take care of yourself – as you matter the most. A simple metaphor for knowing the importance
of self-care might be putting on your own overhead oxygen masks before placing them on to your
children or the elderly or infirm. If you can't breathe, how are you going to help others to do so?

Healing Our Inner Child

This is a subject and a potential learning opportunity near and dear to me. The notion that we have this
little child within ourselves that still has unhealed hurts and sadness is very powerful. Close your eyes
for a moment and think back to those times in your childhood when you felt hurt, abandoned, scorned
by a parent or an adult, unloved, not good enough, lonely, scared, vulnerable, confused, abused or
traumatized in some way. Even though you are an adult now, perhaps you still flash back on these
feelings that there is something missing. You still dwell on those moments in your childhood that still
live on in you disturbed and unsettled. I believe that those wounds are forever active and exist
somewhere on a soul level. Until you choose to heal and make peace with them, with those unsettling
moments that still leave you angry or vulnerable today, these feelings will continue to live on inside you
and fester. This, in turn, detracts from your ability to become whole and grow emotionally, spiritually
and consciously.

During my incarceration, I took a Parenting course, because I have grown children and know that the
trauma of my Alcoholism and eventual incarceration really hurt my children, my ex-wife, and our
families. I wanted to see what I could do to help them forgive me and to become a better and more
meaningful parent and life partner.

The truth is, I learned more about being a child than I did about parenting. My marvelous instructor had
me write a letter to my parents, my ex-wife, my children and to the child who still lived wounded within
me. He also had me visualize that little boy who felt abandoned, lonely, not loved and never good
enough. He had my adult self talk to that little, scared and sad boy and assures him that he would never
have to feel this way again. That his adult version of himself would also be there to help, protect and
guide him. That he was loved and good enough.

Some of you may protest that real men don't do these things. Hogwash! Between the letters, which I
never sent, but did spend some time writing and contemplating, and the visualization exercises, I finally
started to heal and let go my anger, resentment, frustration and feelings of inadequacy. Today, I am
happy to report to you that I feel free from the anger, sadness and emptiness I felt as a child. While
feelings aren't necessarily facts, they are powerful triggers and often come from irrational beliefs that
we still hold as adults. We both need to challenge these often false and misleading beliefs and to
correct them to heal and create better outcomes for ourselves. This is one of the ways that we can
leave our unhappy pasts behind and free ourselves up for much deserved peace-of-mind that will allow
us to experience the amazing life that is right in front of us!

While I have just touched on this powerful healing tool, there are many excellent books and even therapies that you can avail yourself of. I suggest you put this on your "To Do" list and allow yourself to be freed from your boo-boos from childhood. You won't regret the time it took to examine something today that took place years ago.

Taming King/Queen Baby

Many of us can identify with the King or Queen Baby syndrome.   Our self-centered, selfish and childlike ways of dealing with the world put us on a pedestal with our crowns and royal ways demanding that life should serve us and not the other way around. We want everything our way, on our terms when we want it. We make unreasonable demands on our peers, family and friends to serve us "Or Way," holding the pickles and the lettuce. We are spoiled and grandiose in our beliefs.

We've all had moments like this – some more than others. Naturally, we can't sustain a healthy life or find balance – let alone keep friends and family - by continuing with this warped attitude. If you have struggled with King or Queen Baby, get off your high horse and come down to smell the roses with us common folk. You will be far better served learning about humility and how to show gratitude and to be a servant rather than a royal. Positive Attitude and right thinking will take you far when you are both humble and grateful. You are now the adult and it's time to let the King and Queen rest in peace – and to allow your truth, authentic self to rule!

Lighten Up; Don't Take Yourself Too Seriously

Nothing is worth getting bent out of shape over – really. I, for one, have always been way too serious. I think I must have been born that way. Being overly serious has a lot to do with being emotionally over-sensitive or just plain ill-equipped to handle adversity. Perhaps it is our personality's defense mechanism to protect ourselves from hurtful situations or is just a permanent state of hurt. Certainly, it has something to do with not being emotionally well balanced. I would love to lighten up most all the time, but it just seems so hard to enjoy myself and experience life with a sense of levity.

There is a saying in 12-step culture that one of the goals of living a sober life is emotional sobriety – which goes along with physical sobriety. Being emotionally balanced, accepting of life as it is and not necessarily as you would have it, dealing with life on life's terms and not necessarily just on your own is emotional sobriety. Not getting too angry or too elated – not being so up and down (or for some bi-polar), but somewhere in the middle is my goal. So, the saying goes like this: "Learn to life like a set of loose clothes."

Humor as A Way of Life & Lightness

I love to laugh, but don't do it nearly often enough. Humor and laughing has been found to elevate the healing process in sick people, as does being and staying positive. It provides hope and instills inspiration in those fighting for their lives. Laughing is contagious and a good belly laugh is worth its weight in levity. So, learn to laugh, to embrace humor as a way of living your life. It shows your appreciation for the lighter side of things.
There is nothing more satisfying than a good belly laugh – one that brings you near to tears. For me, laughing is often the best therapy for a dull and drab day. Give yourself permission and the time to listen to someone else's jokes, watch late night talk shows or just enjoy a good joke and someone else's humor at a cocktail or dinner party. Laugh and be happy.

Stepping Out of Fear, Anger, Resentment, Sadness, Self Doubt, Guilt & Remorse

All emotions that are serious and formidable road blocks to your own life recovery and reboot. Negative emotions that pray on our sense of self-esteem, being comfortable in our own skin, and our ability to embrace and enjoy life are one of the many goals of "How to Love Yourself"-Reboot. In order to make a decision to take positive actions in our life, we must learn to manage and deal with these negative emotions. This book provides a variety of life tools and methods, as well as programs to do so. It is not something you can expect to conquer and eliminate instantly, but with repeated effort and the concerted power of Honesty, Open Mindedness and Willingness ("HOW"), anything is possible. As we will address later, you can't have trust and faith in a Higher Power while you are sitting in Fear, Anger, Resentment and Sadness. So, building a healthy relationship with self, getting out of self, and stepping into life on life's terms are the steps we need to take to conquer our often irrational feelings and state of emotions.

Anger Management

Anger is a difficult and irrational emotional reaction to situations and events that happen to us that we feel we can't control. Often, anger is caused because we have a false belief that something should happen when certain situations arise and we become disappointed when they don't. Anger is a problem when we get stuck in it and our feelings of Anger linger or reappear when we are triggered by some internal or external event. Anger can also be a harmful weapon that we used against others and ourselves. If we allow anger to go unmanaged, it can manifest as violence towards ourselves and other in several forms. Abuse towards ourselves and others can be physical, emotional, psychological, and can cause enormous spiritual damage.

Learning to manage our anger is critical to achieving emotional balance. There is not much happiness and joy to be experienced while in a fit of anger or rage, or sitting in your own feelings and feeling like acting out physically, emotionally or in some other damaging way either towards yourself or others. So, if you struggle with being angry and not being able to manage what or when you might act out, consider a series of anger management tools available from behavior modification, cognitive behavioral therapy, quieting your mind through meditation, yoga, breathing or other physical and mental exercises that have been proven to be effective. But, don't choose to be angry and stay that way. Again, life is 10% what happens to us and 90% what we do about it. A lot can change within that 90%!

Giving Yourself Permission

For What? How about for finding the life you always dreamed of and deserve! For living your life that you were always intended to live. For being the person who you really are and for allowing yourself to be you. We can be our worst own enemy. So, you can give yourself permission and make a decision to take a chance, use the tools that are so freely available to you, drop your resentments, and other road blocks to change that might be getting in your way of positive change and try and test this new life of yours out to its fullest. Sometimes we have to make a conscious decision to undo what we unconsciously blocked!

Learning to Love Yourself

Perhaps a higher and critically important goal and purpose of Self-Care is making yourself your number one priority in life. When you finally get to know yourself, understand who you really are and what makes you tick, set and work to achieve your own goals and purpose in life, you will like what you see, how you feel, and confirm that you are doing those very things that will create a higher sense of self-esteem. Continuing to do esteem able things and the next right thing with your thoughts and motives, attitudes, actions and behaviors create so many positive benefits. As you stop loathing the person you became and start appreciating the person you are becoming, your ability to be the person you've always wanted to be that others are now seeing, perhaps for the first time, you are going to like and eventually love yourself.

Our ability to receive and express love is, perhaps, the most important emotion and experience we can have in life. The more we love others, the more love we get back in turn. The better we feel about ourselves, the better we feel about others and our prospects to live a happy, joyous and purposeful life with meaning and immense satisfaction. If you can't love and appreciate yourself, how can you possibility truly love another? Love is always the answer – inside and out – and Love is all around you – you just need to learn how to see and take your share.

Many of us not so well adjusted types are plain uncomfortable in our skin. We do everything we can to avoid and stuff, even deny our feelings. Why? We don't believe that we are worthy or deserving of to feel good about ourselves. That we need to continue to punish ourselves for perceived – real or imagined – inadequacies. It might be fair to say that we're not very nice to ourselves. In fact, we inflict a great deal of harm by self-flagellation, anesthetizing our feelings and avoiding situations that make us feel inadequate or bad.

Why do we shoot the messenger? Remember, feelings aren't always facts, but are important signposts that we still have work to do on our thinking, behavior, intentions, attitudes. We might need to depend upon our spiritual practice to get better results. We need also to take stock that it's OK to be less than perfect, to not be the best and to give ourselves the occasional pat on the back for a job well done.

As we get to know ourselves better and find more positive ways to live and actualize our lives, we start giving our self permission to get comfortable in our skin. As we get to like ourselves more, we begin to accept who we really are and feel empowered to take those necessary actions that will lead us to emotional and spiritual freedom from our old selves. Like learning to love ourselves, we also need to learn to be kind and gentle with ourselves, take care of ourselves when needed, maintain a good and healthy lifestyle balance and be our own advocate in life. If we won't or can't do this, than how can we expect others to do it for us? Being a good friend to yourself makes it much easier to build healthier, more sustainable and rewarding friendships with others. We all need friends as part of our true purpose in life. Share, love, give and receive.

Feeling Your Feelings

Many of us have learned to "stuff" our feelings and we all know where that gets us: Full of anger, resentment, self-pity, and grief. When you are flooded with powerful emotions and feelings, I am a big believer in sharing them with others who understand you and will consider your feelings the most. They'll also be the same people who will call you on your "stuff" when they feel you're doing damage, misinformed, not focusing on facts (feelings aren't necessarily factual), walking off an emotional or behavioral cliff or something worse. Sharing our feelings with the people who know us best is a safe way to find land and a safe haven in often stormy waters. When we don't deal with our feelings either rationally, empathetically, sympathetically or at all we run the risk of doing even more damage to ourselves and others.

Self-help or communities of people who share your issues and know you best is always a good choice. If your problems are especially severe and are bordering on unmanageable, seek professional help through therapy, coaching, or even a medical professional.

Managing Your Feelings

On a similar note, as you get better at recognizing the typical suspects that trigger your emotions, you will build the tools to manage your feelings and emotions. Later, we will talk about challenging your false beliefs and thoughts which can easily distort and trick your emotions into feeling things that are not based on fact. Managing your feelings would also include better self-care, taking a time out as the dangerous waves of emotions can easily overwhelm you. Sharing your feelings and emotions is another way to cut the power of the feeling in half and to gain perspective on your particular situation. Another excellent way to gain what I call emotional sobriety or balance is to move a muscle and change a thought and don't sit in your feelings for too long, but do something different to also change the way you might be feeling. Lastly, getting out of self and helping others is one of the most effective ways to tame your emotions, which are often self-centered and part of our self-absorption. Help another with their problems and share with them how you dealt with similar situations. Show them your strength, focus on the positive and solutions and watch how quickly your feelings of self-pity, self-wallowing and eventually anger and resentment to build to a dangerous and very uncomfortable crescendo.

For those of us that are emotionally sensitive, managing your emotions to get more productive results that will also serve as important situational and life teaching lessons is critical. As we will talk about later, trials and tribulations in life are God's way of telling you to pay attention and give energy to more important issues that may be underlying your feelings. Our goal is to become emotionally balanced and healthy. Our larger goal is to experience more happiness and joy in our lives as we script how to also make them more meaningful and full of purpose. You can master your emotions by learning how to manage them better.

This Too Shall Pass

We've talked about how negative emotions are often the result of not being present – but rather obsessing about the past or fearing the future or some future loss of something you cherish. Most of these feelings are not real and, almost always pass in due time. Since we are not really known for our patience, we fret that these feelings and emotions will last forever. They won't.

It's very much like grief. When the trauma of death of a loved one occurs, we must go through a grieving process. For some of us, it can happen fairly quickly or even very slowly. With work and support from others to heal our feelings of loss, grief eventually passes. It is not necessarily healthy to grieve for long periods of time, as it can retard your own growth and happiness which is not negotiable in my book. Not to be callous with others' and your own feelings, but it is important to recognize that you are holding on to something very natural, it is not about you and that perhaps there is something far deeper going on with you. Maybe it's your own unhealed or incomplete relationship with that person, your inability and failure to express your own heartfelt feelings and love to that person while they were alive or some other unfinished business. Today, there is nothing you can do about it, as the person is already passed. The only healthy thing you can do is heal yourself and let it go. It's natural and, like all feelings, will pass in time.

Handling Negative Emotions

There are many ways to deal with anger, resentment, self-pity, self-doubt, remorse, fear and the usual other suspects. The main idea is to deal with them and not sit in them. That's the destructive part of the feeling – it continues to hurt you and in turn you continue to hurt others.

Learning to let go and let someone other than you – even your Higher Power – to handle these problems for you. When I had overwhelming legal problem, I was instructed by my personal mentors to make my lawyer my higher power and to make it his job to handle my problems.

Taking the Sting Out of Anger & Resentment: Pray For the Other Person

Sounds crazy, but it works like a charm if you can hold out long enough. So here's what I was taught that helped me: When you are holding on to a strong resentment, are stuck in your self-justified anger and have already started feeling sorry for yourself through your own self-pity, pray for the other person to get the help they need to heal and resolve their issue or problem for 10 days. If your feelings haven't diminished or disappeared by the end of 10 days and you have honestly put in the effort to sincerely and unselfishly with holding onto your own anger pray for the other person to get better, then try it for another 10 days.

Praying for the other person serves several purposes and comes with added fringe benefits: 1. it gets you out of self. 2. It puts the focus on your attention to helping and not just hurting and punishing the other person, 3. It creates both actual and spiritual good will. The best part, when you do it sincerely, honestly and without reservation it take the focus off your intense feelings and allows the cool down period to occur and to give you the time to build a healthier and more sustainable distance between you, your feelings and the target of your emotions.

Living A Day-At-A-Time

"How to Love Yourself" is all about thoroughly evaluating your life and priorities as if today were your last day on earth. There is much wisdom, too, to focus on doing your life a day-at-a-time, in "How to Love Yourself"-hour time segments. We can handle most anything today, but projecting into next day and even further into the future to next week, month or year gets us in trouble and can easily make our life and emotions feel out of control and unmanageable. Just for today is a great way to think about your current experiences and reframe your life. It really makes everything that much more do-able and far simpler.

The reason why alcoholics and addicts are taught to re-frame their lives into "How to Love Yourself"-hour segments is that it is far easier to deal with the urges and cravings of your addiction a day at a time rather than anticipating stopping forever. Not picking up that first drink or drug today, now, at this very urgent moment is the way we are taught abstinence. This incremental minute by minute, hour by hour and day by day existence is the way we put distance between ourselves and our drug of behavior of choice. We may need the help of a detox or rehab to do so, but once the initial and often dangerous withdrawal period has passed, we retrain ourselves by changing our habits by introducing new tools, ways of socializing and re-education for the rest of our lives. Change is incremental for many of us, but there is nothing we can't do a day-at-a-time.

Framing Your Day with Thanks & Asking For the Help You Really Need

I begin each day with a simple prayer that My God gives me the guidance and the strength to deal with all my current challenges and tasks. As importantly, I ask God to help those I know also need his help, that are still sick and/or suffering and don't have much light in their own life to help them illuminate the solutions to their own problem. I ask For God to help the medically and emotionally sick and to bring painless end to those that are terminally suffering. I also ask God to help guide those that have recently passed on their spiritual journey to their next destination. I ask for God's grace to bring a smile to their soul. When needed, I ask for God's help and strength throughout the day when I feel pressed or am in need of a solution to a problem. I also ask that God help me to stay clean and sober and not to act out in any negative ways. The second part of my daily rituals are about giving and expressing heat felt thanks to my Higher Power and to those that have been kind with their time and other resources to help me or another. I show my appreciation by saying "Thank You" when it is deserved. At the end of the day, I thank God from the bottom of my heart for all the blessings I have received and for both the good and the bad that has happened to me that day. The bad are always signals from above for me to correct some behavior, attitude or bad intent/motive that is negative, selfish, unlawful or just unethical or immoral. I ask for His forgiveness and ask Him to help others forgive themselves for hurting another. I mean every word of it. This took me a long time and gets better with practice. I have included some simple, not religious, just spiritual prayers and affirmations that you can use and adapt for yourself and your own particular needs,

Stop Taking Everything So Personally: Give Yourself A Break!

As I've discussed earlier, I have long struggled with being emotionally over-sensitive. I had a bad habit of allowing things to rent space in my head. I would mistakenly think that others' were always pointing the finger at me.

Most all the time what people say or do has nothing to do about me. I just think so and take it too personally. I am always impressed when others allow things to roll off of their shoulders. They don't get emotionally embroiled in what other people say or think about them or anyone else. Frankly, what other people say or do has nothing to do with me, and has far more to say about them. It's all about my level of Acceptance of things as they are, and not as I feel they are because of my sometimes distorted perceptions. So, my advice, just doesn't take things too personally, lighten up and enjoy!

Finally, Let Go, Let God and Stop Sweating the Small Stuff

Life is far too short for us to sweat and angst over every little detail. Those of us who are emotionally challenged tend to let everything affect us. We lack perspective and can't see that many things really don't matter in the scheme of things. Why do we expend so much unnecessary energy on all the little things in life when the big things are what we should be paying attention to?

Some people are really good with doing all the small things and taking the small steps in life; others are big picture people and can see the forest through the trees. I believe that we need to appreciate both but find ourselves sometime in between: understanding and appreciating those many small things that are necessary to make bigger things happen in our life (the Micro) while understanding and not losing sight of the bigger prizes that await us by achieving our bigger, perhaps more important goals (the Macro).

Dropping the Rocks of Anger, Resentment, Self-Pity, Remorse & Fear

There is both a need and an art to letting go and letting of the heavy burdens, guilt, self-pity, anger and resentments of your past. Part of this comes from acts of forgiveness of yourself and others. But, it also comes from letting go of the wreckage of your past. Part of this is just growing up and getting past your negative feelings and emotions. This is something you need to do on your own or with the help and support of others more capable. Let me introduce yet another way:

Turning Your Anger into Something More Positive & Powerful

The emotion of anger can have tremendous power over you and others. Imagine being able to better control and manage your anger and then turning all the negative energy and passion for self-destruction into something good and positive. Passion can have two sides – one far more attractive and lasting then the other. Learn how to develop an outlet for your anger – whether it be hitting the gym and pouring out your negative feelings in to an aerobics, yoga, spin or cross fit class and sweating your negative feelings out on the mat. Or, perhaps, turn this power inside by meditating and transform those negative feelings into something more productive and satisfying and feed your soul while calming down.

Accepting Tough Love as a Compliment and a Sign of Love and Caring

We tend to be fairly defensive people and don't like to be told that we are wrong. But, in times of deeper distress, we aren't always in our right mind and get caught up in our emotions and mental anguish and turmoil. These feelings, while not always facts, can end up hurting us and others – or take their form in something even more destructive.

So, when someone is trying to help you by being firm with you or telling you something you probably don't want to hear, you end up putting up the wall that keeps them out. Tough love, while not easy to swallow, is sometimes the very medicine that we need to get out of our own heads and see things for what they are – not as we would like them. Expressions of tough love by those who care from us is sometimes the only way that people with thick heads like us will actually be able to hear what is often best for us. An extreme version of this might be doing an intervention with someone who is self-destructing with drugs, alcohol or some other behavior that might take them to the grave or just keep them in misery. Consider it a God-send or wake-up call from someone who deeply cares for you and your welfare.

"Letting Go and Letting God"

What does that mean? It's a huge spiritual and behavior modification tool that I've learned to not become sucked down into an emotional maelstrom when things get tough. My job is to do my best and to continue to take the steps and actions to reach my goals. When I can't handle it all (who can all the time), I allow myself to give it over to the God of my understanding to handle. He or she is far more equipped to deal with the often tough stuff in life. When the tough get going, they share their burdens and responsibility with others and with God. Sometimes, in a pinch, when I need to the most, I need to let things go that I can't control and let my Higher Power step in. Sometimes that higher power is spiritual, sometimes it's my lawyer, doctor or some other professional that I deem my Higher Power on any given subject, but it is most definitely not me – thankfully. I've finally come to know the difference – hence the essence of the serenity prayer: "God, grant me the serenity to accept the things I cannot change, the courage to change the things I can and the wisdom to know the difference." Amen for that!!

Accepting the Help You Need

Pride, ego and grandiosity block us from getting the help that we both want and need. The help is there, but we are too damn proud or stubborn to accept it. How can you ever expect to change if you don't let the people in who can help you the most? I was a perfect example of this. I was getting sick and sicker with the disease of alcoholism and addiction, had a gaping hole in my soul and struggled with near all the ills I described in the Introduction. But, I was too in denial that I had a problem and felt that I could solve everything on my own power by myself. I didn't need anyone else's help – until I finally got so ill that I could no longer function. The doctors, therapists, family and best friends had all been telling me. I didn't want to hear it. I just hadn't had enough pain yet and was so accustomed to feeling pain that it became a well-grooved habit. It nearly killed me. I don't advise this for you!

Stop Trying To Control Everything

Many of us are control freaks. If we don't run the show, it will never go right or according to our expectations. Some of us are even blinded by our need to control everything in our environment that we end up hurting ourselves and keeping out others. Or, perhaps we don't hang around with those people that we can't control. Even worse, we are threatened when people challenge our need or attempt to control them and their relationships. Clearly, this is not healthy and a sign of some greater insecurity and weakness. Thankfully, there is hope, but the first step is your own awareness.

Be a Friend When Someone Reaches Out For Help

When you aren't especially good at the relationship game, it's often hard to be a friend in need. Being available to others also means being accountable to yourself and allowing yourself to become more vulnerable. This means taking a risk and that could be painful. This is part of what you need to let go. If you want to be a good friend when others really need and want your help, then you need to demonstrate your willingness and open-mindedness to caring for others the same way that you would want them to care for you.

Life is 10% What Happens to Us and 90% What We Do About It!

It's not what happens to us, it's what we do about it. Stuff is always happening to us. If I do nothing, then probably nothing will happen except what I already know and expect. This is part of gaining certainty, even if my responses are illogical or half-assed. Am I going to remain a victim or take this 90% of possibility and do something meaningful with it to change the potential outcome of the hand of cards I was just dealt. This is our choice, isn't it?

Do we choose to sink or swim, fight or flee, move a muscle and change a thought, or make the most of a potentially bad situation? Here comes the free will stuff again. We can do many things to change our situation and its many possible outcomes, but we must make the first move or we become victims. It is within our capability to make the right choices in life that is what makes us informed humans and not a member of the animal kingdom where base instincts rule.

I'd like to think that I can manage the outcome by shifting my beliefs, or as Coach Tony Robbins insists, "changing my story." If I want to hear a different story, then I must tell a different story. This is how we change. By choosing those strategies that will create the optimum outcomes for us based on our realistic needs and goals.

Progress, Not Perfection

You are anxious. You want results yesterday. You can't wait until tomorrow. You've waited your whole entire life to end your misery and get some peace-of-mind and clearer sense that things will finally be OK. Sound familiar? It is. We all struggle with impatience and setting unrealistic expectations for ourselves and others. All this creates is a world of negative emotions: Anger, disappointment, resentment, self-pity, poor self-esteem, guilt and a host of other life eroding feelings – none of which are real – but just created in your mind.

The solution is to give yourself a break, a pat on the back for making small, incremental improvements. It's the turtle and the hare syndrome. The turtle always wins with the sure and steady pace. You've waiting your whole life to change. You are not going to get miraculous results overnight.

Learn to acknowledge small, slow and positive incremental improvements as you move towards your goals. And, stop measuring yourself against others. What they do and accomplish or not is none of your business. Keep the focus on you and calm down. In time, you will see results. After gaining some perspective and experience on the matter, if you feel that you could realistically improve your performance and sense of accomplish, go for it. But, first pass it by your support network, then forget it and stop all the worrying. You will only make yourself miserable again.

Measuring Up: You Are Always Good Enough

While this might sound suspect, if not impossible, you are already good enough. So, why beat yourself up comparing yourself to others? They don't matter. The only thing that matters is for you to start giving yourself a break.

Many of us suffer from poor self-esteem, feeling that we will never be good enough, smart enough, qualified enough, loveable or good looking enough, strong enough or successful enough. What an utter waste of time even thinking about the prospect that we are not good enough and will never measure up to others or the Joneses. The only one you need to please is yourself.

Easier said than done. Right? Building good self-esteem takes time. You have spent much of your life without it. The first thing we need to ask ourselves is how realistic are our goals or benchmarks as to what is good enough. But, it is something you need to work for if you are ever going to eliminate the distortions you have of yourself and your self-worth.

The first thing we need to do is to stop measuring ourselves. Everyone is different. It's like our strengths and weaknesses, likes and dislikes, assets and liabilities. If you want to become a more positive person, you need to begin stop being so negative and hard on yourself. Look at your better qualities and highlight those. Stop worrying about what you think you are not so good at and your perceptions will change and the problem of being good enough or not will fade away.

Another way to change your perspective on any given situation is to change time frames: How did you deal with the situation in the past? How might you deal with the challenge or problem in the future? What would or could you do differently? Similarly, changing the pace. Either slow things down or speed them up. Either approach can make a world of difference and either solve the problem that you are grappling with or give you a better outcome.

We are all trying to change for the better. Take stock of all your natural talents and strengths and stop worrying about what other people think. We are working on building our sense of self worth, but like everything, this takes time and practice. Your estimation that you are not good enough is a lie and you are the one who told it. Stop believing what isn't true and focus on those things you can do today like making yourself happy and working on your own particular desires and needs for improvement.

You Are NEVER Alone

Whenever you're feeling down and out, keep in mind that you are never alone. We all think that our problems only relate to us. But, of the six or so billion people on this planet, guess what? Many other people have gone through the same types of difficulties and challenges that you have. The hard part is seeing and knowing who they are.

There is a saying in the recovery world. And, that is: "Let us love you until you can love yourself." When the hand of kindness and empathy comes your way, all you have to say is that you'll grab onto the hand of help that so many of us want to freely offer you. There are so many self-help and support groups both off-line and on-line. Just Google your most recent sadness or feeling of despair and help is often that close.

Putting One Foot In Front of the Other

Seems so easy a child can do it! When we're stuck, very much like learning to do life one-day-at-a-time, we also need to put one foot in front of the other. That is how we get around the world, one step at a time. It's so easy to overcomplicate everything that we often forget the simplest and shortest path to our goals is typically a straight line. So, when you're feeling down and out, just start walking, see where you're feet are and keep on walking. You will always get there in time. Remember, no destination, just the journey is what we really care about.

You're worth it, so Work It

There's a rally cry we often say at the end of AA or NA meetings about giving ourselves a pat on the back for working our 12-step recovery program. There is no better satisfaction than giving yourself credit when credit is due for taking full responsibility for your recovery. It's all about YOU and the wok you are doing is for your ultimate benefit. Naturally, all those you love and who love you that surround you will also benefit from your many actions to get and stay clean and sober. But, it is good to remind yourself how important it is to honor and acknowledge that what you are doing is for your own good and is the best incentive to working hard to keep and stay recovered. Without this, it is hard to impossible to live a happy, long and purposeful life, let alone ever be able to get out of your misery and life-struggle.

Hard work and repeated willingness, honesty and applying the skills you are learning here will go a long way to building your own stock in your own happiness – the best investment you will ever make!

Move a Muscle, Change a Thought

I learned about this concept and saying in 12-step addiction recovery programs, and it has always stuck with me. I share it with many others and it always seems to resonate. Here's the way this beautiful, little slogan works: When you are stuck, don't know how to think out of the box, are getting anxious or depressed that nothing is changing, you're feeling the discomfort and dis-ease of inaction or even sloth and procrastination, then try something different. Take another or different kind of action or change the way you are thinking about a situation, challenge or problem. Don't just sit there and do nothing. Get out of that bad neighborhood you call your head!

The way you change your reality on any given situation is to actually change. Not doing so brings us back to the definition of insanity: Doing the same thing over and over again and expecting different results.

So, do something different, think about the problem in another way, get perspective as we discussed earlier and try to look at the solution and the way you are approaching your frustrations in a different way. What's the worst thing that could happen? Nothing changes, but you are already used to that.

Get off the couch, out of the house, take a ride or a weekend away in the country, take a long walk, meditate, go to the gym and sweat it out, take a nap, eat a healthy snack or meal, pick-up the phone and call a friend or trusted advisor and try a different approach. You will be amazed at how just simply changing your environment, starting a new activity, having a conversation or being social with other people will get you better results and stop the anxiety and frustration which will eventually lead you to other negative emotions and results.

Surround Yourself with Positive People

If you want to be positive, surround yourself with positive people. If you want to live your life without the need to take mind-altering substances, then spend your time with people who are clean and sober and not in bars or clubs. If you want to learn how to meditate, don't hang out with anxious and depressive types. The point is, surround yourself with like people that will foster a positive environment for you to model and change your own behavior. What better way to support your new habits and attitudes about your new life than to put yourself at the heart of the wisdom and support network that will make this more possible. We've all heard the saying: "Birds of a feather flock together." If you want to be a goose, hang out with other geese. Likewise, if you want to be happy, joyous and free from your misery and unhappiness, surround yourself with people who can best help you to do that.

Positive Self-Talk

We've spent some time earlier on the consequences of negative self-talk, which we know leads to many harmful and damaging consequences like anger, guilt, poor self-esteem, shame, resentment and a host of others. The way we talk to ourselves about us and our world is the way our reality is formed. Negative, attitudes, thinking and beliefs eventually gets us negative actions and results. And, we're certainly not making any friends in the process!

So, now we're going to flip the coin to the other side and look at the benefits of learning how to talk positively to our inner self. Rather than telling "The Committee in Our Heads" that things are bad and we will never succeed, we are losers once and forever, I want you to reframe your discussion with your own internal committee and tell that useless chatter that what they are saying is all a lie. You will never win by rewarding yourself with the negativity and self-doubt that will words create a self-fulfilling prophesy. If you think you can't do something, you deserve to be unhappy, that you are not good enough, that you didn't do enough or did the wrong thing, that you are guilty of something that you may not have done – in other words – if you keep judging yourself negatively, things will continue to turn out the way you think they will.

This vicious cycle of negativity will continue to produce negative results and your feelings will match your beliefs and thinking. It's all irrational and not based on fact or reality. If you do believe or your own negative self-talk, then you need to think again. Positive people think positive thoughts and get more positive results in life. And, as confirmed by researchers, live a longer and far happier life. So, let's be clear that our negative thinking produces negative thoughts and gets more negative results.

So, why not try something entirely different: Praise yourself for even small achievements well done, show that you are confident in your own abilities, think more highly of yourself and your self-worth. Look at your life as a glass half-filled and not half-empty. Be kind to yourself and for once, give yourself a break! You are worth it and you are already good enough. So, why not begin saying it? Eventually, you, too, will start believing it. And, then the problem will begin to fade away and your positive attitudes, thinking and beliefs will overwhelm your negativity. It all starts with changing your unkind attitudes about yourself first!!

Build & Maintain a Support Network

We will spend some wonderful time in a later chapter talking about the importance of having trusted advisors, mentors, coaches, sponsors and even counselors as part of your brain trust. Considering that many of us have had a bad track record living our lives well, having others to help us build perspective, good orderly direction, and create more meaningful and positive results in our life is a must.

We can't and needn't do life alone. Part of healing ourselves is becoming part of the world that we were always meant to be a part of. We tried solving our problems on our own for way too long and the results are pretty predictable: Not good! It is very important to become a part of something larger than yourself: Support groups are an excellent way to be with other like minded or purposed people confronting a crisis or major transformation or issue in their life.

I like to think about having respected and smart friends and professionals around me like my "Board of Advisors." Later, we are going to talk about how to find and get your own personal "Board of Advisors" to help you through difficult transitions, decisions and help you build perspective and gain wisdom on a host of critical issues. These are people you can depend on for solid, sage advice and counsel when you need it. Ask for help and get it. Don't expect it and be disappointed with yet again poor results.

Creating Good Habits, Routines and Rituals

In his bestselling book, "The Power of Habit," author Charles Duhigg gives a brilliant insight on how we can change old "Keystone habit loops" by changing "routines" that come from us following certain behavioral cues and then the rewards we come to expect by these old behaviors. The book explores some key concepts that can help us change old and stubborn habits to new and more desirable ones with better results by reconditioning ourselves with new, more desirable routines – whether it be with personal struggles like weight loss or addiction, reinventing old products into widely successful new ones, or introducing behavioral movements that are changing the world like Alcoholics Anonymous and Rick Warren's Saddleback Church. The "hard" part about change is embedded in our human nature. We don't like to change and find most change hard. Some people are better at adapting and quicker to change than others, but anyone can change if they apply some of basic tools available. Whether your goals are to exercise more, lose weight, build a revolutionary new company or invent a groundbreaking new product or service, deal with anxiety and stress better, whatever your choice, Duhigg talks about learning to reprogram our lives. He talks about identifying the "keystone" habits we all have in our lives that can often be make the difference between life and death. He then talks about breaking old and negative habits by changing our "cues" in order to respond with different results. For example, he shows how Alcoholics Anonymous "…reforms lives by attacking habits at the core of addiction," or how Coach Tony Dungy "reversed fortunes of the worst team in the National Football League by on his players' automatic reactions to subtle on-field cures. He gives another example of how Proctor and Gamble transformed "Febreeze" from a product flop to a multi-billion category changer and new market by taking advantage of consumers' habitual urges. I highly suggest you study this book to understand how you can effect habit change in your own life.

Neuro-Linguistic Programming (NLP), made popular by Tony Robbins, and a host of other Behavioral Therapies and Coaching Modalities are also very helpful in changing old habits into newer, healthier ones.

Creating good habits comes from understanding and recognizing how bad or unhealthy habits negatively impact our lives. We all have them to varying degrees. Some of us are lazy, impetuous, and moody, can't make a decision, or spend too much time doing whatever isn't good for us. When you have finally gotten sick and tired of being sick and tires and have finally had enough, you will hopefully develop the willingness to try something different and correct the damaging old behavior. Part of the solution to doing so is changing your attitude about the problem and focusing on new solutions.

Practice makes perfect and you will be trying and testing many new, more positive possibly life-changing and enhancing tools in your life. When everything changes then you have finally made the decision that it's time to try something different and create new and more permanent and positive habits in your own life.

For me, I have formed mostly good, productive and positive habits that have helped me to live a more meaningful and positive life. All of the suggestions, tactics and proposed solutions in "How to Love Yourself" are intended to help you to change your old ways of thinking and doing things in order to find more effective solutions to living your own life. This book is all about changing old habits and routines now and for the remainder of our lives.

Building Self-Esteem; Doing Esteem-able Things

Many of us have long struggled with poor self-esteem. We don't think well or highly of ourselves and our capabilities. We don't like who we are or the person we are becoming. We struggle with a poor self-image.

Lack of Self-esteem is painful and creates many negative struggles of ego and negatively impacts our personality and ability to become our own personal best. It is a major roadblock to our recovery and stems the tide of positive change. We can no longer accept not thinking well of ourselves and loving the person we really are.

On the flipside, building a strong sense of self requires that we start to do esteem-able things. If we feel less than, then we need to do more of those things that make us feel good about ourselves, fulfilled, happy. We need to start doing things well, taking small steps to measured success. We must build our confidence by doing those things that will make us winners. It doesn't have to be monumental achievements, but small things like losing a pound a month, joining and going to the gym, buying some new, modest-costing clothes, taking some time for ourselves, participating in a hobby, going to church or temple, practicing mindful meditation or yoga, getting a haircut or hanging out with our best friends.

We feel better about ourselves when we start taking care of ourselves and our needs. It also requires that we stop all the negative self-talk that we've bought into and come to expect and start to reframe our experience and lives with positive self-talk. Rather than telling yourself or someone else that you or they are a "loser," either say nothing or focus on a positive attribute or achievement the person has done.

I am confident that if you continue to practice the strategies and techniques you are learning in ""How to Love Yourself"-Hour Reboot," you will most definitely begin to feel better about yourself and your prospects for peace-of-mind, happiness and a more fulfilling life.

Learn to Please Yourself

Healing and happiness are an inside job and only you can make this happen and take responsibility for the process. Nobody else: Not your parents, siblings, children, teachers, authorities or your therapist or health care professional. You are doing all this hard work for you and you will be the first one to reap the rewards for a job well done. Naturally, all those who touch your life in some capacity will be welcome and happy recipients of your healing and new found happiness.

So, when you choose to get well and put your past behind you, do it for yourself first and the rest will come in time.

Be Your Authentic Self

You don't need to wear masks or put on airs for people to like you. Many of us are socially awkward or uncomfortable in our own skins. That's OK, However, the only person you really have to be with yourself or others is YOU. Just be yourself – good, bad, warts and all. That's the best way to be happy is to allow your own true self and all the gifts that come a long with that to shine through in their finest hour. You will be happier and so will everyone else for you allowing them to get to know the real you!

Rebuilding Old/Broken Relationships

You will never be able to repeat and repair the past in exactly the same way it was. That is now history. Those relationships that you still value and seek to salvage require healing first. Taking responsibility for harms done, making appropriate amends and restitution where appropriate comes first. People, like elephants, have long memories. The good news is that like the Higher Power, most people will show sympathy and compassion – and most importantly will forgive you in time for wrongs done. You, too, must forgive them and yourself for perceived or actual harms done. Time takes time as does healing. So, allow it to do its job without forcing it. That is not realistic or a good idea. You know that you can't make anybody do what you want or think is right until they are ready – if ever. And, with certain people you will never repair old relationships. These are the folks you should be praying for so that they may heal on their own.

Living with Others

Not always so easy, right? Consider your history of unhealthy relationships. Some of the more common issues people struggle with is 1. Self-centeredness and selfishness – thinking only of yourself and not about others. 2. Understand your communication style and learn to listen as we explored earlier. 3. Identify your communication style – there are four basic styles with respect to relationships: a. Aggressive, b. Passive-Aggressive, c. Passive and d. Assertive. You want to be Assertive with others which mean not overwhelming the other person and being considerate and thoughtful in your approach and what you say. You will get a lot further and find greater meaning and satisfaction by adopting a more assertive communication style with others. Ask for what you want and need, but be respectful and appropriate at all times. Always think about how you want and expect others to treat you.

What Are The Benefits of Healthy Relationships?

There are many. For starters: **1.** We get emotional support from others who understand us and can be empathetic with us. **2.** We get instrumental support to provide us with resources and strategic help when we need it. **3.** Companionship is a human need and something that healthy relationships give us – whether it's a friend or partner. **4.** We also get a sense of connectedness and belonging – which satisfies another common and important human need. We feel a part of something when we have solid and sustained relationships. And, **5.** We get honest feedback, which we both need to get clarity on our particular situation and to also get the truth!

Learn the Art of Effective Communication

We all like to be heard and understood by others – as that is a basic human need. But few people really know how to listen. What's more, fewer know how to communicate effectively and to get the results that they really want. The truth is that few people really know how to communicate effectively.

So, first consider this: "The meaning of a communication is the response that it receives." Translated simply, it doesn't matter what you say or how you say it, the person you are saying it to may actually hear something radically different than what you believe you actually said to them. It is not important what your actual intent was. Instead, it is what the other person comes to understand and interpret. For example, play the telephone game. You start out by saying something to the person next to you, and then they do the same until everyone has whispered the message to everyone else. The last person repeats what they heard and then compares it with the person who initially sent the message. Rarely are the two ever the same or even close. It's usually pretty comical and illustrates how distorted communication can be between two or more people.

So, how do we ensure that people are actually hearing and getting what we want them to hear? That's what makes marriage counselors and even family counselors and anger management teachers so highly valued. There is an art to communicating well.

Also, mean what you say and say what you mean. How many times have you heard this before? Learn to take the time and pause to think your thoughts through before you speak. If you are nervous, take a deep breath or two. Develop good eye contact with your audience, use non verbal communication to enhance your message and "close" your point. Body language is an amazing way to both read people and to better get your message across. Do you smile, look genuine, in command and excited about the material you are presenting? Have you engaged your audience by asking them to participate or express their views on a subject or issue? Ask for their experience with the subject matter and watch how much more engaged your audience is and relevant your communication and presentation becomes.
When you are speaking to another, take the time to make sure they actually understood what you said. Ask them to engage with you so that the meaning of your communication actually gets the response you intended and desire! Watch how improved your relationships become. Nobody likes to be talked at. They want to make sure that you are also taking them into account and consideration. This also demonstrates your respect and civility when you consider the other person, their feelings and their listening abilities into your conversations. This is also especially helpful when you are talking with children or people that may not have a grasp on the material that you are presenting.

Step one: Learn **Active Listening** Techniques. There are five steps and they require that you actually practice this with others to learn how to do it right. 1. Look into the other person's eyes you are talking to and develop strong eye contact. 2. Communicate what you want to express to them. 3. Then, the recipient has to repeat back to you what they believe you said in as clear or exact a manner as possible. This is called "**Mirroring.**" 4. The person who started the communication then provides any correction or elaboration to you, the recipient. 5. You repeat this process until you both have "heard" each other by confirmation by the other. Each person on the listening side must be completely quiet until the other person is completely through what they want to say to you. No interruptions or corrections whatsoever. You must discipline yourself to be both the sender and the receiver. Try also doing this after someone has given a talk or spilled their guts to you on some emotional or important issue. Don't interrupt them, but to ensure that you heard what they have to say, ask them if it is OK to mirror back to them what you think they said. Ask them at the end of your recitation if you got all this correctly. Let them correct you or add to whatever they believe they wanted you to hear and understand.

You will find this to be very difficult if you are not already a good listener. Even if you are a good "Active Listener," you can always improve your skills and probably should. Many of us are so bent on telling people what we want them to hear and then get upset when they feel misunderstood or something was misinterpreted. If we all just took the time to become better listeners, be considerate of the communication process and check to see that they got it all, we might all be better understood, much happier and have more friends.

Also, mean what you say and say what you mean. How many times have you heard this before? Learn to take the time and pause to think your thoughts through before you speak. If you are nervous, take a deep breath or two. Develop good eye contact with your audience, use non verbal communication to enhance your message and "close" your point. Body language is an amazing way to both read people and to better get your message across. Do you smile, look genuine, in command and excited about the material you are presenting? Have you engaged your audience by asking them to participate or express their views on a subject or issue? Ask for their experience with the subject matter and watch how much more engaged your audience is and relevant your communication and presentation becomes.
When you are speaking to another, take the time to make sure they actually understood what you said. Ask them to engage with you so that the meaning of your communication actually gets the response you intended and desire! Watch how improved your relationships become. Nobody likes to be talked at. They want to make sure that you are also taking them into account and consideration. This also demonstrates your respect and civility when you consider the other person, their feelings and their listening abilities into your conversations. This is also especially helpful when you are talking with children or people that may not have a grasp on the material that you are presenting.

Confronting and Leveling

Feedback can have a positive or a negative effect. Destructive feedback can really hurt other people in ways you can't always see. So, when you want to give criticism to others, rather than insulting them or harming them, consider this first: 1. Talk about the behavior you are commenting on in others without labeling the person. Speak calmly and respectfully when giving criticism. 2. Remember to examine your motives to why you are criticizing another. Are you hurt and you're acting in some passive-aggressive manner or you seek to retaliate, or are you really trying to give constructive and helpful commentary on the other person? 3. Identify the consequences of the person's behavior to them in ways they can best relate to. 4. State clearly what it is about the person's behavior that you desire them to change. Provide an alternative or suggestion for them to follow. 5. Do it out of caring and concern for the other person, not to just get in the last word and to prove yourself "right."

Become a Good Listener

I was stunned at how poorly I and others communicate. I learned this from my beloved mother. My heart and soul were in the right place. I knew how to be empathetic and show compassion. I cared about people. People told me how well I communicated and wrote. Yet, here I am a Human Communications and Journalism Major in College and I discover at age 59 that I don't really know how to listen. And you wonder how I became an Alcoholic and eventually dysfunctional?

I was more interested in being heard and making sure I was understood than I was in actually hearing what others had to say. Being the impetuous and insecure person I was, I found it easier to just cut someone off in the middle of a sentence thinking I could mind read what they were thinking or were going to say. I just wanted to make MY point! How completely off the mark, insecure, insensitive and grandiose this is. People had been telling me all my life that I need to let them finish their statement before interrupting. I just never took the time to hear them.

Learning how to listen and listening to learn are two key components to good communication and healthy relationships. How do you feel when people don't really "hear" you or give the impression that they really care for you? Not good. It's insulting and beyond frustrating. On the flipside, how good do you hear or comfortable to do feel when somebody really understands you? You feel validated, OK, considered and respected. When another is able to touch your heart and soul and create meaning in their communication with you and you to them, you have arrived. This is how you are supposed to feel.

I am strongly encouraging you to practice the "Active Listening" skills I introduced earlier in this section. You will be amazed at the results and it will be a game changer for you.

Anger Management

One of my favorite topics. I used to be a very angry person – especially during my last 10 years. I have since learned the art of taming my anger and not acting out. I'm by no means perfect, but with practice of the following tools, I'm a lot better. So, here's how this works: 1. Examine your thinking: Is it irrational and emotionally charged. Do you need to challenge your thoughts and understand the integrity and accuracy of your beliefs that are influencing those thoughts and impacting your feelings and subsequent behavior? 2. Seek Compromise: If you discussion is getting heated, consider asking another for help or perspective, or try a little give and take. You can't always win an argument and sometimes compromise is that the best solution to a win-win. 3. Take a time out: Same as taking a few deep breaths and not saying or writing something you may end of regretting (like writing that heated email in a fit of fury and then pushing that send button with great regret! 4. Check your attitude: If you're sitting with a negative and toxic attitude, drop it now and see what's really going on. Then adopt a positive attitude and approach. 5. Keep your options open, including running for the hills in retreat or finding a safe haven and the help of others. Escalation and heated argument usually don't end well. Also, try adding a little maturity and adulthood to your style -- it often goes a long way to just grow up and not be so childish. Nothing good comes out of the heat of the moment except maybe passion and love!

If you really struggle with bigger anger issues, there is a lot of help for you and I have included some additional resources in the Appendix. Feel free to use them and see what works best for you.

Three Roadblocks to a Positive Attitude

There are three big ones: **1. Resentment** is the number one offender. Deal and then drop them. **2. Self-Pity** – being absorbed in our own negative self-talk and emotions keeps us from getting un-stuck. **3. Grandiosity**, or thinking too much of yourself and not enough about others.

Understanding and Dealing with Our "Blind Spots"

Self-awareness is one of our greater goals in ""How to Love Yourself"-Hour Reboot." While in prison, I learned about this nifty tool called "The Johari Window" – developed by a philosopher, Charles Handy. What it is a technique used to help people better understand their relationship with themselves and others? [Pix of Johari Window here] So, imagine a window pane with four panels. One panel says **"Open"** and includes information that is visible to you and that you might share with others, which might include your hobbies or your love for your children or work. The next panel says **"Secret"** and contains those things that you know about yourself, but don't choose to share with others. If includes your personal problems, addictions, bad habits, secret behaviors or the stuff you will take to the grave before sharing with another. The next window pane is your **"Blind"** pane, and this includes those parts of yourself that others see in you, but you don't. For example, you may think you are a caring, smart and wonderful leader where others might see you as selfish, grandiose and full of yourself. And the final pane is your **"Potential"** – those things about you that are unknown both to you and others. But, with work, you can develop your awareness and focus on those things that you want to include in the new you. I have included some simple exercises you can do to develop your own awareness of your blind spots in the Appendix so that you can amplify the good traits and minimize or eliminate the bad ones. It's a great way to get to know yourself in the context of your world and to increase your awareness of how you communicate yourself to others.

Become Your Greatest Fan

We advocate for so many others in our lives – our kids, significant others, good friends, underdogs, heroes that we admire, top producers and chieftains in business. But, when it comes to ourselves, we fall short. Why? We've already talked about the need to know that you ARE worth it and that you have to work for it. In the inspirational song written by Deniece Williams, "Let's Hear It for the Boy," she sings "Let's hear it for the boy...Let's give the boy a hand...Let's hear it for my baby...You know you go to understand...." She's working hard to empower her significant other. You need to also do this and also cheer out loud for yourself!

If you don't advocate for Numero Uno, who will? I'm not suggesting that you suddenly become a narcissist, but I am arguing that you need to make a best efforts attempt to give yourself a five star rating in all matters pertaining to you.

Becoming an advocate for yourself means having solid self-esteem, strong self confidence and a meaningful self-care program. When you place yourself right up front on the rating scale and do what will serve you best without being selfish or self-centered, you are taking responsibility for yourself and managing those things in your life that you can control. Once you've done this, your family, friends and support network will begin to see your sense of pride and self-respect and they will respond in kind with cumulatively positive effect.

Setting & Maintaining Healthy Boundaries in Personal & Business Life

People violate all kinds of boundaries every day. It might be your physical personal space, your privacy boundaries, violating friendship or an intimate relationship. Perhaps you've been lied to and not dealt with in an ethical and moral fashion. Maybe somebody has violated your trust or not followed through on a promise. Or perhaps your boss treads all over you at work or in certain situations maybe violates your own privacy. Maybe someone has not apologized or made good on something, or perhaps a verbal or legal contract was not honored and you feel taken.

People experience being violated most every day and aren't always aware when they've violated something about someone else unless it is brought to their attention. In other cases, perhaps it's more serious like being robbed, raped or emotionally battered.

Civility, respect and honesty go a long way towards ensuring healthy boundaries in your personal or business life. If you are uncomfortable with someone and feel that your boundaries are being violated or not respected do something, say something or accept it. But, don't beat yourself when you continue to feel uncomfortable. If it's serious, get the advice of respected others. You need to have an action plan and be willing to implement and honor it.

One last thought on healthy boundaries. And, that is, do your best to leave your work life at work and not bring it home. More good relationships have been broken by people who bring their jobs home with them and sometimes the negative attitude and problems that still linger from the day. I have long admired people who can leave their work behind and just be home and present for their families. It takes practice and learning how to let go of those things that you can't control. Work is work and your personal life should not be ruled by it. If it is and your feeling overwhelmed by your job or profession and it carries over into your personal life, then you need to take a hard look at your priorities and see what you must change to make the separation between your two lives more workable. Life is too short and your family is precious. Don't go out of your way to muddy the waters of a good thing.

Yes You Can! Taking Charge of Your Life Today

I tell my kids and those young and struggling that there is nothing within reason that they cannot do in their lives if there's a will and a way. I don't believe in living my life with regrets and have always subscribed to the notion that if things don't work out, I can try and try again until I finally succeed.

If you think you can, then you can. It's like the fabled story of the "Little Engine That Could." About the animated little train that was challenged with the monumental task of going up this gigantic mountain. It kept building its self-confidence by assuring itself and repeating "I think I can, I think I can." And, it did eventually and proudly make it up the hill

Having a "Yes I Can" attitude about life will get you a lot further along on your path to success and freedom if you are considering realistic and achievable goals, managing your risk with a measured reward, and have an action plan in place that you have vetted through others who have sought and experienced similar achievements.

Invite your valued and respected friends and mentors, become part of a group of like-minded people, take the time to learn all about the task at hand – what it involves and strategies and tactics others have used. Become educated, aim and then shoot with confidence. Watch how your life soars as you try, try and try again and then finally succeed in your own pursuits and dreams. If you tell yourself you can do it, you can do it!! Miracles happen every day. May you live to celebrate many more, while you encourage others to do the same!

The Importance of Momentum

How many of us struggle with stagnation and plain old being stuck? Many of us feel depressed or even anxious when we are not moving forward to our liking. The answer to nearly all our problems with things going to slow or not at all is gaining traction and momentum.

We are looking for profess here, not perfection. As long as we are taking little steps to get to where we think we need to go, we feel OK. Once we are stuck, good feelings are off the table. So, once again, we have three choices: Do something, say something or accept it. If you can't accept it, you will revel in the positive endorphins of progress and forward momentum.

Mentor, Counsel and Coach Others

One of the most rewarding aspects of growing up is learning how to help others help themselves. This is also one of the highest forms of charity: "Give the man a fish and you will feed him for a day. Teach a man him how to fish and help him to feed himself for life."

There is great pleasure and importance in helping others. I will save my discussion for a later chapter on getting out of self. But, teaching and guiding others is one of the most important and satisfying things you can do for your own growth – let alone what it does for the person you are helping! Mentor young people on life and career issues. Help them to build a plan that will include satisfying realistic and sustainable short- and long-term goals. When you're ready, sponsor other men and women in 12-step or other recovery programs, lead a spiritual or religious retreat or class, be a big brother or sister, a Den Leader for boy scouts or girl scouts, a counselor and coach for the YMHA or YMCA, a camp counselor the 4H Club, Volunteer for Habitat for Humanity or one of your other favorite charities, take people under your wing at work and mentor them. Teach people what you know and do it with love, compassion and without expecting anything in return. In other words, make it a selfless passion to truly give yourself to others and be of service and not a selfish self-centered pursuit to make yourself look good.

Prayer:

I can't say enough about the importance of prayer. For me, it's not about religion, but a non-denominational way to develop a conscious contact with my Higher Power, the spiritual and divine universal energy of the universe. It has taken me 40 years to develop my own prayer practice which, in its simplest form, invites God to come into my life, to help and guide me through the challenges of my day and life, to help me to do the right thing and to better live a good, moral and honest life, to keep me humble and useful and to help me discern His Will from my own and for me to understand what that Will is and to perform it. In addition to being a practice of request for help, insight, wisdom, courage and hope, it is also a sincere acknowledgment of thanks and gratitude for all the many blessings and grace that I do receive on a regular basis.

There are many ways to pray and no right or wrong way to do it. The important thing is to develop a regular prayer practice with your higher power and to have a conversation with him like he was right in front of you and also your best friend. You can tell Him or Her anything that's on your mind or of concern to you. Talk about your wants and needs, innermost desires, dreams, concerns and worries. Ask for all the help you need in your own words in your own way. Get to know His power and watch His presence in your life grow.

Meditation:

This is different to prayer, but they work especially well together – although not necessarily one after the year in any order. What meditation is is a way to explore and discover your inner dimension and your soul. Wikipedia defines meditation as a practice where an individual operates or trains the mind or induces a mode of consciousness, either to realize some benefit or for the mind to simply acknowledge its "content" without becoming identified with that content, or as an end to itself. It includes a wide variety of practices that promote relaxation, build internal energy or life force and develop compassion, love, patience, generosity and forgiveness. It promotes deep relaxation and a wonderful sense of inner calm and serenity. I have been practicing a number of different types of meditation for years from mindfulness, kundalini and transcendental meditation with tremendous results. It is a key and necessary component for anyone who seeks inner and outer healing from life struggle and pain.

For every culture and country, there is a healing tradition that has its roots in ancient history. They run the gamut from spiritual to scientific. The exception might be Western style medicine that was built on science and scientific proof that it actually works. There are many other healing modalities that exist that I may not have mentioned. Please accept my apology now if I have offended you in any way for not including them in ""How to Love Yourself"-Hour Reboot." You can contact me at my email address fenton@lifecoach911.com to update me with practices that you may have found especially effective and helpful.

Doing Life without Mind Altering Substances:

As you have gathered by now, I believe in sobriety for me. I am not suggested it may be right for you. My point is that if drugs, alcohol, pills or some other mind altering substances are interfering with the quality and integrity of your life and happiness, you need to seriously consider what your priorities are. If you need help from withdrawing and abstaining from these substances, then there is much help available to you. Get help and when you are willing and truly ready to quit take action and get help. Only you can judge this issue for yourself.

Forgiveness

Forgiveness is a central concept and a way of life for those that are trying to heal and become spiritually connected. We have addressed forgiveness or our inability to forgive as a roadblock to change.

On the flipside, learning how to let go of your past, and dropping the rocks of resentment, anger, guilt, self-pity, shame and the host of other terribly negative and harmful negative self-talk that we abuse ourselves and others with is key to finding true and authentic happiness both inside and out. Learning how to forgive others for perceived or real harms done can take a lifetime of concerted effort. Forgiving ourselves for those real or perceived harms done by others to us is even more difficult.

How to we learn to forgive? First, we must recognize the importance of doing so. If you possess the "Honesty, Open mindedness and willingness to heal yourself and get to true happiness, you must start the process of forgiving yourself and others. We do this by taking an honest inventory of our character defects and harms done to others. We focus on cleaning up and correcting our side of the street. We stop blaming others for our problems and start taking those actions that will make amends and rectify the wrongs we have done. We embark on a path of forgiveness by being able to move pass the emotions and the pain of our past. The past is history. We can only change it in our minds. The quality of our present day will determine the quality of our future days, so it is well worth taking the time to do inventory – an important subject and technique that we discussed earlier in this section.

Give time time, be patient with yourself and others, don't have unrealistic expectations and focus on your actions and don't worry about what others do or don't do. What matters is how you walk the walk each day going forward. It is a process and there will never be any destination. The rewards of honest acts of forgiveness are huge and the lifting of these huge burdens of guilt, remorse, shame, will slowly dissipate as you walk on the road to healing and happiness. Share your burden and guilt with others and let others in to your life to help you help yourself. You will also gain the unexpected gift of helping others in the process – as they will feel your pain and identify with your experiences.

So, how exactly do we forgive ourselves and others? For starters, whether we are guilty of hurting someone else or not, we always work to clean up our side of the street. Here's an email I recently sent to my ex-wife and children as I was exiting the Federal Bureau of Prison system, which was truly liberating and amazing. It was the first time I had been physically free for nearly four years. It was also a very stressful time with my family and I had been experiencing some of the real effects of the damage I had caused them. In an effort to help move everyone forward as they became able and willing, I wrote this:

"Dear Family,

It's been a difficult and emotional few days for me and I suspect some of you. As you all know, of the several important things I am currently involved with; one of the most important spokes of my efforts has been my Strategic Intervention Life Coaching Training. Besides writing 3 hours/day on my book, working at my friend Tom Ingegneri's business (The Cranbury Inn) and completing my stressful obligations to the Bureau of Prisons, I spend 5 hours/day training to be an Addiction Recovery & Life Trauma coach -- something that is very dear to me.

I received this email today which is entitled "The Power of Love" co-developed by two of the most renown therapists and coaches, Chloe Madanes and Tony Robbins. The 1-hour video is one of the best I've seen on how the strategies that I'm learning to practice actually work in real life. The session is about a married couple and their separation and discord. It's complex, but much of it will resonate with you all.

I hope you will accept my deepest apologies for having recently acted out with your mother. I accept full responsibility for my actions. I love you all and want nothing but happiness and success for all of us. I am still flawed in many ways and am a work in progress. I take my change as a man, ex-husband and a father very seriously.

I know the past decade has been painful for all of us. I have long struggled with the disease of Alcoholism & Addiction and it is real and very alive even when I don't drink. It takes rigorous daily maintenance for me to stay well. If I don't attend to it with all my efforts -- I will die -- as it already nearly killed me twice. I hope none of you ever have to struggle with a killer disease or disability as I did. It ruined my life and tortured all of you. I was very sick and alone for a long time.

I am working so hard on my recovery and making a good, honest, meaningful and productive life for myself. I have much work to do, but I am optimistic. I have spent the last 4 years in hell and many years prior to that getting there. I can't imagine a life without my children and a respectful & civil relationship with my ex-wife, your mother.

I have changed, really, but none of you know that since we have spent so little time together. I want to tell you how sorry I am for what has happened to all of you -- to all of us. It breaks my heart to think about how much pain and suffering I've caused you all. That is now history if and when we learn to let it go and put it all behind us. The only way I know how to make good is for me to become a power of example and live a good, sober life. I have also worked hard to live in the present, and not regret my past or project and worry about the future. Each day brings progress and that is what I focus on.

I hope and pray that you all will focus on and ultimately succeed in forgiving me for all the hurt and trust that you feel was broken. I have had a lot of time to think about it and understand it. I have first had to forgive myself for harms that I perceived done to me. But, forgiveness and not dwelling on the past is paramount to me staying happy in the present. I hope you will continue to forgive me for your sake. I also want you to know how much I want to build new relationships with all of you. It has not been easy for any of us, but if we can't give each other a break, then who will? I'm hoping we can all finally bury the hatchet and begin to move forward. The actions of the past week or so have moved us backyards, and for that I am sorry. I'm certain you feel the same way.

Trust and Faith

Two of the most important actions and qualities one can take to growing your spiritual life are developing faith and trust in others and with an entity greater than yourself. Faith and trust in the process of healing, of the wisdom of the truth, of Good Orderly Direction in your life, of a permanent life of happiness and finding meaning and purpose requires a concerted effort to acquire faith and trust. First in the truth, in honesty, in positivity, in doing esteem able things, of building good character, of trusting that things will turn out alright as long as you do the right thing and do your best.

For all of us that have paid the price of our struggles and the many trials and tribulations that have come with that and with learning how to live differently – better, we've tried to do things our way, because we believed that our way was the best way and always right. That turned out to not be completely true and we have suffered with much pain through the years.

As we move into the next section, I want to underscore here the critical importance of acquiring these two skills in two of the most rewarding levers to change in your own life. Have you learned to trust somewhat since going the course on ""How to Love Yourself"-Hour Reboot?" Have you begun to find your way and see how you might go about changing your life by taking charge of it? If so, taking even the smallest of baby steps to trusting me, others in your life that you can trust to lead you in the right direction; this is how you will grow in these qualities.

To trust is to rely on the integrity, strength, ability, and surety of a person or thing. Have confidence in an authority greater than yourself. Acquiring faith is taking a leap of understanding and trust that someone or something else other than you is right; that all will turn out well if you come to believe that everything is going to be OK.

Giving Back to Others

We have spent considerable time talking about the rewards one gains by getting out of self and giving their time, money, skills, or just a helping hand to those in need. The act and even the intent to give and help others is one of the key ways that we also receive God's grace and feel better about ourselves.

Helping others and giving back to your community and to those who also struggle is one of the best ways to grow, become far happier, build solid self-esteem, become a better friend and partner to others and to become a vital and valued partner in your world. We will revisit just how we can do this in a later Chapter.

Chapter VI.
LIVING HAPPILY AFTER EVER (Staying Changed & In the Healing Process Forever)

Sound like a fairytale? Well it is! We all know that life isn't a fairytale, but it doesn't have to end like a nightmarish horror story either. The gift lay somewhere in-between – or what I call the middle ground. Living a good and noble life is a labor of love. It takes, time, tons of effort, determination, lots of guidance and a great deal of humility and gratitude. The negative self-talk and self-sabotaging attitudes, thinking and behaviors need to end. Positive self-talk, good attitude and right action need to take its place. There is no room for doubters. It is necessary in you first to believe in yourself. You literally have to get out of your own way, open the blinders and let the sunshine in. that is all around you – not necessarily deep within you – at least yet!

All the power and wherewithal you will ever need are already inside you. You don't have to covet externals like money/bling, power or prestige to get it. Your heart, soul and mind are fertile ground for drastic change. But, first you have to want it and feel the pain to know that something big is missing. There are no quick fixes or magical cures.

To underscore what it really takes to change, let's review my original observation from the introduction: "The majority of 'cures' by themselves, while helpful, don't work and last for most. Brutal honesty, accurate self-assessment, willingness, hope, raw courage, sufficient pain and an honest desire to discover our deeper spiritual truths are needed for successful and permanent change. So are learning how to ask for and receive help from others, getting out of self and a deeply rooted and acquired trust & faith in a source of strength greater than oneself. These keys to success require an-going support & commitment throughout one's life-cycle for true and lasting healing to occur."

We begin by making the decision that we have finally had enough and that things have to change or else. We are learning how to make small, incremental conscious choices a day-at-a-time. We are not looking perfection, but measurable progress that we can see and feel. We put one foot in front of the other to get where we need to go, and we learn to smell the roses and enjoy the beautiful view along the way. We stop regretting the past and fearing the future. We feed our spirit and soul. We feed our head and get out of self. We heal our relationships and let go of our resentments, remorse and all things that are signs that we are still stuck in the past. We stop fretting about the future and begin to enjoy our day. We spend our time with people who struggle like us and learn how to extend our helping hand when needed. We are finally getting out of our own self-centered selves and learning how to contribute to the world around us. We are learning how to live and contribute in the flow of life and love. We are finally on the journey that has no destination and we find peace and happiness in the process.

Healing From the Inside Out

Ultimately, the only way to get and stay healed and permanently happy and fulfilled is to change from the inside out. Our core problem is a spiritual one. We are restless, irritable and discontent. The rest of our problems we can be fixed by changing our attitudes, our beliefs, thinking, habits and behaviors. It is amazing what we can change by doing things differently and following the directions of those others who have discovered their own purpose and happiness in life.

Is the Student Finally Ready?

I believe you are and I want you to believe that I believe are. Why? Because, I have experienced the many fruits of my own labors and have seen the miracle of transformation happen to myself and in so many others. Anyone can do this, no matter how low your bottom, deep your pain, or how large the absence of happiness and fulfillment in your life. The hard part: I'm not just asking you to change, but I'm imploring you to change everything.

We have covered a lot of territory in a short period of time. As we reviewed earlier, time takes time and the pace and amount of change you will experience is directly proportional to your willingness to make the key decision that you've had enough pain and are willing to do whatever is necessary to stop the insanity in your life. What do you have to lose? Your misery? This I will happily refund. There really is a better way, but you have to want it and be willing to commit to actually making the decision to get what you deserve: Something far better!

So, let's refresh. What it is the prize here? Learning how to step out of misery and dysfunction into finding and getting meaning and purpose in your life. When you start to satisfy your basic human needs, you will like the way you feel. I know for a fact that you will want more of a good thing. And, in the process of getting your needs met, you will find that the really simple, yet complicated solution is stepping out of your perceived "problems" and learning how to be happy and to live on purpose – to discover your authentic self – your very essence that makes you you. When you choose to live in life's solutions, your problems miraculously go away. Now, we finally have a tool kit on which to improve and grow what we have already started.

Fear and Pain Are Our Greatest Teachers

Life's trials and tribulation determine the quality of your life. Our lives are the ideal theater for learning to live your life. The teacher has appeared and has always been there. The real question remains: Is the student finally ready to learn and to take action on the life lessons that the teacher has presented? Or, is the student unsure and thinking about going back to his or her own ways because that's what they know and are comfortable with. Does fear and that feeling that you are not worthy or capable of receiving this gift still there?

Our journey is unique to each of us, but we all share common experiences. Understanding our own particular situation and those things we need to change and grow is one thing. Doing something about by taking definitive action to change and grow is another.

As we've explored earlier, if we are not growing and actually living our lives, then we are in the process of dying. That is very sad and unavoidable, in my humble opinion.

The reason why you picked up "How to Love Yourself" is because your life was not making you happy. Your needs weren't being met. You felt unfulfilled – maybe even empty. You found the struggles, fear and the pain difficult to cope with on your own. You weren't used to asking for help and perhaps you were just too damn proud to tell anyone just how bad things had gotten. This was your choice, whether you believe so or not.

By now, you have sensed my enthusiasm for living. As a recovering addict and alcoholic, I still struggle with the disease of "more," but now it is healthy stuff like being a good life junky. I am just happy most all the time, even though I struggle like you. I have experienced so much pain that I often have trouble putting it into words. I choose to live my life differently today. It's hard to see that WE are the ones that have made so many bad and unproductive choices along our journey. We became the victims of our own intentions, thoughts, emotions and actions. Those choices, whether conscious or not, got us to where we are today. This is our responsibility, no one else's. Hopefully by now, you have agreed to own, look at all its ugliness and choose to dispose of those parts that no longer work or serve you. The days of blaming and rationalization are over.

If you want to feel different and fill that hole in your soul, you need to build up and re-train your emotional and spiritual muscles that were never exercised properly to begin with. You need to work out each and every day. We weren't just born unhappy. We created our own reality – with the exception of those things that we had no control over like being born, our parents, where we grew up and all the other things that we think victimized us in our youth. That's history now. It's in the past. You can't change those conditions that are part of your story. But, you can change the way you think about them, the feelings and emotions that you experience. As importantly, you can and must change the way you behave – all your actions, deeds, behaviors, as well as your intentions – the true meaning to why you do things in the first place. You are fully responsible now. We've spent the last "How to Love Yourself"-Hours growing up, now it's time to leave the nest and develop your own wings if you want to fly to higher heights with the rest of us. I want you so much to come a long for the ride. Because, if you continue to practice the tools I have laid out for you, you will change your reality in time. Sometimes quickly, sometimes slowly – it's all the same journey that we are trudging together on the road to a much happier, more fulfilling and immensely more meaningful destiny. This destiny is yours for the taking. If you still need help, we will always be there for you and you will never be alone again.

The truth is, while we have made much progress, the work has just begun. You have just been exposed to a new vision of living your life: One that is incredibly on purpose and on point.

Being at the end of your rope is actually a good thing. For, now you are finally ready to accept the change that you always wanted and needed. And, living life is if today were to be your last day forces you to face the own music in your life and to embrace change like never before. And, living-a-day-at-a-time is a beautiful and manageable way to live. It helps you to focus on living in your life in manageable time segments and to focus on the present and not stay stuck in the past or fearful of what the future may bring. Anything is do-able in "How to Love Yourself"-hour time unit.

Chapter VII.
SPIRITUAL GROWTH & DEVELOPMENT

The first is recognizing, acknowledging and honoring the need to feed our spiritual natures in order to find our higher truth. To me, our souls are our true nature, are an illuminated spark of a much higher and amazing universal energy and a reflection of the divine and ultimate source of all things. Much like the snowflake, each of us has a unique and fairly complex soul which powers our entire being. Our personalities are a direct reflection of our souls and our bodies are the vehicles for our souls to evolve and change in this life.

So, in an ironic way, we are spiritual beings living in a physical body, contrary to what our five senses are capable of understanding. Just because we can't see and identify the soul doesn't mean that it doesn't exist. According to Quantum Physicists, everything is energy and most of it is not visible to the eye. It is my personal belief that the soul is eternal as is the universal source of all things – or the divine. Our primary purpose in this life is to heal our souls and become intimate with our spiritual nature, which are complex ecosystems of energy that reflect our many lives, past, present and even future. So, the care of the soul is fundamental to all healing, spiritually, emotionally, physically and cognitively.

When I talk about spirituality, I don't mean religion. This is not about dogma or whose truth is the right truth. It is not about a religious God. But, rather, it is about reframing our lives to discover our own true reality, our purpose and how we can carve out permanent and joyful meaning from our own lives. It is about living our lives on purpose which means taking into account the whole person.

Our Innate Need for Self-Actualization

When we consciously or unconsciously deflect the illumination of light and positive change from impacting our lives, we are not becoming our best possible selves. We are blocking those parts of ourselves that need to be healed and are resisting the often unseen powers that are all around us that want us to heal and live our lives to the fullest. All living matter has an innate and powerful ability to heal its own self. The universe and the divine, compassionate and loving energy that drives all reality, wants and will support us to heal and grow – to evolve to higher and higher levels. It is common knowledge that humans only use a small part of our brain capacity – experts claim as little as five per cent -- and that we have an enormous potential to experience massive change and growth in each of our lives. I believe that we have an innate desire to become fuller, better and more fulfilled human beings. That we ALL have enormous power and capacity to live to our greatest potential. To become a more meaningful and purposeful part of the human race, our families, and to fulfill our own unique and particular mission on this earth. I further believe that with the right attitude, desire and open-mindedness, we can achieve anything that our hearts and minds set out to do. This, in and of itself, is very powerful and amazing.

Finding a God: Developing a Relationship with Something Greater Than Yourself

"Get A God!!" This was the incisive and definitive advice of my second A.A. sponsor, Vee P., who passed away while I was in prison along with two of my A.A. sponsees– God rest their souls. He was both religious (a devout and practicing Greek Orthodox) and deeply spiritual. He had been sober for over 40 years and despite years of struggling with Leukemia, was one of the happiest and most purposed men I have ever met. He also became a life mentor and one of my most loyal and dependable friends.

When he saw me struggling through relapse after relapse with my Alcoholism, I begged him to tell me what my problem was and what I needed to do. His simple, only and unembellished answer was "Get a God. It's the only thing you need to save your life and live it well." I remember telling him I didn't know how and begged him to help me. I was so unhappy and miserable that I couldn't stem the tide of my disease of addiction on my own. I thought I had been so spiritual. Clearly I was wrong. My sponsor told me that this is a journey I would have to take on my own. I just needed to dive in. The water was already there.

That was my first wake-up call to how so very disconnected I was with a God of my understanding, a Higher Power, Master of the Universe, Creative Intelligence, Divine source of everything, God or G-d. I had been trying to battle my "dis-ease" alone and, as with many times before, thought I had the intellectual wherewithal and fortitude, determination and sheer will to do this recovery thing all on my own. After all, I knew how to meditate, was Bar Mitvahed and was schooled in Jewish history, religious and ritual practice, followed Eastern Philosophy and spiritual practices, did Yoga and believed on an intellectual level that God existed– even though I was no longer practicing any of those wonderful tools.

I was powerless despite all this power around me. That was my wake-up call that I would have to go through this necessary process of spiritual discovery and connection, discard my pride and ego and get willing to try something new. This dis-ease was a far more formidable power than I thought and I was finally beaten into submission out of desperation.

This was, perhaps, one of the most difficult things for me to do. For some people, they are very sensitive and aware of their spirituality. Perhaps they came from a religious family that practiced a certain way of life and values. Or maybe you had a spiritual practice that has developed your own innate awareness of your soul. For me, it didn't come easy, even though I have always been a seeker and very spiritual from an early age. Nature and the great outdoors was my introduction to spirituality. I was always drawn to things natural. I grew up Jewish, went to Hebrew School and was Bar Mitvahed at 13 – like most Jewish boys coming into manhood. But, learning Hebrew was difficult for me and I never really understood or appreciated the prayers and rituals because they were taught in a foreign language which I never mastered. I hate being told what to do and had no concept or feeling of God, except one that was punishing and scary.

Upon entering the room of Alcoholics Anonymous (A.A.), I was told to get a sponsor and make the rooms and the people in the fellowship my higher power. Many of my fellows were "recovering" Catholics, Protestants and Jews who similarly had a negative experience with organized religion growing up.

All 12-step programs are predicated on developing a relationship with a higher power - not necessarily a religious one - but something greater than you. It took me nearly a decade to finally get the spiritual angle of the program and another 10 years to come to appreciate the need and importance of having a higher power in my own life. This same higher power has helped me to make all the other critical changes in my attitude, thinking, behavior, heart and soul and to re-orient my thick and stubborn brain become the person I was meant to be.

So, now I'm in prison, and I discover that the Federal Government, which I now loathed, but once loved and admired as a young boy, practices a strict separation of Church and State. Over the many years since I was a child, I have slowly watched the Government move away and escape from the religion business. The many lawyers, who run our government, along with the "nature-nurture" schools of science, were sure to litigate Uncle Sam if they showed any signs of religious discrimination, so the powers that be in Washington, D.C. decided to exit and stage left. Not only did they abandon those very principles that our nation's founding fathers once made us proud of, I strongly believe help to make our country strong, develop a deep sense of pride and remind us that we needed to be thankful and show gratitude to the supreme maker of all things, but they forbid the mention of the "God" word and even spirituality.

Suddenly, the soul no longer exists (because we're not allowed to talk about it), and spirituality which is the primary vehicle to explore our journey to the soul and beyond is taboo and illegal. How could this happen? How could our children be growing up in the public school system not knowing of the importance of the soul in their lives? What utter foolishnesses and misguided leadership! Eradicating any discussion of the soul, foolishly mistaken to mean "religion," is the beginning of the end for our society. Those wonderful, faith-based communities I visited on my many travels through the Midwest and the Southern Bible belt. They would all now have to send their kids to parochial school or to practice Eastern philosophies in Tibet or in yoga class. What utter foolishness.

In prison, we even had to remove our very well and voluntarily attended 12-step recovery meetings to the Chapel, because the Drug Recovery program that is known as "The Residential" and "Non-Residential Drug Abuse" programs were informed by the bureaucratic lawyers were no longer permitted, as was the mention of the word "God." Really. It's one thing to choose to be agnostic or atheist, but another thing to force the large incarcerated population that in their time of need, they weren't allow to depend upon a higher power and that they would have to become closet practitioners in order to find the only strength that, perhaps, could save them from doom. I can go on, but I won't. I think you get the point. So much for logic and behavioral science.

What is this "Higher Power?"

The term "Higher Power" (or "HP") has come to stand for a kinder, gentler description for a non-denominational God -- something not religious, but spiritual and inherently all-powerful in nature and will help lead you to your higher truth. It was coined in the 1930's by Bill Wilson and Dr. Bob, the founder's of the 12-step recovery movement, Alcoholics Anonymous, and is meant to describe a power greater than ourselves that if tapped into, can help to ensure our transformation a day-at-a-time into sober recovering Alcoholics. It has since been used for the hundreds of other 12-step programs that help others with a variety of afflictions and addictions to recover and to stay recovered from the disease of addiction. All 12-step programs are spiritual in nature. In fact, spirituality is the key component and change agent to transforming one's life and ensuring continued recovery a day-at-a-time.

The definition of a god is an image, person or thing that is worshiped, honored or believed to be all-powerful or the creator and ruler of the universe. An example of a god is Ganesha, a Hindu deity.

According to Wikipedia, "some believe that a God is a metaphor for a transcendent reality. Some believe in a female god (Deism), an Abrahamic god, or a god manifested in nature or the universe (pantheism). Many reglions reject the idea of deities and instead speak of the 'spirit of life' that binds all life on earth." **Quantum Physicists** have discovered what they believe to be the smallest identifiable particle known to science recently termed "The God Particle." Science has long denied nor been able to explain the existence of God, though Einstein and others have intimidated the mysterious existence of a God. Other Eastern religions like Buddhism, Hinduism and Sufism all espouse a Creative Intelligence, Universal Power, Master of Creation.

America, known from its founding days 1776 and the American Revolution, has long included the concept of God, Freedom and in something larger than life that we can all trust ("In God We Trust") it is an important and intrical part of our culture as a nation and people. Our founding fathers were all God loving people. Many ancient and traditional monotheistic religions like **Judaism, Catholicism, Protestantism and Islam** all believe in a single, all-powerful and forever great God). Often referred to as "Lord," "King," Master of The Universe," "Sovereign," YHWH, Adonai, Hashed. They see God as a being who created the world and who rules over the universe. God is usually associated with qualities like: holiness, sovereignty, omnipotence, omniscience, benevolence and omnipresence. God is eternal, unchangeable, transcendent and unaffected by earthly forces or anything else in creation for that matter.

Some Jewish **Kabalistic** thinkers have purported that all of existence is itself a part of God, and that we as humanity are unaware of our own inherent godliness and are grappling to come to terms with it. The position that Hasidism, proffers that there is nothing in existence outside of God – all being is within

God, and yet all existence cannot contain Him. Others believe that even the Heavens cannot contain Him. Modern Judaism teaches ht God is the sum of all natural processes that allow mane to become self-fulfilled.

Christianity teaches that God is a single being that exists simultaneously and eternally as the sum total of three entities or persons: The Father (the Source or Eternal Majesty, The Son (the eternal "Word"), manifest in human form as Jesus and thereafter as Christ, and the Holy Spirit (the Advocate).

Islam is a strict monotheism called tawhid. God is described in the Qur'an as: "Say: He is God, the One and Only; God the Eternal, Absolute."

Buddhism teaches the notion of a supreme God or a prime mover. The sole aim of the Buddhist spiritual practice is the complete elimination of distress or pain ("dukkha") in samsara, called nirvana. The Buddha either denies or accepts a creator, denies endorsing any views on creation and states that questions on the origin of the world are worthless. Nirvana (or heaven on earth or enlightenment) is the highest goal of practicing Buddhists.

Hinduism teaches the concept of god as complex and is dependent on the particular tradition. The concept spans conceptions from absolute monism to henotheism, monotheism or polytheism. It also believes in a sovereign God who is the omnipotent cultivation of all Hindu gods and Goddesses. The practice leads to enlightenment – an education or awareness that brings profound change in reality and, In Eastern Religions is referred to as the highest form of spiritual development. God Consciousnesses – or complete joining and awareness, knowledge and perception of God. Universal Spirit, Higher Consciousness, Creative Intelligence.

While I was born Jewish and received an excellent Jewish religious education and was a Bar-Mitvah – when a Jewish boy is pronounced a man, my pursuit of spirituality, or the Higher Power, began early by experiencing nature as a young child. While certainly not judging it, my early experience with a religious God left me longing for something deeper and more meaningful to help explain my purpose, and my help me to order and make sense of my life here on earth. Being in nature was my early portal to something powerful, calming, transcendent, beautiful, amazing and infinite. The Solar system and outer space – the Universe, became my go-to spiritual portal of wonder during my young teen years. Growing up in the 60's and 70's hallucinogens, an abundance of Alcohol and assorted other drugs, kundalini Yoga, Karate was the way I connected with God. I thought I was having a religious experience every time I hallucinated with LSD and certain other drugs.

It wasn't until college and my early adult life that I began to explore the deeper meaning of the soul. I was initiated by teachers of Maharishi Mahesh Yogi into the practice of Transcendental Meditation ("T.M."). I took Karate, Learned to meditate and practice Kundalini Yoga – all of which were very powerful spiritual experiences. In fact, my experience with T.M. was so powerful in early adulthood that I unconsciously stopped drinking and doing recreational drugs because they interfered with the powerful and life-changing experiences I was having. Meditation greatly lowered my chronic stress and anxiety levels and allowed me to think more clearly. Why in the world would I want to muck up this good with drugs and alcohol? I stopped using all mood altering substances for about a year. I enjoyed and embraced the T.M. retreats and advanced teachings. I couldn't get enough of this new wisdom and experience that seemed to feed my hunger for my spiritual nature. I felt alive for the first time since my childhood.

I lost that feeling and the spiritual practice I had embarked on my chase of girls and young adult freedom that College offered and my raging hormones seem to get the better of me. I didn't return to that state of wonder and spiritual pursuit until I became desperate in my alcoholism and addictions – one of the being greed and the other being pride and ego.

Developing Your Own Personal Relationship with This "Power"

For me, who always believed I was a searcher of higher truth and reality, it didn't come easy. My intentions were good. It's different for everyone. For some, it comes easy and they already have a fully developed relationship with a God of their understanding. Perhaps they learned it from their family early on and it became something not just forced, but fun to do. Or, maybe it was part of your family culture and you learned how to live with good, moral, ethical and righteous principles and good values.

When I was an Advertising Director at Sony in my 20's and was traveling around the country to introduce the new Sony Walkman, I observed how certain cities and states had a wonderful family life. Religion was a central part of the family and most people I met just seemed to be happier. Life was so much simpler and calmer and people seemed to know what their purpose was in work and life. Here I was living in the heart of Manhattan, ground zero for city life and culture, especially for a single man, and everything seemed so grand, fast and furious. I had long forgotten about my early spiritual longings or religious upbringing. That had long faded away only to have the rush of success and all that I believed went with that had become my master. I never forgot that experience and all my subsequent years of business travel. As an advertising person, I needed to get out of the myopic world of living in a big city to understand how the rest of America lived. They seemed to know where they were going in a far different way.

So, how exactly does one develop a relationship with a God of your understanding or a Higher Power?

1. Through Religious Practice:

While I hated it growing up, I have now come to love and appreciate the power of spirituality found through Judaism. It doesn't matter what religious persuasion you are. Each has a deep spiritual side and all practices lead to the same place: The Divine source of all things. The place that fires the spark that is your soul. Your higher being and purpose on earth. So, if religion is not for you, take a look at the spiritual roots and dimension of your practice to see how you might reshape it to work for you.

2. <u>**Prayer & Meditation:**</u>

Prayer: Through the repeated and initially tedious practice of prayer and meditation, I began to experience that silence and happiness that came from deep within me, my spirit or soul. Developing your own practice can take time and requires persistence, belief, trust and faith in something greater than yourself. There are many ways to pray and many wonderful prayers to practice. I've included some of my favorites in the Appendix in the back of this book. I have found that practice makes perfect. Acting as if you will get some benefit from prayer will eventually bring real results.

I pray ancient religious prayers, but equally important if not more important is the power of personal prayer. We often referred to them as "Fox Hole" prayers when I was in the throes and desperation of my alcoholism and assorted addictions. Went things seemed desperate and all the walls were collapsing in on me, I begged with all my heart, soul and tears for help. Sometimes they were answered, but as soon as I resumed my old behaviors, my prayers were forgotten.

Praying to the Master of all things and creation is not about religion. It is something that many of us "recovering" Jews, Catholics, Protestants and others of the more religious stripes now have come to understand. I learned to pray three times a day as a Jew. Then twice a day with occasional check-ins during the day as a 12-stepper in recovery. Now, I pray throughout the day, because the practice brings me so many incredible rewards and I am all about Return on Investment – like in business. I love the feeling when I plead honestly to God for help, tell Him everything that is going on to me like a best friend or lover standing right in front of me – both good and bad, apologize for my transgressions and ask for forgiveness and the wisdom and direction to do the next right thing in my life. I am sincere and my prayers are usually answered, not always in my time, though. I've learned to understand how to sublimate my will to a larger Will that is much smarter and wiser than me. It has taken me years to develop this amazing relationship and it continually keeps me in the black and becomes deeper over the course of time.

Meditation: According to Wikipedia, "Meditation is a practice where an individual train the mind or induces a mode of consciousness, either to realize some benefit or for the mind to simply acknowledge its content without becoming identified with that content, or as an end in itself" There are many ways to meditate. Meditation takes many forms and practices. Building a meditation practice of your own or with a group has many benefits, including mental clarity and acuteness, emotional and psychological healing, physical awareness and, of course, spiritual awareness. The physical and emotional benefits are deep relaxation, calming the mind, reduced stress and anxiety, lowered blood pressure, increased alpha (or happy) wave activity, better eating habits, reduced anger and more smiles. I practice both mindful meditation and Transcendental Meditation. I also practice a more formalized religious form of meditation – where I contemplate and show gratitude for the importance of many things such as meaning and wisdom of the many things I learn everyday – both from the external world and from deep within. Here are some more examples of ways to develop a mediation practice. I strongly urge you to start meditating in whatever way floats your boat. Ultimately, a strong practice of mediation is like a portal to what Eastern philosophies like Buddhism and Hinduism called transcendence or Nirvana and enlightenment – where you are powerfully transformed into the invisible world of the soul and higher purpose of your life and existence. I will spend more time discussing this in the next chapter and also have provided some simple instruction on how to meditate in the back of this book. So here is a short list of ways and practices to meditate: Transcendental Meditation, Mindful Meditation, Concentration Meditation, Buddhist and Zen Meditation, Tai Chi, Qigong and even Walking Meditation. Of course, there are many other methods for deepening our consciousness like chanting, dancing,

3. Develop an Intimate Relationship With The Present Moment – The Here & Now:

Most of us have very active minds, where our thoughts are always racing and we can't seem to get out of this "committee in our heads." It is very hard to get a break from what some refer to as our "Monkey Minds." Doing so requires repeated practice of detaching from your thoughts and becoming the observer of your thoughts. This observer is your soul and is the main portal to your higher power. Become aware of your thoughts, and also recognizing and honoring that you are not your thoughts but the one observing them, is the one of the goals of developing a relationship with the now.. These many, fleeting thoughts nearly always have something to do with our reacting to the past or anticipating the future. Doing so does not permit us to experience the very moment that we are in and where our lives are actually happening. Become the observer and begin to detach from your busy mind – which can be very hard to turn off.

Practicing distancing yourself from the thoughts that your mind and personality create in time will create a deep and silent experience which you can broaden and deepen. My three favorite books on developing this practice, which is also referred to as Unified Field, the transcendent, the deep pool of creative intelligence and the path to enlightenment, nirvana, incredible joy and peace, are Eckhart Tolle's "The Power of Now," Michael A. Singer's "The Untethered Soul," and Gary Zukav's "The Seat of The Soul." I rotate reading them along with other prayer and spiritual books that I have found incredibly useful in developing my own practice. Arguably, very few humans have achieved this state of being, but it is becoming more readily available to anyone who chooses to be a member of this new and burgeoning age of enlightenment, which many spiritualists and religionists believe is already upon us.

4. Nature & the Great Outdoors:

The Natural world and the great outdoors has long been a gateway to developing a relationship with the Divine – the power, creative intelligence, master of all creation that created the Heavens & Earth, the Stars & Planets, the Galaxies and all living beings. You already know my experience with nature and how I was able to connect with an amazing power greater than myself by just being and chilling in nature's backyard. I love it all, the plants, animals, insects, all living things. I am amazed, awed and just so inspired by nature's beauty. How can you not be taken by the natural wonders of the mountains, oceans, lakes, rivers, forests, fields, and majestic national parks like Yellowstone, Grand Canyon, Yosemite, Grand Tetons, Acadia, Everglades, Denali and Hawaii's Volcanoes. Perennial and Annual Plants and Flowers of all kinds and their intricate, ornate and uniquely colorful and varied. The natural order of things, sunrise, sunset, night sky, the constellations, and more recently all the amazingly detailed photos that we have received from our exploration by NASA of outer space from International Space Station.

When I was a child, I remember getting chills down my spine watching Neal Armstrong and the Apollo 11 space crew, the first man to land on the moon in the 1960's. I had my first white light spiritual experience while walking in the State Park behind my house while growing up on Long Island. I've sat and watched hundreds of asteroids fly by in blindingly starry nights while living out in the country on weekends, vacations in far away and remote places and even while on the rooftop of my New York City Apartment. Nature takes me where manmade matter can't. There is something alive and I feel the presence of God while experiencing nature's bounty. A chiropractor once told me to walk on the dirt on weekends while living in Manhattan, as it would provide much needed healing from the city of concrete. I have found the presence of God while flying over one million miles on airplanes and looking out at the incredible cloud formations. During my incarceration, I imagined myself many places, but especially enjoyed sitting by the edge of beautiful fields of hay and other crops being grown outside on the prison grounds. The Mountains move me with their majesty. And, of course all the outdoor sports I have enjoyed over the years like camping, canoeing, bicycling, hiking, swimming just about everywhere, skiing in remote places during a powerful winter storm, ice-shoeing on the virgin snow fields everywhere. Even Golfing on a beautiful green speaks to me. Naturally, I could go on, but you get the idea.

5. Detaching From Technology and Getting Quiet:

It is hard to be present in the here and now unless I fully detach from the myriad of technology that begs for my attention. From smart phones and computers, Apps and software, driving in a newer model car with all its many electronic and digital wonders. I need peace and quiet, eyes closed or open, but not engaged on anything that is powered by any energy source. Clearly, technology is wonderful and an amazing enhancement to my life, but I can't focus on the whispers of my higher power all around me while the buzz and eye candy that is electronics walks down the electronic runaway for my eyes to feast on.

6. Exercise & Getting Healthy:

An hour of intense and regularly scheduled exercise every day or other day is an excellent way to get out yourself and connected to your body – an amazing vehicle with 613 organs and body parts – all different and serving a unique function. Our bodies are the temples that house are souls, our heart, and our spirit. Getting in tune with our bodies is a powerful way of connecting with the spirit within – a spark of the divine which spiritualists believe resides in our chest, heart and brain. The human brain alone consists of 86 billion nerve cells (neurons) – the "the gray matter." Billions more nerve fiber and trillions of connections, or synapses. The miracle organ that beats 100,000 times a day on the average and pumps blood, oxygen and nutrients to the body, while returning carbon dioxide and other wastes from the body. Amazing, evolutionary ever since the beginning of man perhaps some seven millions years ago. Random chance? I think not!!

So, where does the higher power come in and how does the body help us to connect with it and to develop a deeper relationship? When you connect the dots of the human creation, it is one of the most amazing creations in the universe. One of the ways I meditate is to close my eyes and to silently thank God from the bottom of my heart for every single part of my body. I do a body scan of my outer organs, and then scan from the bottom of my feet, toes and toenails to the top of my head, skull, skin, hair, brain and every organ, vein, tendon and for all my five senses. I thank God for creating this magnificent mound of matter – as it allow me to get closer to Him. Then, taking great care of the body, my nutrition, what I eat and drink, getting restful sleep, and allowing my body to heal with either Eastern or Western medicine as an assist is the way to keep it all together and to continue to honor the body so the soul can continue to develop, heal and evolve throughout my natural lifespan.

7. Hobbies and Pastimes:

 Finding and engaging in favorite pastimes, whether it be a playing a sport, collecting stamps or coins, playing your favorite computer and video games or board games, cards, movies, reading, hiking, joining a club to be with others who share your special and beloved interests are all ways to learn about yourself, and allow you to practice your spiritual tools with others.

8. *Doing What You Love:*

Whether it be work or play, just being yourself, doing the things you love to do either personally or professionally can go a long way to discovering your inner strengths and your authentic self. Finding yourself and your "happy place" through the work you like to do most, or those personal things you like to do most is part of living a meaningful and purposeful life. The more you do "you," the closer you get to your authentic self, the happier you become and the closer you get to self-actualization.

9. Joining a 12-Step or Other Self-Help Groups/Fellowships:

If you struggle with an addiction and have finally gotten honest enough with yourself to do something about it, there are a number of excellent 12-step programs for whatever plagues you pretty much anywhere in the world. There are hundreds of programs – all members supported and non-denominational from Alcohol to narcotics and especially opioids like cocaine, heroin, crystal meth, compulsive behavior like sex or gambling, even work. Then there are programs for families of those who struggle who also need help, are affected by the addictions of their loved ones and also need a life recovery program for themselves – programs like Al-Anon and many others. They are all spiritual in nature and are hailed as the standard for recovery from any type of addiction. The 12-Steps and 12-

Traditions of Recovery is both evidenced based and works for those who work it. A Higher Power exists in these rooms which are magical and save countless lives from self-destruction.

God speaks through people and just attending and especially participating at the hundreds of thousands of meetings available pretty much anywhere in the world, both physically off-line and now even on-line is an amazing place to hear the voice of God and the power of Recovery in your own life.
Other Self-Help Groups: Perhaps you struggle with the death of a loved-one, a divorce or separation, loneliness, a chronic disease or have a special interest like gardening, reading through book clubs, movie clubs, golf and tennis lessons, outdoor activities of all types, there's a club for that, too. Getting out of self, feeding your thirst to be part of a larger fellowship, club, activity or just having a good time and sharing it with those who have like interests is really important to living a fulfilling, stimulating life, getting out of self and being a part of the larger world and human race that we all need to be an active part of. God speaks through people everywhere, and as you develop your relationship with Him, he will speak to you often through others. You just need to learn how to hear the subtle, but often powerful messages He is constantly sending you through a variety of sources and experiences.

10. Getting Out of Self:

 Volunteer your time, mentor others with your special skills, coach those in need, and be charitable with your time, knowledge and financial resources, give until it hurts. By giving you will find (The St. Francis Prayer or part of it here).

11. Studying and Enjoying Culture, Art and Music:

What better way to feed your heart and soul, and of course feast all your senses than with immersing yourself in your culture(s) of choice. Whether you travel to far away destinations and love to explore, enjoy visiting the many museums and art galleries in your town or in nearby cities, go to concerts of all types, learn about history of your country, people and the way they lived today and in the past through architecture, archeology, food, and of course culture, soak it all up. Whatever your cultural or artistic pleasure, you will learn more about yourself, feed your particular areas of interest and sooth and excite the mind and soul all at the same time. Being an active part of the world around you is not only fun, but also feeds and frees the spirit from the monotony of the day, week and year. Take as many vacations as you can allow in your busy schedule, get the potatoe off the couch and indulge yourself in the rich world of art, music, culture and life. Perhaps if you're bold enough, live abroad for a period of time and see how other people live. God speaks through people of all cultures and their expressions of life through art, architecture and music. Vive la difference!

12. Journaling:

I'm a writer, so I have found and deepened my relationship with authentic self and self-expression through writing. My beloved daughter, Julia, taught me about the value of journaling from when she was a teenager and later as I was hurting terribly following a divorce.

I am very driven, so at the time, it seemed like a good idea to start journaling so that I could use the material for a book. Julia explained to me with love that journaling was for me, not for others. It is a way for me to express myself, my frustrations, my experiences, my passions, my purpose, and those things I love and wanted to remember.

There are so many wonderful reason and ways to journal and I found this to be great solace and a source of comfort and inspiration while I was away at prison. I still have those many notebooks and can't believe the gobbledygook I wrote when I was withdrawing from the 15 medications I had been on. But, that was my journey then and it has morphed into my present journey which has proven to be much richer and more rewarding.

It doesn't matter how well you write or whether your grammar is correct. Just write the way you think and don't worry about the accuracy! You journal as a way to communicate to your very best friend (YOU) as a way to get to know yourself and to commit onto paper those thoughts that are swirling around in your head. Putting pen to paper really helps to organize and filter your thoughts. Each day is different and is easily shaded by your moods and current experiences. What a great way to get to know yourself and to begin an evolving relationship with yourself and your true purpose. What a gift that my beautiful daughter gave to me. I know want to pass that on to those who are struggling to develop a better relationship with yourself and the God of your understanding.

On a final note, while in prison, I also wrote five to 10 letters a week to those few friends and family that I still had a relationship with. It both got me out of self and my head and helped me to grow in profound ways. I also wrote a longer letter to my now 93 year old mother each Sunday as a way to share some rare time with her – thinking that I might never see her again if she passed away before I got home. She is still alive, and though advanced in years and with dementia, she still remembers me writing and our weekly visits. My sister was gracious enough to read her those letters each week – and I am eternally grateful for what she has done to keep the eternal flame of love and respect going with me and my mother.

Sadly, writing has become a lost art and texting in the new world of communication. I can't state it more emphatically how important it is to learn how to write well and to write often. Keep the flame burning!!

13. Love Your Brother and Fellow Human Beings:

 What better way to express your spirituality and connect with the God of your understanding than through expressing and confessing your love countless times to your loved ones and to the people close to you that matter the most – both in your personal and professional life. The Beatles proclaimed, "All you need is love…love is all around you." The bible says, love your fellow man as you would love yourself. Do onto others as they would do unto you. Share the wealth of your deepest love for life and for your beloved. By exercising your heart muscle, building your emotional intelligence and capacity, letting go of your anger, resentments and hang-ups, and just allowing you to be yourself – you open the heart to immeasurable joy and happiness. And, you get to show others how to love you in return. Not a bad deal. LOVE is ALWAYS the answer. You will never go wrong.

14. Self-Love:

We've touched on this in an earlier chapter, but perhaps one of the most important ways to love is to love yourself. Easier said than done and also a labor of love. But, by building your self-esteem, ridding yourself of anger and resentments, learning to forgive yourself and others, giving yourself permission to feel your feelings and express yourself as you really and authentically are, you are building a powerful trinity in your relationship with yourself, the larger Spirit of the Universe and with your fellowman. The more you learn to love yourself, the more love flows to all those around you and of course, always to your Creator!

15. Contemplation:

 Is an ancient practice developed or learned by all major religions – both eastern and western. Its literal translation means the action of looking thoughtfully and deeply at something for a long time. As long as it is purposeful and the intention is to get to know or understand whatever you are contemplating better and at a deeper level, it is all good. It is an amazing form of meditation. In a religious sense, contemplation is usually in the form of a prayer or meditation. In Judeo-Christian circles, contemplation literally means to see God or to have the vision of God. The intent is to reconcile the heart and the mind into one thing. There are many wonderful, important and spiritual things to contemplate about such as who you really are, what is your true purpose on earth, what does your higher power have in store for you, and what is your soul and it's connection to the universe and the divine scheme of the universe? You can contemplate the meaning and experience of love, compassion, wisdom, empathy, joy, happiness or just about anything you want to know better and need to find the inner space to wrap your arms around. I will go into contemplative states often and it is a form of meditation for me. It allows me to consider without the restriction of space and time, those things I really want to get to know better. It is kind of mindfulness where I experience total presence and being in the here and now. I don't have the clutter of noise in my head. The act of contemplation is usually accomplished with total silence and the absence of thoughts. It is a very powerful to connect with the powers of the unseen and the higher consciousness of the universe. It gets me out of self and into a place of joy and gratitude. I have included additional resources in the Appendix.

16. <u>Immersing Yourself in Spiritual & Religious Texts and Study</u>

I have long been a reader of spiritual texts – all kinds – both religious and spiritual. I also watch U-tube spiritual speakers; authors and experts talk about various subjects of interest. This helps feed the intellectual side of my spirituality and heightens my awareness and understanding of my soul and spiritual life. It helps build perspective and frames my awareness of my soul experiences with a deeper understanding of what I am experiencing. Another way of saying this might be that I'm better intellectualizing my spiritual nature. While there is no way to replace direct experience with book knowledge – as that is an absolutely necessary experience for each person to have – helps build my understanding of the world of spiritual psychology and describes my experiences (both current and future) in words that I can understand. It also creates a stronger intention, direction and increases the velocity of my spiritual growth. They work hand and hand. There are so many excellent books and authors to choose from, depending on your particular area of interest and curiosity. I have included some of my favorites in the Appendix.

17. <u>All of the Above.</u>

Mix and match to your heart's content. Just make a decision to do it. I promise you huge rewards if you start the journey and keep at it will morph and change and your Higher Power will never give you more than you can handle, but He will help make sense of your life in a way that we mere humans will never be able to do. So, try and experiment what you think might work for you best. We are all wired differently and there is no one solution to developing a strong spiritual foundation and relationship with your personal Creator. Once you've broken the ice and started on your spiritual journey, you will never be the same again. It may very well be the most important thing you can do about learning to live life on purpose, with passion and with awesome fruits of your labors as you evolve your relationship with the larger powers of the universe.

<u>Your Spiritual Journey</u>

If only we could flip the switch and turn on our spiritual light right away when we need it the most, perhaps our pain would subside all that much quicker. But, as I've discovered on my own journey deep within, the pain and suffering we do endure is our Creator's wake-up call for us to get closer to Him and to his power to heal. He is the ultimate healer and our unique job on earth is to heal and grow our soul and spiritual life. It takes time and practice and spiritual awareness and higher consciousness of the incredible world that we can't see but has enormous sway over our lives is the ultimate rub and goal. We want to go deep within, develop a real and meaningful relationship with our God, and connect to the infinite world of reality and energy waiting to greet us. True power is found within and then you can bring its many benefits to the world around you. Love and compassion, true thankfulness and gratitude for all the grace and wisdom that you will receive and share with others. This is the prize. Not the material bling that attracts and intrigues us like honey to the bee, but an unending and infinite well of joy and happiness that exists for all mankind to enjoy and share.

Have it your way: Hold the pickles and the onions – no problem. Just make the decision to pursue your true wealth and discover your own purpose and meaning as your life exponentially unfolds to its higher purpose. Just do it. You can explore what works best for you in the Appendixes in the back of this book

Good Orderly Direction (G.O.D.)

Again, this is not a religious, but rather a secular way at looking at all the good and eternal wisdom that we want to live our lives by. We are developing a new blue print, a new set of rules and procedures, with which we are creating our new architectural masterpiece that we will have to live in for the rest of our lives. This masterpiece is your ticket to freedom – from pain and struggle. It's the vehicle you can ride to take you on the most incredible journey you've ever dreamed. All you have to do is make a decision to try living a good and right life, based on moral, honest principles, re-educating yourself to embrace solid values, realistic and achievable short- and long-term goals, learn to follow the lead from others that have already grooved this path for you and learn to get out of self and give yourself to others who are pursuing the same path that you started on. Make the commitment and practice the honesty, openness and willingness (H.O.W.) to see this through to continued success – one day-at-a-time.

The concept of Good Orderly Direction, or (G.O.D.) was born in the rooms of Alcoholics Anonymous as a way to provide the fellowship with a non-denominational or non-religious, secular way to refer to a Higher Power -- that special something – that life-giving and saving power -- greater than ourselves. People who struggle with addiction issues have often found that their anger and dissapointment with the God that they were taught to obey and be fearful of as a child, is not a trusting, benevolent, loving God. As a result, they have resorted to use their own will to live their lives, their way.

Here, we are talking about beginning to develop trust and faith in something that presently doesn't exist. Not easy for many, despite the overwhelming need to obtain help from some other source outside of oneself. How can you trust a God that hurt you or just didn't deliver on your wishes as a child or even as an adult? So, I was asked to suspend all that I thought I knew and to initially trust the A.A. fellowship, the meetings, my sponsor, other men and women who provided me with direction and loving wisdom to find my way back to life and away from the chaos I had become accustomed to in my dis-ease. It worked, as did the knowledge I acquired from rigorously embracing and practicing the 12-steps of recovery. They are powerful, and God speaks through the people who are in recovery and have a common problem and proven solution. This is the Good Orderly Direction I learned that also included many benefits from believing in something other and greater than myself. Now, I can just follow this footprint which was made by the many others that came before me and just follow a far more satisfying and easier way to live my life. I hope you find this Good Orderly Direction in your life, too, and work hard to pass it onto others who struggle. That is largely what this book is about and why I set out to write it. You don't need to be an alcoholic or addict to need to find your way to a happier, more meaningful and fulfilling life.

Living In Gratitude; Counting Our Blessings

One of the many ways I've learned to be happy with my lot in life is to internalize an attitude of gratitude for all the many blessings I have received. I believe I have received these blessings, not because of anything I've done on my own, but because I have started to live a more positive and righteous life. The more grateful I act no matter what comes my way, the more grateful I feel deep inside. I know that I have been blessed with so much and that I need to remember to share these blessings with all of you if I ever expect to keep them. That is the price of staying grateful.

Living your life in gratitude means you know that you have someone else to thank for what you have received. As you develop a relationship with your Creator or the Universe or the Master of All Things, you will come to realize that we all have very little to do with our own successes in life. But, when we do receive them, like saying "Thank You" to our fellows, it behooves us to say "Thank You" to the divine intelligence that made our successes possible in the first place. Acknowledging those that make all those good things possible in the first place – whether it be through a friend, spouse, child, parent, partner or professional, being thankful becomes a way of life and says a lot about your level of humility and appreciation for whatever comes your way! It becomes easier over time to express you appreciation for all those things you do have to others who have made that possible. While it takes work for some of us, showing our gratitude and appreciation will get far better results in the happiness department than being ungrateful and negative. Everyone loves to know that other people appreciate their efforts or good deeds. As much as you may like to hear it when others show their gratitude, go out of your way to say "thank you" and I appreciate what you are doing for me. It will go a long way to building a sense of trust and honesty in all your relationships. And, when you least expect it, others will lay their kindnesses and courtesy on you. When you have an attitude of gratitude, you will start to see this positive and attractive attitude in others.

Humiliation as a Path to Gaining Humility

Humiliation and Humility are not the same – not even close. People often confuse the two. Learning how to be truly humble in your life takes a lot of practice and some grace from the man (or woman) upstairs. I know this from direct experience, as I don't believe I had an ounce of humility in me before going to prison. My ego, grandiosity and perhaps even self-centered narcissism made sure that wasn't possible. So, finally, at the heels of defeat, I surrendered to pretty much anyone that would accept me. It took repeated humiliation and relapse for me to finally get and stay sober. I was one of those dyed in the wool thick skulls. After banging my head voluntarily against the wall, it finally started to crack and so did I.

I am not suggesting that you need to experience humiliation in order to become and display humility in your own life. I am suggested that you do what you can to avoid this. But, if you must, understand that being humiliated by others for the way you behave, think or by what you believe is a way to better understanding of your own and the larger truths that operate in this world.

Eventually, everyone reaches their bottom in life and humiliation is a very effective vehicle for getting there – sometimes quickly slowly, but it will always materialize if you work for it! It's kind of like sucking on a tootsie roll lollipop where after much work; you finally reveal the core chocolate-laced gooey ooze that sits waiting for you inside.

We will spend more time talking about the virtues and gifts of triumph that come from authentic humility and the features and benefits that experiencing it can bring to you and those around you. It is a gift and a prize and something to look forward to, if you haven't already experienced it.

Filling That Hole in Your Soul

When you decide to live your life on purpose, you necessarily choose to fix that gaping hole in your soul. This is huge and is at the very center of our sadness and feeling of hopelessness. If I can find the words to describe the way I felt before, during and after my own fall from grace and jump off the cliff into that very dark world called depression and hopelessness, it would have to be that I had this huge hole in my soul. Nothing could seem to fill it, no matter how much experience, alcohol or drugs that I had. At the end of the day, my happiness meter was always on empty and I couldn't understand why. I worked so hard, sacrificed so much, cried so hard. And, the more I tried, the worse I felt until I could feel no more. I became numb and wanted it all to end. How very sad that we can allow ourselves through our own free will to be reduced to such a state of anguish and despair.

I think that we've all learned some hard lessons about our lives and the inadequacies of our happiness getting skills. We need to relearn how to live. But, more importantly, we need to ask why we are doing what we are doing in the first place. What is our true motive for our lives? What do we really want and are we doing what we need to in order to take us to where we want to go?

When you've reached your own personal bottom, have become sick and tired of being sick and tired, know with certainty that you have come to the end of the line and that something big has to give, you are finally ready to make the necessary decisions to change.

So, then we can all agree that there is a better way, and now you can choose to stay the way you are or to change. But, until we create the meaning and discover our own purpose for living, we have not satisfied the question why and we will never be permanently happy. We will not be able to fill that hole in our soul.

Continuing On the Road to Happiness and Self-Actualization

Bill Wilson, the co-founder and inspiration behind Alcoholics Anonymous is often quoted as stating: "We shall be with you in the Fellowship of the Spirit as you trudge the Road of Happy Destiny." The 12-steps of recovery are a core and excellent, proven spiritual program of healing and living." And, if we work our "program" we are guaranteed to experience The Promises, which I will repeat again: "If we are painstaking about…our development, we are going to know a new freedom and a new happiness. We will not regret the past nor wish to shut the door on it. We will comprehend the word serenity, and we will know peace. No matter how far down the scale we have gone, we will see how our experience can benefit others. That feeling of uselessness and self-pity will disappear. We will lose interest in selfish things and gain interest in our fellows. Self seeking will slip away. Our whole attitude and outlook upon life will change. Fear of people and of economic insecurity will leave us. We will intuitively know how to handle situations which used to baffle us. We will suddenly realize that God is doing for us what we could not do for ourselves. Are these extravagant promises? We think not. They are being fulfilled among us – sometimes quickly, sometimes slowly. They will always materialize if we work for them."

You Don't Have To Be an Alcoholic or Addict to Be Unhappy & Feel Unloved

You don't have to be an alcoholic or addict to be unhappy or to have a hole in our soul. Nor do you need to suffer as I did to look for a better way of living your life. In ""How to Love Yourself"-Hour Reboot," we spend much time addressing the true meaning of Good Orderly Direction (or "G.O.D.")

CHAPTER VIII.
YOUR SPIRITUAL TOOLKIT FOR HEALING YOUR HEART

You do need, however, to learn how to live in a way that is going to feed your soul, your purpose and to create incredible meaning for you. You have every right to expect to and to actually become happy, joyous and free of your past. It's there for the taking, but you do have to want and work for it. So, let's continue to build on what is already a really good thing and measurable progress in finding the light and the way out of our pain and suffering.

Retarded Growth & Development

I don't know why I ended up an alcoholic and addict, nor do I fully understand why all the difficult trials and tribulations occurred in my life the way that they did. But, I now understand that it was all part of my necessary journey here on earth. I accept what happened to me to
day, fully and without resentment, self-pity or remorse. They gave me the kindling, tinder and logs to build my own fire and help me understand what exactly I needed to change.

Nobody life's is ever perfect and we all have our issues. Even the President and the Pope. We are all human. We all have our own unique lessons to learn. Some of us get stuck somewhere along the way growing up. We didn't learn the lessons that others learned in our youth. And that is ok.
 If we were "perfect," we would have nothing to change and life would be beautiful all the day – but perhaps a bit boring -- kind of like living in warm weather climates where the sun and temperature are always the same. But, with the four seasons, there is constant variety and opportunity for new experiences. One day it's hot, the next day it's cold, windy and the snow is blowing. Then, peaking through the snow are little sprouts of spring flowers and foliage. God has gifted us with a miraculous bounty of variety and daily surprises in nature.

Everyone travels through life at their own pace and in their own unique way. Some of us are slower. Others are quicker. It really doesn't matter. We must move through life recognizing that whatever we were given to start is ok. But, we can always improve on the givens and make up for lost time and development. So, we know not to beat ourselves up or to act out when we aren't making very good progress. All the important prizes in life are waiting for you when you are ready to receive them.

Everything happens For a Reason, For Our Own Good and For the Very Best (both good & bad)

There is an ancient biblical belief that addresses faith and trust in a higher power and how exactly we are supposed to live as human beings. The concept has a lot to do with healing and growing our souls and spiritual life to ensure that we are doing everything within our power and the free will that we were uniquely given as a species results in a better life in the hereafter.

Whether you believe in the hereafter or not, the point is that everything that happens to us, BOTH good and bad is exactly what our spiritual natures require to learn and grow. And, EVERYTHING that happens to us is for our very own good and growth.

If we learn to pay attention to our unique calling in life to grow, improve, and live a good and virtuous life, we will avoid the vicious repetition of pain in the future. So, life is not random as if often appears. But, instead, EVERYTHING that happens to us, while it may appear unacceptable, painful and intolerable, is meant for us to look to see what exactly we need to change and grow. This is what our lives are all about. But, more on this later. First, a couple of more life lessons to discuss:

Next Steps for Insuring a Really Good & Happy Life...

So, now, it's time to take an insurance policy out on ensuring permanent happiness and peace-of-mind. We have reviewed a variety of important tools and strategies that you can employ any time, any day when you feel you want to make progress in your own personal growth.   The rest of our time together today will involve two main areas: The first is building our spiritual awareness and learning how to access and grow this amazing power within us. And that power is our soul which brings us our spiritual nature to our personality – which is highly unique to us. The second way to ensure permanent healing and happiness is to ask for help and guidance from those many people who have already been where you are now. Mentors, guides, teachers, sponsors, advisors, consultants. Call them what you will, but they are the people who will not only vouch for the content and the techniques that I have laid out for you to explore and test, but also will help you to identify what works best for them and share with you the wisdom that they have learned. More on this in the next section.

Living in the Truth & Staying Empowered From the Inside Out

Developing true purpose and meaning in one's life is truly an inside job. So, is happiness. It usually isn't random, but something we all have the power to create. We weren't born to be miserable and the God of our understanding never gives us more than we can handle.

To build a really good life one has to honor and live their truth. Who are you, what are you made of and what is your true purpose in life? This is what we really want to discover. There is much power in the truth and living with integrity. When we live with integrity, we are also living with integrity and our outsides match our insides. We are no longer wasting energy In making people believe that we are something that we are not. We are authentic in the sense that we are honoring and living our own truth. What you see is what you get.

Seems impossible, considering all the pain and struggle most of us have endured. But, it's not; it's a labor of love and the journeying through our lives well is a sure way to find and keep true happiness and become fulfilled. That's largely what this book is all about. Building on our assets, minimizing and eliminating our liabilities and living the life we were always meant to live, but just couldn't use our own free will to get there.

When we are living in our own truth, we are living consistently with the energy of the universe. We are not fighting and struggling, but we have surrendered to our greater truth, have accepted our lot in life and have chosen to make the very best of the raw materials that we were given.

Healing & Evolving Our Souls

Our Purpose in life is to heal and grow our souls. Period. Everything else is secondary. All our human experiences and physical activities are meant for us to grow and evolve our spiritual selves. The people in our lives, the experiences we have, the pain, fear, love, joy and dis-ease are all meant to teach us the lessons we must learn to evolve as going spiritual beings. Our bodies are uniquely suited to help us to achieve the maximum growth in this life.

Many Lives, Many Masters

You may or not believe you have been here before – that you have had previous lives. In his groundbreaking book, "Many Lives Many Masters," Brian Weiss, M.D. takes us into the world of reincarnation through his unexpected practice of past life therapy. Reincarnation is not just a mystical and something Buddhists and Hindus created, it is actually in all the divine and ancient revelations of the old and New Testament and the Koran.

The main concept is that we are spiritual beings having a physical experience. This "experience" is a necessary episode in the physical five-sense reality for us to move to higher and higher spiritual levels. Our understanding and perception of our spiritual mandates are not revealed to us.

If you believe that everything is energy as Einstein and Quantum Physicists have explained, then the body and the soul are levels of energy. The body and physical matter are very dense forms of energy; the soul and all that is unseen to our eyes have different compositions of energy. All matter – both seen and unseen are manifestations of energy. Like the electricity that surges through the power lines and your house, energy manifests in many forms. Microwaves, cellular phone activity, radio and TV, rainbows, radiation and even photography or all different levels of light and energy.

When you are in a bad mood, in a fit of anger, depressed, anxious, resentful, jealous, sad, or agitated, you are experiencing different emotions which are all manifestations of energy. Positive attitudes, emotions and experiences emit different levels of energy and light.

The soul is pure energy – a small, but incredibly powerful reflection of a larger light. Where this light emanates and is derived is anyone's guess, but I personally believe that it is the source of everything. Some call it God, others creative intelligence or universal source of everything, yet others the Creator, the divine – you name it – somebody's got a name for it. It's far greater than my measly understanding. Some say that by evolving our souls, we can achieve such an immensely advance state of consciousness that some call nirvana, cosmic consciousness, enlightenment. And, throughout history, many prophets, sages and holy ones have been said to have reached this high state of being. If you believe in religion, some call this state heaven on earth. This is what the prophets insist is what we are all going to achieve by the 6,000 year of the lunar calendar. A Garden of Eden like existence where there will be no more pain, suffering, crime, negativity. Only light, joy and love, bliss, compassion and other highly coveted emotional experiences.

Yet, many of us invalidate the soul or spirit because we can't see it. All they can understand is what they can see. The rest is hocus pocus, myth or legend. I'm not here to convince you otherwise, but I would argue that anyone reading this book believes that they have a soul, even if they don't fully understand how it functions

There is a movement in the world of psychology, philosophy and even science of the need for a new study of the soul – call it spiritual psychology. The spiritualist, Gary Zukav talks about a need to better define our spiritual life, needs and experiences.   If we can better understand how this invisible entity affects our being, we can better learn how to heal ourselves and make best use of our time on earth. We can learn to heal our souls, and as a result, fulfill our physical mission on this earth.

Spiritual Guides & Teachers

It is not physical guides and teachers that we have been talking about, but the spiritual guides and teachers that surround us in our spiritual journey that are already here to help you. Every human being has there own private spiritual consultants that are not visible to the human eye, but are ready to help you in your soul development and healing. Your job is simply to ask them to come into your life to help you with your human journey on earth. Guides and teachers are spiritual entities that were sent by the spiritual mother ship – so to speak – to guide you in your choices and understanding what you need to change. Teachers are more developed spiritual entities that are here for you to teach you the life lessons you need to learn in order for you to work out your stuff in the here and now.

The way it works is that you have to learn how to ask for help and for guidance. Not necessarily from your friends and family, but from your Higher Power that you want to develop a special relationship with. We have spoken at length about the Higher Power – your concept and belief is all that matters.

By building and enhancing your relationship with your Higher Power, you are also asking for help. Not necessarily for material rewards like money and riches, but for the help you know you need to become the very person you were always meant to be. When you struggle and suffer, your Higher Power is always there for you with love, compassion and mercy – like no other. The more you experience a relationship with the Higher Power, the greater your ability to access your own internal power – which then helps you to get the guidance and learning that you need to move forward in positive ways in your own life.

This is where your spiritual guides and teachers are ready to go to work. The more you learn to access your own internal spiritual power; you are also accessing the power and guidance of your guides and teachers. That's the way it works. They are there to help. No questions asked, no judgments given. But, are you ready to ask and receive the help that is there for you at any time you need it? Have you begun to understand the importance of asking for help from others, and abandoning the notion that you can take care of your own life with your own free will alone?

Karma & Karmic Debt

Once you begun to understand the connection of your soul to the universe and your purpose here on earth, the more help you will receive and the greater will be your spiritual, emotional and psychic development. That's where the real healing and change occurs. Deep down inside you there's this little flame – or glow – that is ready to be ignited and will help further illuminate your specific journey that you need to travel. It contains all the knowledge, wisdom and DNA code that you require to live your life on purpose. The more you ignore it – as if it doesn't exist – the more you will buck and oppose it. This creates more negative energy and more bad "karma" that you will then have to work out. We create both positive and negative karma through our intentions, thoughts, actions and deeds. When we act out or do negative things to ourselves or others, we are creating negative energy or karma. This will never disappear until we deal with it by paying for it. Karmic debt is an accumulation or an accounting of harms you have done to other beings. Those beings are your mother, father, children, partners, lovers, good friends and even enemies. You have agreed to contract with these people to work out your negative karma – and to learn the lessons you must learn here on earth so as not to repeat the negative and more damaging ones. You carry this debt with you from life to life. That is why we must work hard to change for the better, so that we don't have to continue experiencing trials and tribulations, pain and suffering. This is our primary purpose on earth.

When we finally die, we move on to another life somewhere else – often with the same people – to continue learning the lessons we were given to learn by our Higher Power. Everything that happens to and with us here on earth is about having the best journey we can. When we leave this planet, our bodies die, but our souls live forever and are eternal. Time and space are human constructs meant to help understand our experiences here on the human plane. There are many other planes of energy that exists that are invisible and mostly unknown to us. Higher and lower consciousness is all around us. It's like an energy highway with different energy frequencies. The only ones that we can see are our own. But, all space is packed with energy – even the invisible. We all have our specific jobs to do in a seemingly complex universe. Kind of Star War-ish you might say. Science fiction fantasy might be more real than we think, even if it is a stretch of the imagination. The entertainment and publishing world have been obsessed with it for years.

Developing a Spiritual & Faith-Based Life; Healing & Evolving Our Souls

The primary way we heal our souls is through getting closer and connecting consciously with our maker – the greater spirit that has created us all. Sounds crazy, but I strongly argue that it is true. We grow and heal by developing a personal and grateful relationship with our Higher Power. This is the power that wants us to be the very best version of ourselves that we can possibly be. He or She is compassionate, loving with no bounds, merciful and only wants the very best for us. When we are born, the intention for us to heal and grow is already there and we move according to our specific energy code, our unique plan which defines the experiences we need to have in order to change and grow. When we get stuck – emotionally, mentally, spiritually, we stop growing and begin dying.

To stay in the growing business, we need to develop a spiritual tool kit, much of which we touched upon in the last chapter. Some of us are born with a spiritual sixth sense and some kind call us spiritual. Others develop it through love and devotion to their Higher Power. And, yet others may have experienced some trauma – even near death experience in their life that catapulted them into a higher dimension where they become more sensitized to their spiritual natures. We all have it. Some have a more developed sense of it than others.

Exercising Our Spiritual Muscles

For most, developing a spiritual practice takes time and practice. Developing and strengthening a spiritual life is done much the same way as we build our strength and muscle mass by working out in the gym. We need to create the right habits, rituals and routines that will strengthen and deepen our relationship with our Creator by practicing effective rituals and routines. They don't necessarily have to be religious, but they have to be real and heartfelt.

Building a relationship with your Higher Power has to be something you really want, not just think you need. As I have shared with you, pain and hitting your bottom in life is usually a good place to start to look at your options. You've tried using the sheer force of your will until now. Now, it's time to try something else. Until you desire something strongly enough, you will never put the attention on it that will help it materialize. When you start paying attention to your spiritual side, you begin to develop.

So, practice, practice, and more practice is how we bring our spiritual natures to bear on the here and now.

Building a Trust and Faith in a Higher Power

This has been, perhaps, one of the most difficult things for me to achieve. I only trusted in myself and my own instincts. When that failed, I started believing that I could trust others who seemed far happier than I was. I watched what they did, and most all the people I identified with were faith-based people who were in the rooms of 12-step recovery or my religious friends who had long practiced their religion of choice. They had learned how to pray and meditate from their parents or religious/spiritual guides. It worked for them and they were once like me. But, they had long given up the struggle and fight to do it their way and try something entirely different. They started to believe in this Higher Power. In time, their belief turned to an enduring faith and trust. They taught me how to practice, pray and build a relationship with my spiritual nature and with my Higher Power.

Trust and Faith in something that you can't see or touch is incredibly hard – especially when the expected results aren't necessarily measurable or scientific. Belief in something other and hopefully greater than yourself is the only way to ensure permanent happiness and discovery of your true purpose in life. It's just so damn hard when you can't see the results like dividends on your financial investment or the feeling of falling in love – which is also invisible, but you can virtually see and feel the results – and quickly. Being the immediate gratification people we are who want what we want when we want it, patience is not one of our greater virtues!

But, however you obtain it, trust and faith in the Higher Power is essential to get the results you are truly looking for. More on this later.

Fear vs. Faith. Fear=No Faith

When you are full of fear and this is your normal state, you cannot have much faith. Fear and faith don't coexist in the same space. Faith comes from trusting and you can't possibly trust someone or something when you are sitting in fear. That's just the way it is. So, learning how to step out of fear and replace it with acceptance and positive thinking and attitudes, faith then becomes possible with practice.

Building a Personal Prayer Life

So there are several kinds of prayer. There's the fox hole prayers that you say when you are desperate and cry out in fear for help. Then there are religious or secular prayers that we learn from the traditions of our religion of choice or birth. And, finally, there is a different and awesome type of prayer that is often called personal prayer. Building a relationship with your maker is always personal. It's about you and your Creator. Period. It does not involve anyone else.

How do you develop such a personal prayer life? Start by recalling some of the best and deepest and most heartfelt and honest conversations you have had with best friend or partner. The most real discussions that you can remember are the way we talk to God. You speak to God as if He or She were standing or sitting right in front of you – maybe in your kitchen, den or living room, your favorite outdoor space or even your bedroom at night before going to sleep. I speak to my Higher Power all the time, anytime of the day or night. One of my favorite times seems to be the very early morning – usually between 4:30 am to 6:00 am – right before or at dawn. Everything is very quiet, my mind is becoming more active in consciousness and this is when I find it opportune to talk to God from the bottom of my heart. It's like writing in a personal diary – all those things that concern you, needs that aren't getting met, problems that you are having trouble working through on your own, relationship issues with your spouse or partner, children or parents or even best friend. I ask to better understand what I'm supposed to be doing and what my next steps should be. I ask for clarity and help. I don't necessarily ask for material things – although it is ok to ask for help for you when it is really needed. Anything is fair game: You want a new job, more money, a new house, success with your investments. These are ok if you are asking for the right reasons. God will listen to you pleas and concerns, but does not reward self-centeredness or selfishness. If our intent is good and it is something we really need, it is ok to ask for it. You may be in financial distress and need help. Maybe you can't pay your bills or need help paying for your children's education or for an elderly parent that needs more care. You may also just be hurting and need help. You may struggle with depression or anxiety or some other emotional or personal difficulty. You may want to grow your spiritual awareness and life. You may be practicing some of the many tools that we have reviewed in "How to Love Yourself" and need help with implementing them. Maybe you are seeking help for a friend or another person in your life that has their own problems. These are all fair game.

Have a conversation with God, make it real, do it every day and tell him or her how you are progressing. Let me know where you are disappointed. Tell Him or Her precisely what you are doing to improve your life. Ask for even more help.

As you find a quiet time in your day to talk with God, you will begin to get answers – maybe slowly at first. But, as your relationship with Him or Her deepens and strengthens, you will begin to get answers to your prayers – maybe not in your time, but in His or Her time. Keep practicing your prayer life and talking with God every day. Start with five minutes and increase the time to an hour over the course of the day. Perhaps, combine your personal prayer with religious prayer.

Reading Psalms, Proverbs and other spiritual material is also an excellent way to open up your spiritual channel with your Higher Power. Getting in the mood and hearing of others who have had life challenges that were overcome in part by building an enduring faith and trust in God is a great way to frame your own prayers.

While personal prayer is just that – personal, I highly recommend a bestselling author that I have been reading for years. His name is Shalom Arush and he has written some of the most powerful books on how to develop a personal prayer life. The first book is called "The Garden of Emuna" (which means "faith" in Hebrew) and the second is called "In Forest Fields – a unique guide to personal prayer." The Hebrew word Emuna is powerful and also means having a firm belief in a single, supreme, omniscient, benevolent, spiritual, supernatural, and all-powerful Creator of the universe, which we refer to as God. Personal prayer has changed my life and the stigma I had about prayer in general. Personal prayers are fairly non-denominational in nature and approach – even though the actual practice stems from a more mystical and very spiritual side of ancient Judaism. You will not be disappointed.

Here are two examples of personal prayers that I adapt to my particular conversation with my higher power. I generally just have a conversation with my Higher Power, but I liked to get inspired and warmed up first, so I read some spiritual material to put me in the mood and prime my spiritual pump. You can use whatever readings that float your boat:

Eternal Companion	**Crying Out To God**
"Eternal Companion,	"Oh, how I want to cry out to You,
Help us	God of strength,
Pour out our hearts	to cry undistracted
To you	and with a pure heart
Honestly and sincerely,	help me pray
With these prayers	with all my strength,
As our guide.	To raise my voice
Help us	in resounding supplication --
Feel close to you,	until
Dear God."	My own prayers
	Strike my head like thunderclaps
	And refine the innermost recesses
	Of my heart."

--"The Gentle Weapon – Prayers for Everyday and Not
And Not So Everyday Moments" **– Rebbe Nachman of Breslov**.

God Does Not Require Your Help – Just Your Cooperation

There's a great saying that I found posted on the wall of an A.A. meeting years ago. Its author is unknown. It reads as follows: "Good morning. This is God. I will be handling all your problems today. I will not require your help." Now, if that isn't clear, I don't know what is! What it means is that when you learn to truly trust your maker, you then need to leave all the dirty work up to Him or Her. You need to get out of the way, accept what is front of you and change the things that you can and leave the rest alone. This is true trust and faith when you can do this without interference.

Blocking and Tackling Our Spiritual Natures

Many of us are in denial of God. We may be atheist or agnostic. That is perfectly ok with me. I'm convinced that you need more time and experience with developing your own spiritual awareness and consciousness. The truth is that fear and ignorance are the reasons why we don't have a God of our own understanding in our life. To deny that you have a soul and that it comes from somewhere as do you as does nature and all the incredible world and universe around us is understandable, but at some point of your misery is ridiculous. Whether Creation came from a single event or from evolution is not important. Somebody other than us or your parents are responsible for all of this.

It is fear of the unknown or denial of the non-physical that keeps us from developing spiritually. Hopefully, you will get over your disbelief and get on with your life and allow yourself to grow in all respects. But, stubbornness and denial will get you nowhere fast.

Contempt Prior To Investigation

The 19th Century Philosopher, Herbert Spencer, is quoted in the "Big Book" of AA for having addressed one of the key roadblocks to discovering our spiritual natures. Being someone who grew up hating religion and denying my own spirituality, I have found this passage most useful. I think it worthwhile sharing it with you now:

"There is a principle which is a bar against all information, which is proof against all arguments which cannot fail to keep a man in everlasting ignorance – that principle is contempt prior to investigation."

The Buddha talked about the necessity of direct experience and testing of facts and knowledge. He believed that here say was nice, but had to validated by each person's own experience with it. I wholeheartedly agree.

Spiritual Experience

Recovering alcoholics and addicts…"who grew up spiritually in the rooms of recovery have read about something called a "Spiritual Experience" something that was essential in order to stay recovered from alcoholism and addiction. Some people have reached a sufficient bottom in their life that they can no longer take the pain. Bill Wilson, AA's co-founder talks about a "Spiritual Experience" in the "Big Book" of AA – which is the blueprint of the program of recovery from addiction originally written in 1935. All other 12-step programs have their roots in AA. As follows:

"Yes it is true that…many readers got the impression that these personality changes, or religious experiences, must be in the nature of sudden and spectacular upheavals. Happily for everyone, this conclusion is erroneous.

In the first few chapters of "Alcoholics Anonymous," a number of sudden revolutionary changes are described. Though it was not our intentions to create such an impression, many alcoholics have nevertheless concluded that in order to recover they must acquire an immediate and overwhelming "god consciousness" followed at once by a vast change in feeling and outlook.

Among our rapidly growing membership...such transformations, though frequent, are by no means the rule. Most of our experiences are what the psychologist William James calls the "educational variety" because they develop slowly over a period of time. Quite often friends of the newcomer are aware of the difference long before he (or she) is him/herself. He finally realizes that he has undergone a profound alteration in his reaction to life that such a change could hardly have been brought about by himself. He finally realizes that he has undergone a profound alteration in his reaction to life that such a change could hardly have been brought about by himself alone. What often takes place in a few months could seldom have been accomplished by ears of self discipline. With few exceptions our members find that they have tapped an unsuspected inner resource which they presently identify with their own conception of a power greater than themselves.

Most of us think this awareness of a Power greater than ourselves is the essence of spiritual experience. Our more religious members call it "God-consciousness."

Most emphatically we wish to say that any alcoholic capable of honestly facing his problems in the light of our experience can recover, provided he does not close his mind to all spiritual concepts. He can only be defeated by an attitude of intolerance or belligerent denial.

We find that one need have difficulty with the spirituality of the program. Willingness, honesty and open mindedness are the essentials of recovery. But these are indispensible."

You don't need to be an alcoholic or addict to acquire a God consciousness, but you certainly have to be willing to do whatever is necessary to acquire and grow it.

The Light That Shines Within All of Us

Once again, developing your spiritual nature does not mean that you have to believe in or practice religion. Our spiritual natures are one of incredible light and energy. Once we acknowledge and begin to discover our true spiritual natures, we help fuel the fire of our own light. This light is a reflection or spark of a much higher or intense light – kind of like the small flame of a candle vs. a bonfire. Our spiritual growth illuminates our path and shines the light on our negative natures and gives us the knowledge and wisdom that we need to grow and heal. As we grow spiritually, we develop this "god consciousness" or higher self. Some of us will eventually reach such an advanced state of consciousness like Maharishi Mahesh Yogi, Abraham, Isaac and Jacob, the Prophets, Jesus and Buddha, that we will live in a permanent state of enlightenment or God consciousness. This is a healing and wonderful, compassionate and loving power within that we all have available to us if we choose to acknowledge and access it. It can also be achieved by Eckhart Tolle teaches by accessing the "The Power of Now."

God Speaks Though People, Places and Things

I first started believing in a higher power by watching the other people in the rooms of recovery experience a psychic and spiritual change in their own lives. I saw the smiles on their face, the hope and the endless possibilities that I could find joy, happiness and peace in my own life. I was inspired and followed in their sober footsteps toward my own sobriety. They freely gave me the same gift that they received from their sponsor. I continue to give that gift away to others who reach out for help.

Today, I am keenly aware of how God speaks through people and through my own life experiences. I have learned to listen to His messages and to see when His grace and direction are shining through others that I meet and befriend.

Attending fellowship meetings in the rooms of recovery, in faith-based environments like churches and synagogues, in nature and even in the New York City subway, I see God's expression everywhere. I hear Him through other people sharing their experience, strength and hope in my life. I can tell when He is talking to me. The message just seems to resonate and I can identify with the messenger and their experience. It happens in so many places. Sometimes, it just seems so coincidental. But, I know that it is not. The more I learn to listen, the more I see. Being observer of people and day-to-day transactions has been such a gift. Learn to listen. Listen to learn. You'll be amazed at what's staring at you in between the lines!

Living In the Here and Now – Where Time Flies...

I have spoken at length on the need to begin to frame your life and experiences within the present moment. By holding on to resentment, anger, self-loathing, self-pity and holding on to the past, you are missing the point of your life which is occurring right here and right now. Similarly, by worrying about and fearing the future, you are also missing the amazing experience of your life right this very moment. Most all of our misery, dis-ease and dis-content come from not being able to experience the present moment.

Think of those really wonderful times where you lost your fear or anxiety in the moment – when time seems to fly and before you know it, an hour or two have gone by. Maybe you were crying watching the bride and groom go down the aisle, you feel deeply in love with another, you were in sexual union, your breath was taken away by some majestic scenery or incredible journey in nature, you woke up refreshed after a couple of weeks on vacation and had a memorable day – forgetting about the worries you left back home. Your child was born or you went skydiving and forgot about your fear. Those are the feelings of escape from the past or future into the present moment. They do happen, but for most of us, they are the exception, not the rule.

As you build your reference in life, time and space to present moment experiences, you are getting to know your authentic self. This is who you really are. Not the worry wart or basket case that you were or might be. When you let go entirely your fear and worry and drop the huge weight of anger and resentment you are carrying over past disappointments, you are opening yourself up to discovering your true nature – which is all very positive, full of light and love. This is where you find passion, color, lightness, intensity, compassion, gratitude and, of course, love and even blissful joy. Practice mindful meditation or just plain any kind of meditation, get out in nature and experience your life. You'll be amazed at what you find when you learn to live out of the box!

Eliminating Your Personal Character Defects and Atoning For Your Wrongs and Sins

We have spent considerable time talking about developing positive character assets and working to eliminate defective and negative character defects. This must be a life-long practice in order to develop strong spiritual muscles and habits.

By now, you should know a thing or two about yourself. You have looked deep within yourself to examine who you really are, taken an inventory of your assets and liabilities, and set more realistic life goals and expectations for yourself. Now, you must keep practicing by truly apologizing and then correcting your mistakes.

It is so very important to become accountable for your negative thinking and behaviors. When we have harmed another – even if we just think we might have – we owe an apology. We need to say "I'm sorry" out loud and sincerely to the person(s) we have harmed and really mean it. Then, we must change our behavior so that we don't ever repeat it again. In other words, we need to change whatever it is that we thought or did that resulted in hurting someone else. Saying you're sorry are empty words if they are not accompanied by sincere change of behavior. Not doing so will eventually result in loss of trust and credibility and will further complicate an already difficult situation. You must own your stuff or it will continue to come back to you in negative ways.

Religion and Religious Practice

While this book is not about religion, it is about building a strong spiritual life as well as mastering the many practical tools available to us to improve our lives. Happiness is here for us all and it involves both living a good life, being the best person you can and building a spiritual dimension to your life that will enhance all your human activities and endeavors.

I hated growing up Jewish. I experienced firsthand anti-Semitism, discrimination, hate and loathing. When I traveled the U.S. and overseas for business, I felt the impact of white supremacists and skin heads who hated Jewish people. Some people wanted to know where the horns were on my head that they had heard about from others. The amount of ignorance and bias that still exists in many parts of the world – including right here in our own backyard is real and horrible.

Compounding my personal experience with bias was the fact that I never understood Hebrew and found it to be difficult to understand let alone appreciate as a young person. As an adult, I have found it far more than mechanical. Now that I have studied and practiced in my own way, I can really appreciate the many wonderful dimensions of my history – both cultural and religious. However, I never push religion on others. Religion is there for those who want it and believe in it. I both admire and greatly respect those that have built their faith in religion and practice it proudly.

For me, I have found the need to explore my spiritual dimension through several inputs: In AA, I learned of the importance of developing a relationship with a Higher Power as a way to help keep me clean and sober a day-at-a-time. In meditation and yoga, I discovered my spiritual side by learning transcendental meditation and other forms of meditation. I have practiced and enjoyed the many benefits of yoga. I have studies Buddhism and Hinduism and have absorbed some of the basic principles of eastern religions and philosophies into my own life. Many of these same principles and truths exist in Judeo-Christian religions. I have attended Mass, prayed in churches everywhere and been on secular spiritual retreats. I love going to Catholic Mass and have been on many secular meditation and 12-step retreats for weekends or longer. I have enjoyed the benefits of a regular meditation and yoga practice now since I was in my 20's, but more consistently in the last five years as I got clean and sober. My experiences going deeper into my practice have brought me closer to my Higher Power. So, my particular brand of tools and formula for building and maintaining my spiritual life works for me. You will also develop your own preferred way of living your spiritual truths. The point is to just start and do it. Once you have made the decision, you must take the action until you have gotten the results that you want. If you still aren't getting the desired results, keep practicing, ask others for help and keep up the good work. Good things come to those who wait and want it!

Learning To Listen To Your Inner Voice: Intuition, Instinct and Inspiration

Some of us are more attuned to their inner voice than others. Most of the voices I heard that were not my own were swirling around in my head – my committee upstairs. I am not talking about the incessant clatter of those little voices that sometimes just won't shut up. I'm talking about the voices and whispers that come from listening in silence to the messages and inspiration I get from my spiritual teachers and guides. I have come to trust my intuition – though I must say that I still spend time passing my thoughts and ideas through my personal board of advisors. Wisdom is a rare and wonderful thing when it comes my way, and my intuition or inner instincts have greatly improved over time. I also get much of my inspiration by listening carefully to the voice inside my heart, not my head. It isn't necessarily just my feelings and emotions that are causing me to react, but sometimes it is knowing that what I am hearing quietly inside is the wisdom and answers I have been seeking. The better we get at trusting our instincts, the more we will access them.

Spiritual Elevation and Growth

This is what comes from spiritual growth. Reading, studying practicing and experiencing first hand my deeper inner spiritual side is how I grow. I need to feel like I'm spiritually grounded, but I can only do this by continued and diligent practice. When I lose my spiritual connection, which I sometimes refer to as falling off the spiritual beam, I feel off and not myself. I tend to rely on fear and focus on the past or the future. When I practice daily prayer and meditation I grease the wheels of my spiritual life.

Being Grateful & Becoming Wealthy In the Process

We have talked about acquiring an attitude of gratitude in your life. Being thankful for all the many gifts that we receive is one thing. But expressing this thanks to our maker and to those around us helps to keep us in gratitude. Gratitude is an action word, not a concept. It is a way of life. When you are a grateful person, you are in deeper appreciation for life itself and communicate that positivity to yourself and to all those around you. It is contagious and all part of good positive self-talk.

When I was in the throes of my addiction, homeless, penniless and very distraught, social services had me see a therapist/social worker. The man asked me what I was grateful for. I couldn't answer him, because I couldn't imagine what I could possibly be grateful for. When he pushed me to answer, I muttered, my sneakers – which were torn and worn out but were red. He had me repeat the process as he worked his magic on me. My life started to change from that point forward – even before I went to prison. By the time I got to prison, I was incredibly grateful for my life and had already developed an attitude of gratitude.

Gratitude is not about taking and getting. It is about giving. The way we develop an attitude of gratitude is as follows:

Step 1: Think of just one thing that you can be grateful for. Your life, health, children, spouse or partner, your job, house – anything. The less material the better, but we're just starting, so not to worry.

Step 2: Give thanks to the universe, your Maker or whomever you believe has more power than you (I'm not talking about the bully next store or Guido from the restaurant downtown). Do this for that one thing first thing in the morning and then before you go to sleep. Make it your morning and pre-sleep ritual.

 Step 3: Each week, write down one more thing that you are grateful for and add it to your list. Repeat Step 2 until you've got at least five items on your gratitude list. Continue practicing this till it becomes a regular habit. If you forget one day, start again tomorrow. Practice makes perfect.

Step 4: As you begin to develop a true sense of being grateful for your many blessings in life and not take these for granted, you will deepen your heart appreciation and growth, which in turn grows your feeling and appreciation for gratitude. Do this with your partner or family. See how it begins to turn negative attitudes, thinking and behavior to more positive self-talk. It really works if you work it!

Step 5: By the end practicing this for one year, you should easily have 10-20 items listed on your gratitude list. Keep going and enjoy the many benefits of living in gratitude.

How to become wealthy? What is wealth? Is it money, happiness, peace-of-mind, emotional balance, the ability to love and be loved, to have brought up healthy and happy children and grandchildren. Or does it mean material wealth? To me is can be all of the above, but without satisfying the other parts of my life that I have to see really matter, I am broke and will eventually lose my "wealth" by becoming miserable and unhappy. That is a fact!

Humility as A Way of Life

Humility is also an action word. To be humble does not mean to think less of yourself and to think more of others. It means to eliminate your sense of self-importance, grandiosity and big ego and to get "right sized." It means helping others and truly caring for your fellow man.

When we are truly humble, we have recognized the importance of our Maker as the leader of the pack, the Master, the boss. We are small in comparison. Not unimportant, just not the bloated person we think we are.

We are all born equal and remain equal in the eyes of God. Our self-importance really gets in our way to understanding clearly what our mission and purpose is in life. That purpose is to give unto others and to care and love our fellow man. It means to be of service, not of self-importance. It means to make a true contribution in life – not just to give money to charity – though that helps!

Mother Theresa, Gandhi, Dr. Martin Luther King, Jesus, Moses and many more throughout human history are examples of living with humility. They have a higher calling – a higher purpose. They added value not just to themselves, but to many others. They were heroes, prophets, saints in the larger scheme of things. They changed themselves and in the process changed the world.

Everything's Connected – Everything We Do Impacts Others

The world was not created just to serve us. We live in a complex ecosystem of life, not just on this planet, but most likely on others out of our planetary system. We are all part of the universal soup of life and are incredibly interdependent on one another. When we destroy forests or pollute oceans, life dies. When life dies in one place, it affects others both in visible and physical ways, but also in non-physical means.

We can easily see how the eight billion people on mother earth are affected when others suffer. Drought, floods, and famine, earthquakes, over population, disease, and political upheaval – all this affects people, communities, countries and the planet.

If you have bought into notion that living a purposeful life has meaning for you, then you also believe that what we do as individuals impacts others. This impact can be felt in our relationship with significant others, families, children, grandparents, and out towns and larger communities. When somebody dies, it affects others. When a family is struck with not being able to buy Christmas or Holiday gifts or becomes homeless, others suffer, too.

My point is that our motives, attitudes, emotions, thinking and behaviors affect not just us but those around us. This in effect cascades like dropping a small stone in the middle of a glass like pond and radiates outwards. So, when we are sick and suffering, it affects others around us, which in turn affects others around them. On the flip side, when we are healing and happy, when we smile and help others, when we build strong relationships and friendships, when we give of ourselves, we have a positive impact on our world. So, think of yourself as a center of influence – both good and bad. And, think about how others impact you. This comes down to the following: We are responsible and accountable for everything we do. This leads me to our next point:

Do Unto Others As You Would Have Them Do Unto You

Once again, when we step-out of our self-centered fear and myopic selfishness, we are learning how to treat others with the respect, dignity, love, caring, empathy and compassion that we want to receive from others. So, positive out, positive in, negative out, negative in. Think before you act. Step out of anger and resentment. Walk away from your fear and self-pity and think of how you might affect others by your actions. Even if they don't reciprocate, you have done the next right thing by considering them in your life. You might not get a "thank you" right away, but in time, the appreciation will come from within and also from without.

Adopting Permanent Qualities of Our Higher Consciousness

We all know what he means to live in the grips of our lower consciousness. We are busy satisfying our base survival and procreation needs. As we slipped into more negative states of sadness, despair, depression and anxiety, we certainly weren't living as good citizens of the world – no less our families or communities.

So, what are the qualities one demonstrates when living a good, purposeful and meaningful life. Here's a short list to consider, expanded upon from the Dictionary:

- **Love:** That intense feeling of deep affection. Not necessarily sexual, but felt from the heart and deep in the soul. The BEST way to get love is to give it. When you are "in love," you are merging yourself with the heart and soul of another. Love, though, is a higher quality of consciousness. It is spiritual in nature, but manifests in our feelings and emotions – usually based on our beliefs and understanding of love. It can be temporary or permanent. Building one's experience of love comes from both loving others and being loved. Love can be grown and nurtured. It is the quality of your highest power emanating through the spark of life and light that we all possess. Loving your Higher Power is, perhaps, one of the highest forms of love. Like being loved and loving another, it is unconditional and pure. It has no agenda but goodness. But, like all our muscles, if we want to grow our sense and experience with love, we have to exercise our heart muscles and build it into our daily attitude and behaviors.
- **Tolerance:** The ability or willingness to tolerate the opinions, attitudes, thinking or behavior of others – even if we don't agree with them. It is a level of allowance for the

differences in our lives and the world. When we are tolerant of others, we are accepting of the many differences that exist among us. Tolerating those differences increases our understanding and compassion and even love of others. We build a larger understanding for humanity.

- **Respect.** A feeling of deep admiration for someone or something elicited by their abilities, qualities or achievements. This can apply to other persons, places or things, events. It can also be something like love that we feel for our self.
- **Wisdom:** The quality of having experience, knowledge and good judgment, the quality of being wise. It does not mean being smart, but it means taking our knowledge and interpreting it at a   higher level of analysis and learning. "Wise men" are those that can think in larger ways with the knowledge they have acquired. We greatly admire people that are wise and can teach us and the world about things that we couldn't possibly know on our own.
- **Compassion:** A feeling of deep sympathy and sorrow for another who is stricken by misfortune, accompanied by a strong desire to alleviate the suffering. Compassion is one of the highest qualities that we can experience in our motives, attitudes, thinking and behavior.
- **Empathy:** The ability to understand and share the feelings of another. Also, one of the highest qualities of human consciousness. Being empathetic toward others is showing all the qualities mentioned above and requires a higher level of maturity and a well developed heart.

"To Thine Own Self Be True"

According to William Shakespeare's fictional Greek character in "Hamlet," Polonius, "This above all: to thine own self be true, and it must follow, as the night the day, Thou canst not then be false to any man. Polonius believed that a person can be harmless and good to others when he/she himself/herself is financially sound. The literary reference has to do with living a good and balanced life. In the context of ""How to Love Yourself"-Hour Reboot," it has more to with being virtuous and honest and living a good moral life. If you have adopted a set of beliefs that you choose to live your life by, then do so and be consistent with your actions and attitudes. It can also refer to being authentic in that your insides match your outsides.

Wearing Life Like a Set of Loose Clothes

I first heard this saying in an AA meeting, where slogans and catchy phrases are popular because that is sometimes the only thing an alcoholic and abused mind can mentally remember. It has always stuck with me. It means to not sweat the small stuff, don't take yourself too seriously and become comfortable in your own skin. Life is too short and we need to all lighten up somewhat and learn to enjoy ourselves and "Chill."

<u>Learning How to Take The Middle Path</u>

Many of us have been manic in our approach and reaction to life. Things are either great or terrible.
They are good or bad. We are either exuberant or miserable. We are either way up or down low, rich or
poor, happy-sad. But, we never seem to get the pendulum to swing in between the two consistently.

As we get better and more skilled at the game of life, we will want to place ourselves in a more neutral
position of somewhere in-between. It takes far less energy to swing the pendulum from one side to the
other and then back, when all a long, all you have to do is stay in the same position to achieve the same
goals. It's like the turtle and the hare. They both end of finishing the race. Which one do you relate to?
Do you think you could be happier, more stable and less volatile by gyrating all over the place? If so,
then you are on your way to living a more sound and consistent life.

<u>Treating Others with Honor & Respect</u>

We have talked earlier about the need to respect others – especially if you expect to be respected.
Honoring and respecting others are valuable character traits. It shows a level of maturity and good
character when you respect and honor others you feel deserve it.

<u>Death as A Part of Life – Grieving and Death</u>

Most people are afraid of death and are intimidated by it – especially when it happens to someone close
to them. This is cultural and learned. In ancient cultures and throughout history and in nature, death
has always been a normal and expected part of life. We honor and respect those elders who have
acquired wisdom and imparted it those in younger generations.

The truth is that death is a very natural and normal part of the living process. I personally believe that
the soul never dies and is eternal. That being the case, death is purely physical and a natural process of
our own spiritual evolution. We can't escape death and we all will die one day when it is our time.
There is nothing to be afraid of. Rather, it is something to honor and a perfect occasion to celebrate
someone's life with dignity and admiration for the jobs that were well done. There is always something
good or a lesson to be learned from those who pass on. We should come to be grateful and not fearful
of death.

It is OK and natural to grieve when someone passes. It is not ok to get stuck in our grief at the expense
of our own growth or happiness. When someone gets stuck in grief over the passing of a loved one, we
need to carefully coax them to move on with their life or get them professional help so that they can
complete the grieving process successfully and not carry it forward to their detriment.

Living With Reverence, Passion and Awe

Life is and can always be so damn good. It has so much to teach us and give to us. We need to be fully engaged in our own life and to come to appreciate it with reverence, admiration and to live it with passion and awe to the fullest. This gives us every reason to become whole, healthy emotionally, spiritually, mentally and physically.

Doing an Act of Kindness or Good Deed Every Day

I teach people I sponsor, counsel and mentor to be grateful and to get out of self. One of the ways I was taught to do this by my father, who strongly believed in charity to the poor and hungry on the streets, is to intentionally and consciously go out of your way to do something nice for someone else. Bring someone coffee or tea in the morning without being asked, compliment someone on their smile or nice clothing or hairdo when they are looking down. Tell someone else how much you appreciate them and love them for just being them. Give accolades to someone for a job well done. Do a charitable act without taking credit to someone in need. Help an older person with a chore. Say "thank you" and show your appreciation for those things others do for you. You get the idea. Each day for a month, train yourself to do at least one simple thing each day. You will find that it becomes contagious and will reap far greater rewards than it cost you in time or resources. Positive out, positive in. This is one of the best ways to learn how to be grateful, by also learning to be humble and kind.
Love with all your heart, soul and mind.

Using a God Box

As a Jewish boy, I learned about a Tzaddaka box – which is a charity box. But, my Catholic friends taught me about using a God Box to help me with difficult challenges or unresolved emotional feelings.

We have talked about the concept of "Letting Go, Letting God" as a way to bring our Higher Power into our lives. Letting God handle the tough stuff when we need help. I sometimes have used my lawyer as my higher power when confronted with a difficult legal issue, my accountant as my HP when trying to reconcile sticky accounting issues, and my sponsor and mentors when tackling other life issues. When I was in prison, my friend Ira P. showed me how to use a God Box upon receiving some very difficult news about two of my children. I was devastated and powerless to do anything and I felt I had nowhere to go or nobody to really dump my stuff with. The God Box has proven to be a great tool. So, here's how it works: When you are struggling and are unable to resolve the issue or problem on your own, get a little tissue or small cardboard box and label it your God Box. Write on a piece of paper exactly what you are struggling with, ask God for help with all your heart and soul and put the paper in to the box and simply forget about it. The physical act of giving your problem, at least on paper, to God, is very powerful and will help you to let some of your powerlessness and strong feelings and emotions go. Ask for help and you shall find it.

<u>We're Never Alone -- Avoiding Loneliness and Isolation</u>

By now, we have become more aware of the need to avoid isolation with others. Many of us have struggled with loneliness and isolating from others and our problems is a good way to stay lonely. We tend to let the committee in our head rule our reality. When we are lonely, we can't really receive the kind of help we need and stay immersed in our negative feelings, self-pity and our inability to form sustainable and healthy relationships with others.

The truth is, we are never alone when we develop a meaningful relationship with our Higher Power, and we can always ask for help from our Master when needed. The "50% Rule" also applies when we learn to share our feelings and concerns with others in fellowship or among our friends and family. Don't be a stranger!

<u>Learning To Be Happy, Joyous & Free</u>

This is a state of life you want to achieve. It is a state of emotions, attitude, acceptance and behavior that clearly and wonderfully demonstrates that you are done with your old life and have embraced a higher and far more desirable and attainable state of existence. For real, this place in life requires you to be free from the anger, resentment, self-pity, and pain and fear that you have long been holding onto and to let it go for good. It also assumes that you are willing to not anticipate the what ifs of your life going forward. You have nothing to fear as it hasn't happened yet. And, if you have now begun to live in and participate fully in your day – today – not yesterday or tomorrow, you will be present and truly living your life fully in the moment for all that it has to offer you. There are so many gifts in the here and now, most importantly, you can now be yourself and your insides match your outsides. You are a new person living your life on purpose, with unbelievable meaning and high value in the current experience of the moment. You have arrived and need not go anywhere else to find your true worth and value. Congratulations. What a gift and a joy!

<u>The Problem W/ Worshipping False Idols</u>

We have spent much of our life seeking false Gods like drugs, alcohol, sex, gambling, money, fame, success and much more in the ego-gratification department. These are not real and will never make you happy. They are a fool's errand and have misery marked all over them – especially when you tire of worshipping and coveting them and need some other false idol to replace them. The only "idol" worthy of worshipping is the one that brings you life and universal love and compassion. This is the light and source of all creation that is worth being grateful for and thanking with all your heart and soul each and every day in your own special way.

Unplugging From Technology – Unstressing Your Life

We who loved and fed on the excitement of stress when we were younger have eventually become overwhelmed by it. Technology is truly one of the greatest man-made inventions that continue to rise in value and sophistication. The problem is that our obsession with technology, from cell phones to computers to virtual games to apps has us so focused on everything but the real prize, which is being human and living simply and without interference. Technology is amazing in so far as it enhances our life. But, when it begins to interfere and consume our attention that would be better placed on growing our spiritual life and taking care of our basic needs, something is wrong. We are missing lifestyle balance and need to focus on rejiggering our focus on those very things that will make us happy. Everything is good in moderation, even technology. Understand its value and also appreciate its liability and addictive quality. Take a walk in nature, the park, the meadow, the forest trail, by the sea where nature will fill your senses and take you places that technology can't. Also, be a friend to your friend, a child and parent to your children to your family. Don't lose the human touch.

Getting & Staying Right With Yourself

When you are off the spiritual and emotional being, take care of yourself, your soul and your basic human needs. Life is complicated and we need to put our spiritual needs first. If we feed our spiritual nature, we will also be working our lives in balance and harmony.

Living With Abandon in an Age of Abundance

My parents were immigrants and we grew up fairly blue collar. I learned the value of a dollar and working for those things we want. As most parents today will attest to, we are more economically able and rich with resources that most of our parents never had. In some cases, our children have most everything they need and want. When we lose our hunger and desire for growth and contribution, we lose focus on what is truly important in life.

Let's be grateful for all the bounty that society has given us and for all the opportunity that has come our way. It is our responsibility to use this time of abundance to enrich not just our lives, but the lives of others who have less fortune than us. Live with abandon, but never forget where you came from and what gifts life has passed your way.

Finding & Receiving Grace

What is grace and why is it so amazing to be gifted with? Grace is unwarranted good from your Higher Power. It is undeserved and unearned and unexpected. It is the ultimate reward for working to get closer to your Creator and living a good and purposeful life. Some people might refer to an act of grace a miracle of sorts. Perhaps it is, but those who seek it will eventually reap its many incredible rewards.

Coincidence when good things just happen like your terminal condition is miraculously reversed, your basic needs are taken care of by others, you enjoy a level of success that you just can't explain, you experience bliss and joy on a regular basis, you are gifted with children when you were told that wasn't possible, an important relationship was suddenly healed and changed your life, a natural disaster was averted and saved thousands of lives, a baby is found in the wreckage of an earthquake after 11 days. The list goes on. Grace is God's gift and way of Him saying thank you to you. Clearly, if you experience such an amazing and unwarranted gift, you deserve it. This could very well be one of the ultimate prizes you will witness and receive in life. Congratulations, Mazel Tov and enjoy!

Examining Your Real Motives for Doing Things

A motive is a reason for doing something. It can be conscious or unconscious. Criminologists and Police investigators look for a motive for a suspect(s) committing a crime. Why did they do it? What provoked them to violate the law and harm another person or property or to break a law? What causes you to do certain things that perhaps you just can't explain?

Take the time to get in the habit of exploring your true and honest motives for your negative and positive behavior, thinking, attitudes and beliefs. When you understand why you do what you do, you will better be able to fix the real problems in your life. Like losing weight, stopping self-destructive behavior like addiction and self-abuse, self-loathing and self-pity, hanging around the wrong people and the wrong places. Think your beliefs, actions, attitudes, feelings and behaviors through to understand what exactly is driving it. Become self-aware. Keep a diary, if this helps for you to document what's lurking behind a bad habit or behavior.

The Power of Choice Revisited

Nearly everyone has made poor choices during the course of their lives. Some of these made have been made consciously or unconsciously. But, they were choices, nonetheless.

As we grow and mature in our lives, we learn to make more informed, educated and appropriate choices. This is the power of living a good, meaningful and purposeful life. Our ability to choose is uniquely human. Animals only respond to their animal instincts. We have free will to choose.

During our sadder days, we may have made choices that either weren't healthy or perhaps best met our needs. Today, we are blessed to be able to choose wisely. And, when we are unsure of the choices that might be available to us, we have advisors to ask, the internet to Google, and people who care about us to bounce our ideas off of. Choose wisely and enjoy the optimum results. If, if all things fail, try and try again until you achieve the outcomes you seek. Each time we time we choose, we have something to learn from the experience – both good and bad!

Here are the top 25 things that I would get to work on right away:

1. Change Everything: I would immediately resolve to change EVERYTHING that no longer works or has no permanent and redeeming value in my life immediately. I'd waste no more time contemplating what I had to do and I how I had to do it. I would hold nothing back and put everything on the table for consideration. All of it, no whining and with complete surrender!

2. Just Do It & Without Regret: I'd just start doing it now, without hesitation or delay! I'd stop all the procrastination and denial that has held me back from being happy, joyous and free. It suddenly becomes clear to me what my short list is. Don't dare die with regrets!

3. Say "I'm Sorry" & Mean It: Now, it is time to clear up the wreckage of my past. To take responsibility to clean-up my side of the street. To own what I did, and who I am. I'd apologize without hesitation to anyone and everyone for any harms - real or perceived - that I've done to them – not expecting to get anything in return.

4. Stop Beating Myself Up. I'd put down the bat and stop beating myself for not being perfect while accepting the good person I really am – warts and all.

5. Focus On Forgiveness: I first must forgive myself for all real and perceived failures and transgression. Then, I must forgive everyone else for real or perceived harms done. Forgiveness is a huge step forward to growth and healing, and it takes a lot of willingness, honesty and open mindedness. You will never be happy until your self-and other-forgiveness is thorough and complete. This is a major "rock" to drop.

6. Drop My Resentments & Stop Living In Fear: I would stop regretting the past or being fearful of anything in the future – because it doesn't really matter anymore. I must drop my fears, which have been at the root of many of my problems and develop a trust and faith that all will be well!

7. Accept My Lot In Life: The faster I accept that I can't control everything in life and is "what is," the more time attention I can focus on the many gifts I already have. I don't need to change the world, but just those things in my life that prevent me from being my very best. You can be happy without whatever happens to you in your life, whether you're poor or rich, in good health or poor, a doctor or a garbage man – you need to make peace with who you are today and not be so concerned with what happens tomorrow or what didn't happen yesterday. You have everything you will ever need to be happy with what you've got today – no matter what!!

8. Stop Worrying About What Other People Think: It clearly doesn't matter unless we're hurting someone. The only thing that matters from now on are what I think, do and how I act and behave. Living well and always doing the next right thing means I won't have any concerns what others think about me. My self-esteem is high, confident and my strengths and satisfactions come from within. I don't need others to define how I feel or who I am.

10. Get To Know Thyself: The truth will always set me free. Self knowledge goes hand-in-hand with the other real prize – true peace-of-mind, joy and happiness. I would acknowledge and know with conviction who I am, my unique talents, gifts, special qualities and strengths, values and own it! I now know that I am good enough and that that is more than OK. While I would acknowledge and thank them for serving the purpose they did, going forward, I would have no mercy on my character flaws that limited or hindered me from being my true and best self.

11. Identify & Let Go My Character Defects: I would lovingly look at my past roadblocks, character flaws and personal liabilities, acknowledge them without guilt, blame, shame, or resentment and resolve to turn them into personal strengths and character assets. I would also honor them for their huge value in allowing me to finally see the path to personal freedom. I would then finally get out of my own way.

12. Redefine What "Success" Really Means : In this final day, success no longer means accumulating things and material wealth, career & professional acknowledgement, self-importance, but being happy, true to myself, being of service to others, being an active and modest part of life – not always being right. Success also means having meaningful relationships and actively and responsibly fulfilling my role as an adult male, father, son, partner, mentor, coach, friend and member of my community and the world.

13. Forget Money, Power, Ego, Pride and all Other External Pursuits: None of them EVER made me happy for very long and almost always caused more pain than good because, they deflected me from being present in my life and focusing on all the amazing things that were right in front of me. Focus on the internals, not the externals as that is a fool's errand.

14. Don't Take Yourself Or Anything Too Seriously: Lighten up. Nothing is that important as to keep you down and out. Stop taking yourself and everything that happens to you so seriously. Stop being a victim and remember that you have the choice to let the world control you or for you to let the world's struggles roll over your shoulder. There are more interesting and important things to focus on.

15. Become a Power of Example: Change is powerful when it works and is contagious. I would strut my stuff and start walking the walk today. Watch what happens! Lead by example. Become that person that others admire and want to be. Become the "show me" state – and show the world what living a good, purposeful and happy life looks like.

16. Give Thanks & Show Gratitude: I'd thank the God of my understanding, the creator of the universe, and all things for all the blessings I've received and for the life I've been allowed to experience. I would take stock of all these many blessings and gifts and express my heartfelt gratitude and deep appreciation. I would adopt and attitude of gratitude and hang on to it for dear life.

17. Be Present and In The Here & Now: I would focus all my attention on being present for the people I cared about most in my life -- my children, my partner, my mother, my closest and best friends. I would no longer spend any time stuck in the past or worrying about the future – as they are sure to bring me more pain. Rather, I would choose to always live in the moment – where my life is really happening and where all real and permanent change takes hold. The past is history, tomorrow is a mystery; all we really have is today.

18. Fall & Stay in Love: I'd love all those close and important to me to death. I'd celebrate their life and our precious time together. I'd tell them how much I love really love them – often and always, appreciate them, and honor them as having touched my life and mine theirs.

19. Focus on the Positive & Smile From the Inside Out: Ever since Dr. Norman Vincent Peale wrote the groundbreaking "The Power Of Positive Thinking" 70 years ago, nothing has ever been the same in the motivational and executive training world. His point is that results in life – both external and internal – are just so much better when you focus on the positive and deflect the negative. Nobody likes to be around negative people – especially when you yourself are down and out. If you want to be more positive, watch people who are positive and begin to smile a lot in your own life. Start to mimic what they do and eventually become positive yourself. There is tremendous personal power in thinking, believing and acting positively. Eventually, if you continue practicing the principles you will learn here, you will start to exude a deep sense of positivity and possibility from deep within yourself – from your soul, your true being – where true happiness and joy emanates. People will begin to notice this in you and respond in kind. We're talking quantum physics here: The laws of attraction and the laws of karma.

20. Live With Passion & Curiosity: Enter into the stream of life with all the energy, excitement, wonder and curiosity of a child. Make this a way of life in everything you do. Explore, try new things, experiment, break new barriers, be bold, be open and present and watch what happens!

21. Write & Own My "Bucket List": There are at least 10 incredibly wonderful things that you would love to experience before you die. Start doing them today and plan and schedule the rest. There's nothing holding you back now except for you.

22. Focus On The Prize: Healing, Care, Growth & Love For The Heart & Soul. When you heal and learn to care for your soul, it pays huge dividends and repairs and strengthens your physical, emotional, mental and psychological development. You heal and evolve from the inside out. Physical maladies? The rehab, sponsor, doctor, therapist, healer and coach are all "In." Focus on discovering and healing your soul and the rest of your ailments will surely fade away. Dig deep! Do it now! No longer be afraid!!

23. Live In Gratitude and Humility: When you acquire an attitude of gratitude and become truly thankful for the many gifts you receive each and every day – both good and bad, you will come to realize that everything happens for a reason, for your very best and for your own good. Living in true humility is, perhaps, the highest level of achievement for any human being. Be thankful and think of yourself less, not less of yourself.

24. Give It All Away: The only way to truly appreciate and keep those things in your life that really matter, love, wisdom, helping and doing for others – and a life well lived and not just full of material things is to give it away. You can't take any of your toys or prizes with you when you die. Those things don't really matter in the short- or long-term. Give of yourself everything you've got and you get to keep even more.

25. Finally: Now that I've reframed my life, I would resolve to continue living my life as if each day was the most precious commodity, a gift and my last. I am now living on "borrowed" time.

The Gifts of Good and Evil

The amazing thing about free will is that it can take us to nearly opposite ends of the happiness – misery scale. Like trials and tribulations, good and evil can be our greatest teachers. Once we learn enough about what is truly evil and how not being or feeling like a good and deserving person, we get a little taste of what hell must be like.

As we build our own measure of good values, good character traits, personal strengths and likes, we already know what the opposite of those values, traits, strengths, and likes are to us. We have seen them in other people through our own life experiences. We learn by seeing in others what we like and dislike what we admire and disdain, what makes us feel good about ourselves as opposed to feeling worthless or not good enough. Experience can be our best teacher and teach us about what is good and what is also evil. This helps us to define our own value system and adopt those character traits and beliefs that can change our lives. We don't have to be an evil person to know what we don't want to be. But, we can learn by seeing good and evil in others what will best work for us and bring us to an emotional and spiritual state that will bring is more joy and happiness.

Not Judging Others

By now, we've gotten out of the judging business. This is not easy, but necessary if we are going to put the attention and analysis to change our lives on us. Other people are not our concern, unless they require our help and with express permission. Otherwise, stop creating negative energy and hurting other people by falsely accusing them of something they may or may not have done. You aren't the judge. It's bad enough that we falsely judge ourselves. There is only one judge and we will all meet Him or Her when it is our time. Until then, stick to your own knitting and life. The Funny Thing About

If You Are Not Truly Living, Then You Are In The Process Of Dying

""How to Love Yourself"-Hour Reboot is about improving and participating in the stream of life. When you aren't growing or changing or doing, you are stuck and in the process of dying. If you're hope is diminished, re-ignite it. If you passion has been dulled, polish it off and get excited again. If you are not making a contribution to something greater in your life or giving to others, then you are not living to your full potential.

Depression, anxiety, remorse, resentment, anger are all signs that our expectations for life are not being met or are in need of modification. Negative states and emotions take us out of the stream of life, light and love. We've talked about taking full responsibility for our lives – both good and bad. When you are stuck, ask and get help. But, don't stay stuck for long. You are doing yourself and those who love you and need you a big disservice.

One Day at A Time as a Way Of Life

We have spent considerable time talking about the concept of not projecting too far in the future. That's where we continue to get in trouble.   Keep your expectations, acceptance, plans and the hard work you are doing on yourself for yourself in the "How to Love Yourself"-hour period that lies in front of you. Behind that is none of your business and certainly not yet a reality. So, slow down and pace your progress in "How to Love Yourself"-hour discreet segments of time. That is the appropriate amount for anyone to handle.

The Passover Metaphor (Freedom Is an Inside Job)

The Jewish Holiday of Passover teaches us about the importance of faith and freedom. Since being incarcerated, I have come to understand that true freedom is being freed from prison, but is freedom from the bondage of myself. I was enslaved in my limited emotions, fear, anger, anxiety and a host of other negative emotions and behaviors. I did that to myself. Nobody else. By accessing the power that was always was in me, I found the key to unlocking my own door to spiritual and emotional freedom. I was freed from my old self far before I was freed from the prison gates. I will never be imprisoned again as freedom is truly a state of mind.

Hope Is Eternal & Necessary

Life without hope is a very dark place. It is a personal bottom, the end of the line, the last stop before some insane and undesirable harm is done either to us or to others. When we lose hope, we lose sight of light and its many possibilities for growth, expansion and happiness.   Hope is eternal, but it takes determination to keep it in the midst of pain and struggle. It is always there, but sometimes not always visible to the eye and heart. Don't lose sight of the one thing that we all need to keep moving forward to success.

Attraction, Not Promotion

There is a reason people are attracted to positive, loving, caring and giving people. Because good deeds and acts attract other good deeds and acts.   Living a good, purposeful, fulfilling, and meaningful life without the use of mind-altering substances or negative behaviors is very attractive. When you see it, it does not need to be sold or pushed on anyone. Others will naturally be drawn to your goodness and positive change and you won't have to convince others of its value. They will be knocking down your door to get some of this good thing that you have found. Share and share alike.

Become a Powerful Servant

Sounds like contradictory. Actually, it's not. As we become more humble and grateful in life, we really that we are using our God-given talents to help others achieve for themselves what they could not do on their own. We are doing God's work and serving the larger purpose of our life. That purpose is to serve and empower others. To be a servant in the truest form of the word is really an honor. We have now matured so much in all the key cylinders, metrics and measurements of our life that we can now use this new life, purpose and happiness to help others achieve their purpose. So, once a follower, now you have taken on the larger role of being a servant. This sounds bizarre, but, in time, you will come to realize this is true empowerment. It is unselfish empowerment. And, this is how we change the world, one person at a time!

Heaven On Earth?

Heaven is right here, right now for those who want it. It is a state of mind and spirit. We don't have to wait to "get" to heaven to be happy, joyous and free. We have to live our lives in the present moment and travel our journey on a daily basis to know what true freedom is for each of us. We don't have to wait to find what is already available to all of us. Enlightenment and spiritual growth is something that anyone can obtain by developing the awareness and skills to find what they already possess. You don't have to travel anywhere to get what already exists.

Yes, we are still in our bodies, but our souls have always been here, are here now and will always be here in the future. Our Higher Power put us in this body to discover and live our higher purpose. We don't have to take an I.O.U. out to get it. So, being here now and learning to live your life on purpose is the farthest you ever have to travel. You must be willing to let go of your past and adopt a new way of life – just for today.

So, How Do You Know You've Changed??

Change comes from having made lots of little and some really big decisions along the way. Once you've made the decision and have started exerting the necessary energy and resources to reaching your goals, you will begin to notice changes in how you feel. When your emotional state starts to elevate and the fog from your brain begins to lift, you will notice that something feels different. You are making progress – maybe just a little to start. One step forward, two steps back may be the reality in the beginning, but you will begin to notice incremental change. As you begin to feel better about yourself, others around you will begin to notice the difference.

Change is good and very contagious. Once you experience its momentum, the forward motion of progress starts to feed on itself. Be prepared for setbacks and more challenges, but this is excellent progress. Keep going. You are finally moving in the right direction. Your internal GPS will take over from here.

What Does It Take To Finally Get the Job Done?

While I accept real, demonstrable progress as a way of life, I can't accept inertia. When nothing changes, nothing changes and that is not good when you are desperate and really trying to change your life for the better. So what are the specific qualities that you need to continue to demonstrate to reach your goals and make the changes that you so sorely crave?

- **Determination:** The overwhelming desire to see your goals through. Definite signs of a winner attitude.
- **Willingness:** Whatever it takes, you have chosen to be ready and to begin to move forward to a new way of doing things and your new life in freedom.
- **Honesty:** The truth will always set you free, and it takes brutally honest to call yourself on your own stuff. Be rigorous and thorough and catch yourself when you get lost in shades of grey.
- **Goal & Progress Evaluation and Assessment**: You have set real and achievable SMART goals for yourself and your life and you and your peer group and loved ones will help you to evaluate and adjust your goals as you continue to move forward
- **Asking for Help and Taking it When Needed**: Getting out of isolation and aloneness and taking a chance that someone might say not. But, the next person you ask for

help might actually say yes, and, if they don't, you will start finding friends and confidants that will provide you with the help you need. Keep asking!

- **Endurance and True Grit:** Like an intense physical workout, you are in for the ride of your life. Be willing to see this process through until you reach your goals. You can do it, so just do it!
- **Being Unstoppable and Demanding Excellence In Your Own Life:** Set the bar high, but be realistic. Strive to do better, make it your mission to do the very best you possibly can, don't beat yourself up if you aren't "perfect," then keep going. Join the winners.
- **Indefatigable:** Even when you have you say you can do no more, be determined and keep going. You can and will do this.
- **Stick-to-It-ive-Ness**: The difference between excellence and mediocrity is knowing how to see things through to their conclusion. In order to make the changes you have envisioned for yourself.

Chapter VIII.
GETTING OUT OF SELF

"You make a living by what you get, but you make a life by what you give"
- Winston Churchill

"The best way to find yourself is to lose yourself in the service of others"
- Mahatma Gandhi -

Imagine being so self-centered and selfish and then reading the following:

"Lord make me an instrument of thy peace;
That where there is hatred, I may bring love;
That where there is wrong, I may bring the spirit of forgiveness;
That where there is discord, I may bring harmony;
That where there is doubt, I may bring faith;
That where there is despair, I may bring hope;
That where there are shadows, I may bring joy.
Lord, grant that I may seek rather to comfort than to be comforted;
To understand, than to be understood;
To love, than to be loved.
For it is by self-forgetting that one finds.
It is by forgiving that one is forgiven.
It is by dying that one awakens to eternal life.
Amen

--Saint Francis – born in the town of Assisi Italy in 1182 A.D.
(and written after a long period of silence in retreat).

Doesn't compute does it? Why would anybody that is so self-absorbed and the center of their own little universe want to hear this? It's utter madness and a total disconnect. What's in it for me?? I'm certainly no saint, nor do I aspire to be one!

This prayer is, perhaps, one of the best ways to describe the actions one can take to uncover your own higher purpose. It takes an enormous leap of faith to actually do what Saint Francis of Assisi wrote about centuries ago, but the rewards of his selfless approach to life can only come from years of experience with great pain and struggle – which it is said he did experience like many of us. This is not to say that you need to be a saint to be happy. That's not the point. The point is though, that service and contribution is one of the most powerful ways to get right with yourself and to grow spiritually and in the very best way that you were intended to live.

The Secret To A Happy Life Is...

It was once said, "The secret to a happy life is a happy wife." Since I can't personally attest to this as I am myself divorced, I would modify this to say: The secret to a happy life is the decision to devote yourself to others – to be of service and to get out of self. That is a proven fact and the primary key to living purposefully and with profound meaning.

If you truly want to be happy and free from your painful past, I am going to teach you how to be unselfish and to help others to help themselves. Not that we don't matter. We do and we deserve the utmost of attention in healing ourselves. But, like Saint Francis, the way he discovered his ultimate purpose and happiness is by getting out of his own self and devoting himself to be of service to others. The rewards he received of joy, purpose, meaning and happiness came as a fringe benefit of doing the next right thing and being of service.

The Joy of Helping Others

There is always someone worse off than you. When you stop being so self-absorbed and reach out to others, something magical happens. There is no greater joy and accomplishment than to help someone else, anonymously if possible, to grow and prosper. Being the self-centered and narcissistic egomaniac that I once was never made me happy. I learned about helping others through doing service in the 12-step rooms of alcoholics anonymous. As I began to make coffee, volunteer to set-up chairs and help prepare for scheduled meetings, I began to experience what it was like to get out of my own head and to get involved in the present moment. I learned to greet people at the door, offer help to newcomers who, too, were struggling with their addiction and character defects, reach out my hand to those who needed to go to rehab and/or detox centers, go to speak at meetings to share my experience, strength and hope. In other words, I learned how to get out of my own pitiful isolation and learned hopelessness and to actually become a part of something larger than myself – to become an active and helpful member of society. I began to balance out my six lifestyle spokes and learn that even though I was struggling with my own addictions and personal issues, others often were worse off than I. Imagine that. By being told to volunteer by my beloved Sponsor V and later, Jim S., I began to experience a sense of self-worth and empathy towards others.

What Else Do We Get By Giving?

Here are the top toys and prizes. None of them have to do with money or material possessions. We can't even put a real dollar value on them. Their appraised value is nothing short of priceless:

1. We get a wonderful and amazing sense of purpose: the people around us are our mirrors to reality. When we they see the smile of acceptance and genuine humility on our face, they smile back. We then see their radiance in us. That feels so good.

2. Self-discovery: We find that we actually matter and have value to others. We begin to identify with the experience of others and they with us. We matter and become an important go-to resource.

3. Love & Companionship: Goes without saying. Two basic human needs whose twin tanks always needs to be filled up. We can't get it or sustain them without giving it

4. Self-Esteem and Self-Worth: Something we all struggle with. The way we fix this is by doing esteem-able things that make us feel better about ourselves.

5. Positive Reinforcement: Endorphins and serotonin are flowing when we give of ourselves to others. The momentum of giving is in and of itself reinforcing and positive.

6. We Eliminate the Committee in Our Head: When we give and get out of self, we also stop the mental chatter that want stop talking nonsense to us.

7. We Enter the Here and Now and Become Present: When we start giving, we are no longer obsessed with our dis-ease of the past and fear of the future. We are in the very flow of life that we all covet.

8. We Make a Difference by Helping Someone In Need: We're actually making a difference in the lives of others when we extend a helping hand. It creates a sense of friendship and community when we give and actually makes the other person feel better and well considered by you. You might even be changing or even saving someone's life.

9. We Make Good Friends – Sometimes For Life: We all need true friends, and we conveniently acquire them by extending ourselves and investing in others. You must continue to invest in the relationship if you intend to keep it and grow it.

10. We Save Souls and Save Lives: The way redeems us from our prior misery and pain is to do something good for others. We have spent enough time accumulating bad karma, sins, and other negative acts. There is nothing like recreating the balance sheet by doing good and giving as a way of life. We might even safe and redeem ourselves from our prior lives in the process.

11. We Break The Cycle of Addiction and Suffering Once and For All: When we get out of self and start to contribute to the stream of life, we start taking care of our six basic human needs by changing our negative and harmful patterns into more positive ones. When we're busy giving and doing good, we spend less time obsessing about our selfish needs and addictive wants.

How Does One Get Out of Self?

There are a number of wonderful ways to get out of self and to greatly improve the quality of your life and others. Our goal is to not remain so self-absorbed, self-centered, selfish and grandiose. The true goal is to create your own meaning and purpose. There are lots of way to do this from just being a good son or daughter, a good father or mother, a good brother or sister, a true friend to your friends, good love to your lover(s), and a good citizen of the earth by making a difference in the lives of others. Clearly, you will reap greater rewards and grow as a fulfilled human being while you discover your true talents. As importantly, you will begin to give away what you were so freely given to heal your own life. Some have referred to it as paying forward, but, it is truly the highest form of payback to you as well.

Mentoring

So, the concept of **Mentorship** or what I also refer to as my personal **"Board of Advisors"** will be a big concept that we will explore together as our "How to Love Yourself" hours unfolds. Much of today's corporate world and even social networks are built on this. Arguably, most of the most successful people on earth like Warren Buffet, Steve Jobs and Mark Zuckerberg had mentors. So, did many of the ancient prophets like Moses, Jesus, David and Buddha. And, then speak to the politicians and professionals – all have had mentors and learned to use them well. Don't forget the artists and musicians from Beethoven, Mozart, Leonardo Di Vinci, Matisse and Van Gogh – all had teachers, sponsors and artists.

Just Google "Mentor" or "Mentorship" and you will find hundreds, if not thousands, of organizations that will happily "Mentor" you for a fee or for free. It is both good business and good for the spirit and the soul.

Anyone who has been a mentor will happily and openly tell you that they have received from those they mentored far more than they have ever given. The rewards of reaching out and helping others are unquestionable and simply amazing. It will also bring you great rewards that you just can't put a price on.

I have mentored many young and older people in my life – both personally and professionally. It is something I must and love to do to stay happy, fulfilled and vital. It is a big part of who I am and I'm going to teach you both how to have mentors in your life to be with you in times of need and even ordinary times as well as to learn how to mentor others in the business of life and happiness.

Getting out of self is magical and necessary to stay in the flow of life and learning. I can't imagine ever being alone or isolated anymore. Fellowship with men and woman is a big part of my life today. I'm good at it and believe it is essential to your learning to live your life on purpose, with meaning, joy and happiness. As Saint Francis and countless unnamed others have found, you find yourself by getting out of self and committing yourself in healthy ways to others. This is the highest form of living and giving.

Coaching

When I was a young boy, I had coaches in the various sports I played: basketball, baseball and soccer. Similarly, when I became the adult and the father, I coached my kids in soccer, softball, baseball and tennis. They had other coaches. There were piano and voice coaches, tennis coaches and more. Most were volunteers, but some made a living doing this specialty craft. What exactly is a coach? A Coach focuses on the here and now of your life – today. A therapist deals with your past trauma and life. A good coach will help you to identify the areas in your life that you feel you want to grow. What are your current challenges, your current roadblocks and what is presently missing? What needs are not being met or are being met in dysfunctional and negative ways. How can we change those patterns to positive ones? And, what was your old story and how do we create a new story with real strategies for your life now. It's powerful game changer for people who seek to go farther in their life, happiness and their own success. Other forms of therapy just can't do this as quickly or at all.

Counseling

There are several types of counselors. You may have had or been a counselor in summer camp where you had privilege of working with a small group of children or young adults. To counsel is to advise and is a peer-to-peer type of relationship. Then, there's the mental health counselor that may actually be performing some type of social work or light therapy treatment with you. To counsel is to offer, model and to give advice. I have enjoyed many years of counseling as a teenager and young adult for summer and winter camps, sports and special skills from YMHA, YMCA to 4-H camps.

Teaching and Tutoring

What a gift it is to teach a tutor others. One of the greatest rewards I have every received was being able to see failed men in prison get their G.E.D. high school equivalency and to graduate. I've taught many men and women over the years in career, business and life success skills and to see a student's eyes light up to the possibilities of using a new found idea or a strategy to change their own life is priceless.

When I think of my own teachers through K-12 and even in college who had a big impact on me, I am so very grateful that I was fortunate to have them. Teaching and tutoring sadly are not highly paid professions, but any teacher, professor or tutor worth their weight will tell you how very rewarding their careers are. To be able to impact so many young people at vulnerable and critical times of their life is truly an honor. We who have been on the receiving side consider it a gift and will always be grateful.

Take your skills, talents and wisdom and turn them into a teaching program for others. Even hobbies or personal passions, share them with your family, friends and those who might really benefit from knowing what you know. Grandparents and our elders are so under-appreciated these days. They have so much wisdom and knowledge to share. If you want to get out of yourself, be of service to others and give away what you already know to help another help themselves.

Volunteering

One of the very six important life spokes we address in an earlier session is community or civic involvement. There is such a need for volunteers for so many worthy causes. Volunteering both changes and saves lives. It is one of the higher forms of charity and should be every young and old person's civic and personal duty and privilege. If you're not sure where to volunteer your time, ask others who are already happily doing it or go on-line and Google "Volunteering" and you will be flooded with ideas and organizations that can use your help. It is not a full-time gig, but devote whatever time you can. The rewards of giving and expecting nothing in return are enormous personally, emotionally, psychically and spiritually. You become a power of example when you do so and a model for other aspiring volunteers who are considering doing the same. Once again, when you help others, you also get out of yourself, which is one of the major benefits.

Sponsoring

There are several ways to sponsor others. In former generations – especially in America post WWI and WWII, in order to immigrate into the U.S., you had to have a legal U.S. citizen to come to this country legally. That is still true and we have seen many families coming to America by one single family member sponsoring the others. That is what my parents did and my father did for my mother and her family.

Today, sponsorship is basically done through one person who has experience in an organization, fellowship or some type of member society to take responsibility for another who also wants to join. Essentially, a sponsor becomes an example for others in how a fellowship, organization or even association or club works and functions. They are guides and stewards in teaching others what they need to know to become an active member themselves.

In 12-step and other fellowships, a sponsor is necessary to get and stay recovered from addiction issues. It is something that one sponsor passes down to their sponsors and so forth through the generations. We are told to do what they do, act as they act and follow the rules as they have been shown. This modeling ensures a smooth transition of fellowship learning and practice from one to another. It is, perhaps, one of the most critical pieces in the recovery world. We always look to find a sponsor with ample experience with other sponsees and with their own experience in the fellowship. I have had several sponsors in AA over the years and have sponsored many other men in their journey to recovery.

Big Brothering/Sistering/Companioning

A Big Brother or Big Sister fills the role for some boy or girl that doesn't have one. This is a very important and respected job – one of becoming a role model for someone who needs one. These are not easy shoes to fill and it requires much compassion and empathy for one to be successful in such a role. But, the ability to influence someone in need of mentorship is powerful and it requires a great deal of trust – something that you have to earn. This is, perhaps, one of the most powerful and important ways to get out of self, and the rewards are commensurate with the importance of the role. Senior citizens who are perhaps alone might seek a companion as a paid or unpaid volunteer. It is an equally important role and can provide the tender loving care that would otherwise be absent.

Parenting

One of the most privileged and important ways of getting out of self is becoming a parent. It is a divine privilege and honor to be partially responsible for bringing another life into this world – as crazy and difficult as that may be. Being a parent holds a huge responsibility and requires mature role-modeling for those that you steward into this world. It is perhaps one of the most important roles and most misunderstood roles we will ever have. Like growing up, it would be so nice if we were all just given the parenting manual. Unfortunately and fortunately, one has to experience this role for themselves and learn from what they were taught by their parents and by other parents who have solid parenting schools.

On the flip side, it is so very easy to damage young people by being an irresponsible, bad or non-existent parent. There are so many absentee parents today – something I experience and observed myself by being in prison. It is something I will never take for granted again and something I pride my ex-wife for doing with passion and skill.

Care Giving

Something commonly found in the health care industry, being a care giver requires enormous patience, compassion, empathy, love and skill. It is a really hard job and I have had many care givers for my mother who has been in elder care for many years now. These people are truly saints and are worth every penny and far more than they are paid. They should all be acknowledged and honored for their commitment and endurance. It is perhaps one of the hardest and most important jobs – taking care of a loved one in time of need. I believe it is God's work that these people are doing, but most love what they do and would never do anything else. Ask any nurse or aid and they will all tell you of their love of people.

Being Charitable

Charity comes in many forms, both monetary and time, teaching and services. The giving business is huge in the U.S. and worldwide with nearly a Trillion dollars donated each year for charitable causes. Giving charity makes you feel good that you are helping other people accomplish something that they couldn't do themselves without your resources.

One of the highest forms of charity is teaching someone how to take care of or be responsible for themselves. Teach someone in need a skill or trade.

The highest form of charity is giving your money, time and resources without taking any credit – or remaining anonymous. There is no ego involved and this requires a great deal of maturity and humility.

Grandiosity, pride and ego are sometimes a factor in people giving. A wealthy person might want their name on a school or building. That is ego, but that is the way much of big charity works today.

The point of giving is not to need to get. It is to become an important and ego-less part of something larger and more important and to get out of self.

Become a Member of Others' Board of Advisors

We talked earlier about assembling your own personal board of advisors. You should also suggest that you become a willing and active member of others' board of advisors. You will feel better about yourself, it will help you build your self-esteem and feeling of self-worth, and you will be contributing to the greater good of others when you offer your perspective, knowledge, wisdom and advice to those in need.

Being a True Friend

There are true friends and then there are friends and acquaintances. The former you can count on one hand. Being a true, devoted, caring, selfless and proactive friend is different than just having a friend. A good and even a best friend is someone you can count on to be there for you when you need it the most.

Society really struggles with making strong connections on a personal level. Everyone is so caught up in their virtual worlds these days that people forget to talk, touch and look at each other across the table and actually engage in dialog. You can't do this through texting, fishing for "likes' on social media or through email. You must do this by reaching out to someone and initiated active dialog. You must invest in the relationship if you intend for it to last.

Being a true friend to someone else is perhaps one of the best and easiest ways for us to both connect and get out of self. When you consider someone else's situation and circumstances and offer not just perspective, but actually take a risk by helping someone else with their immediate needs or to solve their current dilemma, you are being a true friend. Your only motive is to help.

By doing so, you are not just thinking about your own self-centered needs, but those of another. This is how you get out of self and find your true purpose. So, get connected and help your fellow man (and woman) by being there unconditionally and let them know you care!

Chapter IX.
CONCLUSION

As we draw closer to the end of our time together, a new, brighter and more hopeful day lies ahead for you. Hopefully, you have made the decision and begun to take the initiative to implement the many wonderful and life-changing tools we have discovered in order to improve and change your own life.

My offer still holds: If you are unhappy with the time we have spent together for now, I will happily refund your misery. It's your choice. I believe you will continue to choose wisely!

Change takes time and the pace is different for all of us. If you've had enough pain, you will be anxious to make the decision to move forward with your life. Fear is the bogeyman and never be intimidated or overwhelmed by it. It is not real, just your reaction to some phantom rationalization. Developing new habits takes -- anywhere from three to six months on the average -- so be patient with yourself and "give time time."

But, change you must, but it will only happen if you make the decision to start and focus on building and maintaining your assets of honesty, open-mindedness and willingness, everything and anything is possible.

Never Forget Your Pain and Your Bottom

The two key points to remember are never forget your pain and your bottom. It should always remind you of how you don't want to live any longer. If you've finally had enough and are sufficiently sick and tired, you are most likely ready to continue your journey forward into freedom.

Living each day as if it were going to be your last is an excellent way to think of your life. It will set you free once you start living on purpose. It will also be more do-able and sustainable when you do it just for today. This you can handle. Anything more and we have already removed our self from the day and relapsed into the past or gotten hung up on moving too far into projecting into the future. Neither will this bring you purpose, serenity or peace-of-mind!

Achieving Peace of Mind

When you are truly living your life on purpose, you will have achieved an indescribable sense of peace and serenity that is priceless and almost indescribable. Once you experience freedom from your past pain and dis-ease and dis-comfort, you will never look back. And, if you continue to trudge the road to a happier destiny with us, you will build a life worth living and worth sharing with those you love and cherish. Happiness and joy are most contagious and this is something that others will want to latch onto. You are now becoming a power of example for others who will eagerly clamor to follow in your footsteps.

The Journey Continues

"Success is…knowing your purpose in life, growing to reach your maximum potential, and sowing seeds that benefit others."   **-- John C. Maxell**

If you have listened to learn and learned to listen, you will never have to worry about reaching some imaginary and illusory destination, because your journey is the destination. You have already reached it, but each day gets a little brighter, clearer and even more enjoyable. Not every day is going to be perfect, but most will surely be a heck of a lot better than what you were used to.

Keep focusing on making incremental progress, practice and be willing to test and try new things, even if it does take you one step back. You will shortly be moving two steps forward and will have learned some valuable lessons for improving your walk and technique along the way. Keep feeling good about making progress. Just keep doing it and never look back. The light will eventually envelope you into something even bigger and better just around the corner. Stay strong and stay focused on the quality of your life and achievement of purpose. You will know you have arrived and are "successful" by experiencing that sense of deep satisfaction, joy and peace-of-mind knowing that you have lived your true purpose for today.

Being that I am both Scottish and Irish, I'd like to share this old Irish Blessing that I have come to know so well:

"May the Road Rise Up to meet you – the wind always be at your back. The Sunshine warm upon your face – the Rains Fall soft upon your fields, and …Until we meet again…May god hold you in the palm of his hand!"

God Bless, and may God be with you each and every day of your journey! We WILL meet again!!

Much Light & Love Always,

Fenton

ONE LAST THING…

If you enjoyed this book or found it useful I'd be very grateful if you'd post a short review on Amazon. Your support really does make a difference and I read all the reviews personally so I can get your feedback and make this book even better.

If you'd like to leave a review then all you need to do is click the review link on this book's page on Amazon here:

Thanks again for your support!

About The Author

M. Fenton Deutsch (61) is an author, serial entrepreneur and Chief Life Coach for his virtual coaching company, **lifecoach911.com**. He has successfully developed and grown several consumer products and business information publishing companies. He began his career as a business Journalist and Author in the Consumer Electronics Industry and then moved into the Advertising and Marketing fields working for a large National Advertising Agency where he ran their technology sector for companies such as Canon and Sony. He then became Advertising Director for Consumer Audio at Sony Corporation of America, where he introduced the Sony Walkman, Boombox and Car Stereo into the U.S. markets. He co-founded what became the largest Books-on-Tape Company, Warner Audio, which was sold to Warner Communications. He spent the next 10 years working and developing a series of national real estate database publishing companies and a consumer products company called Natural Child Care with a bestselling author and prominent Pediatrician. He has held the key sales, marketing, business development and merger & acquisition positions in all entities. Most recently, Mitchell has also experienced several life-changing events that have changed the course of his life. He had his own spiritual awakening as a recovering addict and alcoholic which nearly twice ended his life, and spent the next 39 months in a Federal Prison Camp. He has developed his own non-profit as a way of giving back what he was freely given and is authoring a new book entitled "24-Hour Reboot! Learning to Live Life On Purpose." He is also launching a new nonprofit foundation called 24! Change Partnership which will provide addiction recovery services and housing to the addicted and those at risk for suicide. His first book entitled "Doing Business with The Japanese," was published when he was 25 in five languages in both hardcopy and paperback. Mitchell presently resides in New Jersey, is the father of three grown children and has spent his entire adult life residing in the New York City area.

<u>HIRE FENTON TO SPEAK AT YOUR NEXT EVENT!</u>

Book M. Fenton Deutsch as your Keynote Speaker and you're Guaranteed to Make Your Event Highly Entertaining and Unforgettable!

For over three decades, M. Fenton Deutsch has been educating and helping people and companies help themselves to grow and change to achieve better, more fulfilling and happier lives. His Company, Lifecoach911.com is helping people and businesses worldwide to achieve far better and permanent results in their daily function and bottom-line.

His heart wrenching story of his rapid rise as an author and serial entrepreneur, including his role as Advertising Director at Sony Corporation where he introduced the Sony Walkman and Boombox and then later went on to develop the largest Books-on-Tape Company which he and his partner sold to Warmer Communications his battles with addiction and suicide and finally jail, and then triumph over adversity at 60 is an incredible story of success over life's greatest adversities. His insights and wisdom will bring your audience to tears and then elevate them to incredible heights of inspiration and hope. He can be contacted directly at: lifecoach911@gmail.com or at fenton@lifecoach911. Or call direct at 973-885-2839 to book him.

fenton@lifecoach911.com

Look For My New E-Books and Print Paperbacks later this month

TABLE OF CONTENTS

Copyrights
Dedication
Acknowledgement
Forward

Chapter I. INTRODUCTION
My Watershed Moment
Life is a Choice
Pain & Failure as a Path to Success
Why Me?
We Are Reborn Every Single Day!
The Enemy Within
Lack of Self-Esteem, Self-Pity, and Self-Doubt Got You Down?
What Happens to People Who Don't Feel Loved Enough?
These Statistics Don't Lie

What Does it Mean to Struggle With Feelings of Not Feeling Loved?
What is Feeling "OK" Really All About?
How It Works
Chapter II. MY STORY
Allow Me To Introduce You to Your New Life
The Things We Need To Fix
Time For Change
Learning to Live in the Solution!!
The Help We All Need, But Are In Denial of or Just Too Proud to Accept
The Power of Love & How It Helps to Heal Our Lies and Sustain Us
The Basic Components of This Five-Step Program to Love Yourself
Learning How to Fix Those Things That Are Broken: Your Heart, Your Soul, Your Life
The Power of Choice
Our Failure to Satisfy Our Basic Human Needs
Chapter III. ROADBLOCKS LOVE & CHANGE
Fear
Self-Defeating Fear
Self-Centered Fear
The Gaping Hole in Your Soul
Rationalization and Justification
Pride, Ego, Grandiosity & Big-Shot-ism
Self-Doubt
"Don't Tell Me What To Do"
Self-Pity
Guilt & Shame
Resentment
Remorse
Dishonesty
Denial
Analysis Paralysis (W)
Terminal Uniqueness
Co-Dependancy(W)
Stubborness
Lack of Acceptance
Unmanageability
Arrogance (W)
Unrealistic Goals (No Goals) & Expectations (W)
Distorted Sense of "Success"(W)
Being Judgemental
Stinking Thinking
Negative Self-Talk
Knowing It All (W)

Self-Sabotage (W)
Anger (W)
Poor Self-Image & Lack of Self-Esteem (W)
Emotional Oversensitivity (W)
Irrational Thinking
Rage, Self-Loathing, Jealousy and Bitterness
Impulsivity, Impetuousness, Immediate Gratification
Needing to Always Be Right
I Don't Need Anybody Else's Help
Defiance (W)
Lack of Power (W)
External Focus of Control(W)
Isolation/Loneliness (W)
Poor Risk Assessment & Management (W)
People Pleasing
The Committee in Your Head
Sweating The Small Stuff (W)
Blind Spots

Medical/Psychological/Emotional Issues: (W)
Medical or Psychological Disorder
Depression
Anxiety
Addiction
Abuse
Dual Diagnosis
ADD/ADHD
Bi-Polar
Antisocial Personality Disorder
Anxiety Disorder
Insomnia
Borderline Personality Disorder
Dealing W/ Specialists: Doctors/Psychiatrists, Psychopharmocologists, Psychologists, Therapists, Counselors
Psychosis
Obsessive-Compulsive Disorder
Dyslexia
PTSD
Phobias
Dealing with the Professional Community
Issues of Being Wrongly labeled and/or Diagnosed
Science & Technology Are Great, But They Can't Fix You

Chapter IV. KEYS TO SELF-LOVE & CHANGE
The Power of Change
Change Is an Inside Job
Speed Up, Slow Down
Time for a Major Attitude Adjustment
Honesty
Open-Mindedness
Willingness
Belief
Hope
Courage
Acceptance
Respect & Civility
Coming To Know Our Limitations
Asking For Help
When The Student is Ready, The Teacher Will Appear
"Don't Worry, Be Happy!"
Facing Your Fears
Life Is a Journey
Building a Durable Foundation
Making a Decision
Becoming Accountable
Life Is a Practice Test
Trials & Tribulations
Stepping Out of Your Comfort Zone
Try, Test, Experiment, Take Calculated Risks
Build Perspective, Get Information & Knowledge, Educate Yourself
Read, Study & Learn With Passion
Become an Observer of Life
Hope & Inspiration
"Just Do It!"
Lighten-Up & Don't Take Yourself So Seriously
Identify, Don't Compare
Take the Pause That Refreshes!
Chapter V. LEARNING THE TOOLS OF THE SELF-LOVE & HEALING TRADE
Making a Commitment to Making Life Work
Treating the Whole Person
<u>Emotional Tools:</u>
The Importance of Self-Care
Healing Our Inner Child
Taming King/Queen Baby
Lighten-Up, Don't Take Yourself Too Seriously

Humor as A Way of Life & Lightness
Stepping Out of Fear, Resentment, Sadness, Self-Doubt, Guilt & Remorse
Anger Management
Giving Yourself Permission
Learning to Love Yourself
Becoming Your Own Best Friend
Feeling Your Feelings
Managing Your Feelings
This Too Shall Pass
Handling Negative Emotions
Taking the Sting Out of Anger & Resentment: Pray For the Other Person
Practical Tools
Living A Day-At-A-Time
Framing Your Day with Thanks & Asking For the Help You Really Need
Stop Taking Everything So Personally; Give Yourself a Break
Finally, Let Go, Let God & Stop Sweating the Small Stuff
Dropping the Rocks of Anger, Resentment & Self-Pity, Remorse & Fear
Turning Your Anger into Something Positive & Powerful
Accepting Tough Love as a Compliment & a Sign of Love & Caring
"Letting Go, Letting God"
Accepting the Help You Need
Stop Trying To Control Everything
Be a Friend When Someone Reaches Out For Help
Common Sense Tools
Life is 10% What Happens to Us and 90% What We Do About It!
Progress, Not Perfection
Measuring Up: You Are Always Good Enough
You Are NEVER Alone
Putting One Foot In Front Of the Other
You're Worth It, So Work It
Move a Muscle, Change a Thought
Surround Yourself with Positive People
Positive Self-Talk
Build & Maintain a Support Network
Creating Good Habits, Routines, and Rituals
Building Self-Esteem; Doing Esteem-Able Things
Learn To Please Yourself
Be Your Authentic Self
Rebuilding Old/Broken Relationships
Living with Others
What Are the Many Benefits of Healthy Relationships?
Learn the Art of Effective Communications

Confronting & Leveling
Become a Good Listener
Anger Management
Three Roadblocks to a Positive Attitude
Understanding & Dealing With Our Blind Spots
Become Your Greatest Fan
Setting & Maintaining Healthy Boundaries in Personal & Business Life
Yes You Can! Taking Charge of Your Life Today
The Importance of Momentum
Mentor, Counsel & Coach Others
Prayer
Meditation
Doing Life Without Mind Altering Substances
Forgiveness
Trust & Faith
Giving Back to Others
Chapter VI. LIVING HAPPILY AFTER EVER (Staying Changed & In the Healing Process Forever)
Healing From the Inside Out
Is the Student Finally Ready?
Fear and Pain Are Our Greatest Teachers
Chapter VII. SPIRITUAL GROWTH & DEVELOPMENT
Our Innate Need for Self-Actualization
Finding a God; Developing a Relationship with Something Greater Than Yourself
What Is A Higher Power?
Developing Your Own Relationship with This Power
Good Orderly Direction (G.O.D.)
Your Spiritual Journey
Living in Gratitude; Counting Our Blessings
Trust & Faith
The Secret to a Happy Life Is...
How Does One Get Out of Self?
What Else Do We Get By Giving?
Mentoring
Coaching

Counseling
Teaching & Tutoring
Volunteering
Sponsoring
Big Brothering/Sistering/Companioning
Parenting

Care Giving
Being Charitable
Become a Member of Others' Board of Advisors
Being a True Friend
VIII. YOUR SPIRITUAL TOOLKIT FOR HEALING YOUR HEART &YOUR SOUL
Retarded Growth & Development
Everything Happens For a Reason, For Our Own Good and For the Very Best (both good & bad)
Next Steps for Insuring a Really Good & Happy Life…
Healing & Evolving Our Souls
Many Lives, Many Masters
Spiritual Guides & Teachers
Karma & Karmic Debt
Developing a Spiritual & Faith-Based Life; Healing & Evolving Our Souls
Exercising Our Spiritual Muscles
Building a Trust and Faith in a Higher Power
Fear vs. Faith. Fear=No Faith
Building a Personal Prayer Life
God Does Not Require Your Help – Just Your Cooperation
Blocking and Tackling Our Spiritual Natures
Contempt Prior To Investigation
Spiritual Experience
The Light That Shines Within All of Us
God Speaks Though People, Places and Things
Living In the Here and Now – Where Time Flies…
Eliminating Your Personal Character Defects and Atoning For Your Wrongs and Sins
Religion and Religious Practice
Learning To Listen To Your Inner Voice: Intuition, Instinct and Inspiration
Spiritual Elevation and Growth
Being Grateful & Becoming Wealthy In the Process
Humility as A Way of Life
Everything's Connected – Everything We Do Impacts Others
Do Unto Others As You Would Have Them Do Unto You
Adopting Permanent Qualities of Our Higher Consciousness
"To Thine Own Self Be True"
Wearing Life Like a Set of Loose Clothes
Learning How to Take The Middle Path
Treating Others with Honor & Respect
Death as A Part of Life – Grieving and Death
Living With Reverence, Passion and Awe
Doing an Act of Kindness or Good Deed Every Day
Using a God Box
We're Never Alone -- Avoiding Loneliness and Isolation

Learning To Be Happy, Joyous & Free
The Problem W/ Worshipping False Idols
Unplugging From Technology – Unstressing Your Life
Getting & Staying Right With Yourself
Living With Abandon in an Age of Abundance
Finding & Receiving Grace
Examining Your Real Motives for Doing Things
The Power of Choice Revisited
The Things I Need To Change To Feel Loved, Happy & Fulfilled
The Gifts of Good and Evil
Not Judging Others
If You Are Not Truly Living, Then You Are In The Process Of Dying
One Day at A Time as a Way Of Life
The Passover Metaphor (Freedom Is an Inside Job)
Hope Is Eternal & Necessary
Attraction, Not Promotion
Become a Powerful Servant
Heaven On Earth?
So, How Do You Know You've Changed??
What Does It Take To Finally Get the Job Done?
Chapter IX. GETTING OUT OF SELF
The Secret To A Happy Life Is…
The Joy of Helping Others
What Else Do We Get By Giving?
How Does One Get Out of Self?
Mentoring
Coaching
Counseling
Teaching and Tutoring
Volunteering
Sponsoring
Big Brothering/Sistering/Companioning
Parenting
Care Giving
Being Charitable
Become a Member of Others' Board of Advisors
Being a True Friend
X. CONCLUSION
Living Your Day as if It Were Going To Be Your Last 24-Hours
Never Forget Your Pain & Your Bottom
Achieving Peace-of-mind
The Journey Continues